Italian Women
in Basilicata

Italian Women in Basilicata

Staying Behind but Moving Forward during the Age of Mass Emigration, 1876–1914

Victoria Calabrese

LEXINGTON BOOKS
Lanham • Boulder • New York • London

Published by Lexington Books
An imprint of The Rowman & Littlefield Publishing Group, Inc.
4501 Forbes Boulevard, Suite 200, Lanham, Maryland 20706
www.rowman.com

86-90 Paul Street, London EC2A 4NE

British Library Cataloguing in Publication Information Available

Library of Congress Cataloging-in-Publication Data

Names: Calabrese, Victoria, author.
Title: Italian women in Basilicata : staying behind but moving forward during the age of
    mass emigration, 1876-1914 / Victoria Calabrese.
Description: Lanham : Lexington Books, [2021] | Includes bibliographical references
    and index. | Summary: "This book examines the women who remained behind in
    the southern Italian region of Basilicata during the age of mass migration. While
    thousands of married men left, their wives remained in Italy, taking on a new role and
    challenging stereotypes"—Provided by publisher.
Identifiers: LCCN 2021020478 (print) | LCCN 2021020479 (ebook) |
    ISBN 9781793607782 (cloth) | ISBN 9781793607805 (paperback) | ISBN
    9781793607799 (ebook)
Subjects: LCSH: Married women—Italy—Basilicata—Social conditions—19th
    century. | Married women—Italy—Basilicata—Social conditions—20th century.
    | Wives—Italy—Basilicata—Social conditions—19th century. | Wives—Italy—
    Basilicata—Social conditions—20th century. | Basilicata (Italy)—Emigration and
    immigration—Social aspects—History—19th century. | Basilicata (Italy)—Emigration
    and immigration—Social aspects—History—20th century.
Classification: LCC HQ1644.B37 C35 2021 (print) | LCC HQ1644.B37 (ebook) |
    DDC 306.872/3094577—dc23
LC record available at https://lccn.loc.gov/2021020478
LC ebook record available at https://lccn.loc.gov/2021020479

Contents

Acknowledgments

The women who remained behind have always been a group that fascinated me. The idea for this project arose from my love of Italian history and personal fascination with genealogy. I first encountered these women when researching my own family history and I discovered various instances of male emigrants who left their wives in Italy. I found myself spending hours researching my own Italian roots, and as a doctoral student at the time, I thought it might be best to incorporate that hobby with my doctoral work. As I began researching the topic, studies on migration from regions such as Sicily, Campania, and Calabria abounded, yet I found no information solely about emigration from Basilicata, where my Calabrese family is from. This inspired me to focus on Basilicata.

Traveling to Basilicata various times to conduct research has been a wonderful experience. The people I met there could not have been more friendly or welcoming. When I told people I met that I am from New York, almost everyone had a story about a relative who had emigrated or who currently lives in America. The archivists in the Archivio di Stato in Potenza and the Archivio di Stato in Matera were more than willing to assist me, brainstorming possible sources, and giving me ideas for further research. I want to thank Francesco, his wife, and their family, who hosted me in their beautiful home in Pignola. Francesco drove me to the archive every day on his way to work and even came to get me for lunch. Visiting Picerno was also especially meaningful to me, as I was able to walk the same streets as my ancestors and see this beautiful village they left behind in search of a better life for their families in America.

Mary Gibson, my advisor throughout my doctoral studies, has been a wonderful source of support and encouragement. She eagerly read drafts of my work, giving feedback, suggestions, and advice that have been invaluable. Her work and career have been an inspiration to me and so many other young scholars of Italy. I could not have asked for a better advisor. Marta Petrusewicz, my second advisor, also always provided helpful advice and comments on my drafts, encouraging me to consider various perspectives. Her work on the Italian south, particularly rural people, has been an inspiration from my early days as a doctoral scholar. I would also like to thank the other members of my dissertation committee, whose comments and feedback have also helped shape this project. Herman Bennet, who always pushed me in my thinking and helped me ask the right questions. Jane Schneider, for her wonderful perspective on the lives, customs, and practices of rural southern Italian people. Timothy Alborn, for his feedback and pressing me to think of Italian migration from an outside perspective and in parallel with other groups.

I have been extremely fortunate to be a part of a few writing groups as I have worked on this project. They have gone through many iterations, but I want to sincerely thank: Sultana Banulescu, Davide Colasanto, Francesca Vassale, Antonella Vitale, Kara Peruccio, and Jess Strom. Diana Moore has been with me in each of these groups and has read my work the most—her feedback has been invaluable and has helped me to become a better and clearer writer. Each of you took time to read my chapters and provide insightful and honest comments. Our meetings gave me encouragement and motivation at times when I needed it most. I can't express how deeply appreciative I am.

I want to thank family and friends who have always been so supportive of me and my work. I can't thank my parents enough for all they've given me. Their never-ending love and support have been a rock for me. I also want to thank my husband, who has been by my side as I worked on this project. Thank you for going to the gym for hours a day and giving me quiet time to get work done.

This book is the result of several research trips to Italy, beginning in 2011. Since then, I've returned to Italy numerous times, visiting various archives in Potenza, Matera, Naples, and Rome along the way. I have received a number of generous grants which funded these research trips, including the Philip V. Cannistraro Award, the Dean K. Harrison Fellowship, the Carlo Bellini Dissertation Fellowship, and a scholarship from the National Organization of Italian American Women. Contingent faculty in general does not have enough financial support from their institutions or time off for producing scholarly work, so the above funding has been invaluable to the completion of this project.

I have been working on this project for a number of years and am happy that I can finally publish its final version. The women in this study are close to my heart, and perhaps my sympathy for them comes through in these pages, despite my attempts to be objective. There are many gaps in the available source material on these women, and I often wish we could know more about their lives and thoughts. I hope readers find this book an informative examination into the forgotten stories of the women who remained behind.

Introduction

A WOMAN LEFT BEHIND

Arcangela L.[1] of Potenza was searching for her husband, Francesco L., in America. The couple married in 1871 and prior to his emigrating had three children: Luigi, born in 1872; Maria, born in 1875; and Rocco, born in 1877.[2] Francesco emigrated in the late 1870s (likely 1876), leaving his pregnant wife and young children behind in Italy. Despite his departure, Francesco was required to provide for his wife and family, and Arcangela likely expected he would keep in contact. After two years, Arcangela had not received news or financial support from her husband. Seemingly desperate and with few available options, in 1879, she turned to the mayor. With his assistance, she composed a letter to the prefect of Potenza, which initiated the process of searching for and contacting her husband abroad. She made her first request in January 1879, stating that two years prior her husband "abandoned the family," and she believed he was presently living in Colombia. Five months later in June, the consulate responded, reporting that Arcangela's husband was in fact living in Cartagena, Colombia, and had saved money to send her some assistance. The letter also contained some surprising news about how her husband was living: "he has a small shop of little value and lives with a black woman." Despite the fact that he was living with another woman, the letter informed Arcangela that an agent from the consulate would urge her husband to return to Italy, or at least to send money to "his poor wife" at home in order to comply with his duty as the head of the family.[3]

Apparently, Francesco did not keep his word, and less than one month later, Arcangela approached the mayor's office to compose another letter to the prefect. The mayor included a note in the margin as he forwarded her request, saying, "the miserable Arcangela L. . . . humbly presents herself to your goodness and finds herself in the most squalid misery." The letter again explained that her husband emigrated, "without caring about abandoning his wife and three children." This was the second time Arcangela mentioned the word abandoned, and she clearly placed the full responsibility for her situation on her husband for not providing for his family. She asked for justice from the prefect, urging him to make her husband "send the money necessary to feed his own children." This second letter also implied that she had written before and had made various requests to her husband for money to no avail. Four months later, she received another response, informing her that her husband would send her a power of attorney to collect 500 Lire. Arcangela likely did not believe her husband's promises.[4]

Not even five days later, Arcangela wrote yet another request to the prefect. This time her language became stronger. She wrote that her husband emigrated three years ago "for the cursed America" (*la maledetta America*) and that he "left her with three children in the most desolate misery, without caring to send them any aid to feed his children bread." However, by May of the next year, 1880, the consulate sent word that her husband left Colombia and could not be located.

Arcangela waited another year with no word from her husband, then in June of 1881, made another request for information. The mayor on her behalf helped to express her desperation, writing to the prefect, "your authority will excuse me if even I insist for a new search for her husband, for it is a just and holy cause of a woman who lives like she has and always will with the name of her husband on her lips."[5] This request also implies that Arcangela had received information about the location of her husband, but he still had not sent any remittance to her or her children.

After receiving no response, in October 1881, Arcangela wrote yet another letter, insisting that she and her three children were living in "extreme and deplorable misery" since her husband emigrated to America. This letter provides a closer look at her thoughts and emotions. She wrote:

> Finally two years ago I received news of where he was and I was still ignored by him. In this time I hardly had any money from my husband that I had to earn it myself selling bread. I have been able to continue on with life miserably. But now, feeling cornered and having written at least ten letters without receiving a response, directed towards countries foreign to me, because I do not know for certain his location, I ask you to find the address of my husband and if he is alive to again implore him to support not me, but at least these poor children who demand to be saved, which I cannot do because I earn little each day.[6]

She continued, explaining that through a friend she sent her husband a letter directly, but had not yet received a response, so she again turned to official means. Arcangela asked the prefect for justice and to have pity on her.

Her desperation was becoming clear. At that point, she was not asking for money for herself, nor did she ask for her husband to return; all she asked for was aid to feed her children. She painted the image, whether accurate or not, of living in dire poverty and suffering greatly because of her husband's neglect. Her anger was also expressed in the letters, as she cursed America for taking her husband away and was frustrated by his actions.

Still not giving up, she wrote another letter in March of the following year, "to know as soon as possible if he is dead or alive, and if alive to obligate him to send any aid to his wife, who with her children lives in a state of deplorable misery." Since she did not receive a response, Arcangela wrote again in July 1882, stating that her husband had been gone for six years now "without having sent a cent to his afflicted wife, who has on her shoulders three kids who are dying of starvation." She again asked the consulate to quickly find news of her husband and compel him to send help to his family, "while barbarically he does not think of his own children." In December 1882, she received word that authorities could not locate her husband in Rio de Janeiro, Brazil, where she thought he was, and they would expand the search for him into Venezuela. The last piece of information from this story arrived in an August 1883 note from the Foreign Ministry, stating that Francesco was presently living in a small town in Venezuela.[7]

The file stops here, and it is unclear what became of Arcangela or if she ever saw or received anything from her husband again. Despite abandonment, her letters and perseverance are very telling and help frame a number of arguments for this book. Her husband left for the Americas and did not send any financial assistance to his wife and children, which he legally was required to do as head of the family. The first response reveals that he was living with another woman in Colombia at one point. However, this fact does not seem to have been a primary concern for Arcangela. In this correspondence, there was little evidence that Arcangela loved her husband or wanted him to return. Instead, she wanted him to send what was rightfully hers. She made it appear that the family was living in dire poverty as a result of Francesco not supporting his children. Although Arcangela presented herself as weak and vulnerable in her petitions, she was a woman who took action in an attempt to remedy her situation and survive. She sent many letters through the mayor to the prefect, and it appears that many times they were not even answered, as she was not always certain of her husband's location in South America. The documents demonstrate the desperation and perseverance of one woman, and how she demanded what was rightfully hers. Not only did she work, selling bread to help feed her children, but also she appealed to local authorities numerous times, demonstrating she recognized the law and the power of the state in her life. Arcangela and many of the women discussed in this book found ways to survive on their own, with or without support from their husbands, and the experience changed the position of women in the region of Basilicata during this period of mass emigration.

WOMEN, EMIGRATION, AND BASILICATA

Between 1876 and 1914, a great wave of emigration from Italy occurred, with men, women, and children from all reaches of the Italian Peninsula leaving in search of a better life abroad. Despite the large numbers of individuals departing, migration was male-dominated, and married women tended to remain behind at home. This study examines the implications of emigration on the women left behind, and the great amount of change they experienced during this time of absence, particularly in the southern Italian region of Basilicata. Arcangela's story above is only one of the many presented here demonstrating how emigration affected women and families during this period of mass departure. Although her situation was quite heartbreaking, not all women went through such hardships. In fact, many had positive experiences, receiving money from their husbands abroad and attaining a sense of independence like never before. Yet, Arcangela's story is indicative of the difficulties—social, political, economic, and legal—that the women who remained behind faced and the various ways they adapted their lives in order to survive.

In looking at the role of the women who remained behind in this period, it is clear that their lives transformed immensely. Marriage, motherhood, economic responsibility, and their relationship to the community were just some of the many aspects of their lives that took on new meaning during the age of mass migration. At the time, the women in Basilicata were doubly subjugated: as women and as southerners. They were the inferior sex living in a region often considered backwards, uncivilized, and disconnected from the rest of Italy. However, even though women were legally dependent on and subordinate to men, emigration modified these legal circumstances. When husbands were not physically present, the state substituted in caring for wives and children, and in doing so helped to integrate women as citizens in the newly unified Italy. Small towns with hundreds of migrants became transnational societies, and inhabitants were not disconnected or isolated from the world despite their location in a rural, southern Italian village. Whether receiving remittances or completely abandoned, remaining at home or migrating themselves, emigration challenged women to become more independent, stand up for themselves, and claim their due in the eyes of the state and their communities.

The married women who remained behind in Basilicata when their husbands emigrated are the protagonists of this book. These rural, southern

Italian women were limited by their prescribed subordinate gender role, and married women in particular had very few political and legal rights without their husband's authorization. The Civil Law Code of 1865, the first legal code of the newly unified Italian Peninsula, upheld the strong tradition of patriarchy and placed a number of limitations on women. Once married, a couple was bound together until death, and a wife depended on her husband's financial support and legal position as head of the household. There was no option for legal divorce in Italy and would not be until the 1970s. These limitations became problematic for many women whose husbands emigrated and subsequently disappeared. Abandoned women could neither remarry nor gain the rights of a widow until they received definitive proof of their husband's death. Yet, when married women were left on their own, they in practice became heads of households and took on many of the day-to-day responsibilities that men normally performed. In some instances, the situation offered married women completely new opportunities and the ability to carve out expanded social, economic, and even political roles in Italy. Despite an increased practical role, women with husbands abroad still relied upon their distant spouses to provide for the family, especially if they had children. Husbands, however, did not always comply with their duty, and sometimes neglected the wives they left behind. In some of those instances, married women appealed to the state to compel their husbands to fulfill their legal duties.

The women who remained behind are often referred to as "widows in white," or *vedove bianche*, because their husbands emigrated and were living abroad, so it was as if they were widowed. Their husbands were alive, however, so they did not wear the traditional black of mourning. Many of the women were young, newly married, or had young children. Historian Linda Reeder has examined the role of Sicilian women in such circumstances and has shown that migration positively affected the women who remained behind, empowering them to seek education and to become more involved in family finances.[8] Yet, these women were not in the same circumstances as widows, who had fewer legal restrictions. The women who remained behind often were in contact with their husbands, whether through friends, letters, or official means, and many men would eventually return. Women also typically had their natal families nearby, so their parents, siblings, and extended family might offer support if their husbands emigrated. Emigration positioned women in a number of new circumstances, unique to each family, resulting in various degrees of hardship. Nonetheless, despite this adversity, the women of Basilicata demonstrated their strength of will and the ability to overcome obstacles and limitations.

Emigration can be used as a lens to study gender and the role of women in relation to their families, the state, the economy, and their communities during this time of change. There were deep ramifications of emigration in Basilicata, and the phenomenon sheds light on events that were occurring within the region itself, and on the experiences of women in similar circumstances all throughout Italy. Examining women, especially those from rural southern Italy who are so often forgotten or neglected in the historical record, significantly contributes to our understanding of the new Italian state and how emigration impacted women's roles in society.

Italy in the Liberal Period

The Italian Peninsula had been divided since the fall of the Roman Empire in the fifth century, and in the subsequent centuries, it split into various kingdoms. Throughout the Middle Ages and the Early Modern Period, including the Renaissance, Italy was divided into small city-states, at times dominated by larger, outside kingdoms. By the mid-nineteenth century, nationalism became an influential force throughout Europe, and those who dreamed of a united Italian state worked toward that goal during the period known as the Risorgimento. Unification was mostly achieved by 1861, and completed with the inclusion of the Veneto in 1866 and finally Rome in 1870.

Governing a peninsula as heterogeneous as Italy posed a challenge to the liberal and nationalistic ideologies that fueled the Risorgimento. Piedmont, a kingdom in northern Italy, led the unification movement and thus the formation of the new state. Piedmontese law would influence the Italian legal code and the Piedmontese royal family would rule the Kingdom of Italy. While plebiscites were held to officially unify the nation, relatively few Italians had political power after unification was complete, as only a small number of wealthy male property owners could vote. Historian Jonathan Dunnage argues that the electorate at the time included only 2% of the male population and thus had little understanding of the people they worked to unify.[9] As further indication of fragmentation, less than 10% of the population could communicate using standard Italian in 1861—most spoke local or regional dialects and few could read the language.[10] Governing a socially, culturally, and linguistically diverse nation would be a great challenge for the new state. Not coincidentally, emigration rates increased in the subsequent decades.

Unification led to the creation of a single Italian state, yet also exposed a number of regional divisions, especially between north and south, creating what came to be known as the "Southern Question." Since the mid-nineteenth century, writers, thinkers, travelers, and politicians viewed the south as backwards, lagging behind a more industrialized and modernized north. These stereotypes began to take shape in the mid-nineteenth century and visitors to the region—social scientists, historians, and even southerners themselves—perpetuated them. The question became more acute after national unification. As industrial expansion in the north increased in the 1880s with seemingly little development in the south, the failures of national integration became more apparent. These observers equated the north with modernity and progress, and the south with backwardness. Politicians and travelers from the north described the south as a homogeneous, uncivilized entity, characterized by brigandage, outdated attitudes, and crime (although unlike other regions Basilicata did not have a mafia presence). Outsiders believed that liberal ideas would "civilize" and "modernize" and thus improve the south after unification. Yet after twenty years, southerners had not yet been fully incorporated into the new Italian state. Some in the north became interested in finding the root of the perceived disparity, and these discussions intensified debate about the Southern Question.[11] Many stereotypes about the south persist today, despite the work of scholars over the past three decades to attempt to move away from blanket statements or labels like backwards or modern, and portray a more nuanced image of the south.[12]

Economic policies caused a majority of the difficulties after unification. Austerity measures and heavy taxation made the rule of the early government unpopular, especially in the south.[13] High tariffs hurt the largely agricultural economy, and generally favored the more industrialized north, specifically the northwest.[14] The agrarian crisis of the 1880s resulted from increased competition in wheat markets and tariff wars. By this period, steamships transported goods, which led to low prices and more competition, especially from U.S. grown wheat, hurting southern grain growers. As a result of these government policies, many inhabitants of the south began to view the newly formed government in Rome with hostility: a far-off entity more concerned with the economic success of the north than the well-being of southerners. To be fair, the government did not completely ignore the south and did invest in development. Yet, as historian Salvatore di Maria has recently argued, the money was not enough, as the problems in the south required much greater investment.[15]

Local loyalties, historical divisions, economic difficulties, and, in some areas, resistance to government rule—all interwoven issues—were early challenges for the new Italian state. Ironically, during the period of building up a new nation, millions emigrated. At the same time, migration helped the process of uniting people from all regions of the peninsula, as outsiders overlooked local and regional identities and saw immigrants from all regions as Italians.

Emigration

Migration was not a new phenomenon in Italy in the decades following unification, and, in fact, local labor migrations within Italy had occurred for centuries. In the eighteenth and early nineteenth centuries in particular, Italian migration was largely internal and seasonal.[16] Yet by the late nineteenth century, emigration to much farther destinations became a feasible option. The growing network of railroads throughout Italy and the rest of Europe over the course of the century made for quicker and easier movement. Steamboats reduced the length of the transatlantic journey to two weeks and tickets were cheaper than ever before. These two advances alone allowed people looking for opportunities outside their village a chance to travel to places farther than they could have imagined. Workers employed many of the same local labor practices and migration strategies when emigrating to locations outside of Italy, including the fact that women participated in the migration process, yet generally remained at home.[17]

During the great wave of Italian migration that occurred between 1880 and 1914, approximately 80% of emigrants were males.[18] As they emigrated to search for opportunity abroad, many husbands left wives and children behind in Italy. Although a number of Italians left permanently, emigration was also seasonal or temporary. Husbands often left home with the intention of sending back money in the form of remittances, and then perhaps returning after making money abroad. Because of the relative ease of travel, many migrants even made multiple journeys back and forth between Italy and the Americas. These migrants were referred to as "birds of passage." The high percentage of returns was a unique aspect of Italian migration, and some estimate the return rate to be around 50%, if not more.[19] Italian migration differed from that of many other groups during the same period, particularly the Jews, Eastern Europeans, or Irish, whose migration tended to be one way and permanent.

Of course, not only men left. Women and children also emigrated, but at a much lower rate. It was extremely rare for women to emigrate on their own, without a male relative accompanying them or having sent for them. Women were more likely to emigrate with their husbands or family, or as widows with adult children. Statistics from 1905 show that 80% of all male emigrants left alone, while 20% left with family, and the regions with the most family groups leaving to settle abroad were Basilicata, Campania, Puglia, and Sicily, all regions in the south.[20] When whole families emigrated, migration was more likely to be permanent, rather than seasonal.

The Italian government began keeping official statistics on emigration in 1876. In that year, 108,771 people left Italy (19,848 transoceanic and 88,923 to Europe). Those figures increased by 1905, when 726,331 emigrants left (447,083 transoceanic and 279,248 to Europe).[21] In that period of just thirty years, the Americas surpassed Europe as the primary destination for migrants. The numbers continued to increase until World War I, and the *Annuario Statistico* reported that in 1912 there were 5.5 million Italians abroad, mostly living in North and South America. Initially, the Italian government saw emigrants as criminals, adventurers, and individuals attempting to avoid compulsory military service. However, as the years passed and the number of emigrants continued to grow, the state could no longer ignore the phenomenon, and took on a much greater legal and social role in emigration, including enacting two major pieces of legislation in 1888 and 1901.

Basilicata had one of the highest rates of emigration. In fact, it was the only region in Italy with a net population loss between 1881 and 1911, amounting to a 10% decline (from 524,504 to 490,705). Large-scale emigration led to widespread fears that towns would depopulate and that no able-bodied workers would be left to cultivate the fields.[22] Some officials were concerned about the large number of women on their own in the village, fearing they may turn to criminal activity or dishonorable behavior. Some emigrants abandoned their families and their hometowns, never to return, leading to concerns over the survival of some villages with such severe population loss. Yet, many emigrants came back bringing money, new customs and ideas, and a changed outlook on life. They returned to make their lives at home better or called for their wives and children to join them to start a new life abroad. Thus, many of the fears surrounding large-scale emigration from the region were unfounded exaggerations.

While migration was a widespread phenomenon in this period, national histories generally do not extensively cover its impact. Historians of Liberal Italy often mention emigration in passing, with little analysis of its social, political, economic, or cultural effects on the new nation or the Liberal government.[23] Some notable scholars of the past decade have argued that migration history should be more integrated into the narrative of Italian history. Although migration was not always part of the national debate, the phenomenon could not be ignored locally, especially among regions with heavy emigration.[24] According to historian Mark Choate, emigration would be one of the most important challenges facing the new Italian nation.[25] The chapters that follow demonstrate that emigration challenged not only the state but also the women living in Basilicata.

Basilicata: *"Una Provincia Sconosciuta"* (An Unknown Province)

Basilicata is a region in southern Italy located on the arch of the Italian boot, nestled between Campania to the west and Puglia to the east.[26] The region was briefly renamed Lucania during the Fascist regime, a harkening back to the area's ancient name, and the residents are still referred to as Lucanians. Few historical studies exist about Basilicata, especially regarding emigration, and information about the region is often tainted by stereotypes related to the Southern Question. The southern part of the Apennine Mountains falls in Basilicata, making much of the land mountainous and hilly, and many of the towns were established and are still located on the tops of mountains or steep hills. While picturesque, some villages could only be accessed on winding dirt roads, making communication and the exchange of good and ideas difficult. Many areas were also prone to earthquakes, landslides, and other natural disasters. These factors contributed to some observers labeling the region "a south within the south," assigning it a double stigma of backwardness or isolation.[27] Basilicata was not a stop on the traditional Grand Tour, made by wealthy northern Europeans as both an educational experience and a journey of leisure, and most travelers or outsiders did not enter the region, mainly because of difficulty traveling through the mountainous landscape. Outsiders who did travel to Basilicata in the eighteenth and nineteenth centuries were mostly anthropologists or others interested in studying local people and customs.

Perhaps the region is best known as the setting of Carlo Levi's book *Christ Stopped at Eboli*. Written in the mid-1930s and published after World War II, Levi's work was not meant as a historical account of the region, but as a memoir of his time as a political prisoner during the Fascist period, when the region was used as a place of confinement, or *confino*, for individuals considered threats to or enemies of the Fascist state. Levi provides insight into the lives and thoughts of the people living in the region, which were deeply impacted by emigration. In the 1930s, he described Basilicata as a place "denied by history and by the State."[28] He portrays the region as cut off from Rome, but he also stresses that the state did not understand the people inhabiting the region.

This isolated region in the periphery was the most sparsely populated in Italy, with only 524,504 inhabitants in 1881. By 1894, the population increased to only 545,021.[29] For comparison, the region with the next lowest population in the same year was Umbria with 602,634, and the region with the highest was Lombardy with 4,007,561.[30] The inhabitants were also scattered throughout the region and not concentrated in one main area, with many villages having only a few thousand residents. There is no major city in the region; Naples (in the Campania region) is the closest to the west and Bari (in the Puglia region) to the east. Potenza, the capital of Basilicata, never had a large population, and only had 20,343 inhabitants in 1881, a number which fell to 16,163 by 1901.[31] At the turn of the century, the towns of Matera, Avigliano, and Rionero in Vulture all had more residents than Potenza.[32] The population of the region as a whole also fell during the same period, as indicated above. Even today, Basilicata has no major airport, rail lines are sparse at best, and the people remain scattered among small hilltop towns.

Despite much unfamiliarity with the region, even today, Basilicata has a rich history. Greek colonies, part of Magna Graecia, were established by the seventh century BCE on the southern coast along the Gulf of Taranto, off the Ionian Sea, most notably at Metapontum (Metaponto). Artifacts from the region, especially Greek pottery, show the ancient Lucanians were part of an intricate network of trade and communication within the Mediterranean. When the Romans expanded and gained control of the region by the third century BCE, they called it Lucania and established various colonies, most notably Potentia (Potenza), Grumentum (Grumento Nova), and Venusia (Venosa, birthplace of the famous Roman poet Horace). The Romans also built the well-known Appian Way from Rome through the region to Brindisi on the southern tip of Puglia.

By the fall of Rome in the fifth century CE, the area, like much of the former Empire, was largely Christianized. Throughout the Middle Ages, Basilicata was the least populated area of Italy.[33] Byzantine culture dominated until the Normans invaded in the eleventh century and introduced feudalism. Little is known about the region in the early modern period, but in the eighteenth century, it became part of the Kingdom of Naples, ruled by the Bourbon monarchy. In 1799, a number of towns in the area of Potenza were the center of resistance to the Bourbons, as inhabitants of various villages fought for republicanism and against the forces of the Sanfedisti and Cardinal Fabrizio Ruffo. The Sanfedisti were a group organized by Cardinal Ruffo who supported the Bourbon monarchy and organized a popular revolt to overthrow the Parthenopean Republic, established by the French in 1799. While the resistance was eventually put down, local folklore still recognizes their heroic efforts. In 1806, Napoleonic forces defeated the Kingdom of Naples and ruled until 1815, after which the Kingdom of the Two Sicilies, including Sicily and much of southern Italy, was created.

After the Risorgimento and the push for Italian unification, Basilicata joined the Kingdom of Italy, but the transition was not smooth. Brigandage (banditry) was widespread in the years following unification, particularly 1861 to 1868. Brigands from the region, including the (in)famous Carmine Crocco,[34] took action against what they felt were injustices of the nobility, as well as the new state, against the poor peasantry by destroying property, wreaking havoc, and causing what many observers label as a civil war in the south.[35] The Italian government considered brigands criminals who represented a direct threat to state authority and sent in the military in an attempt to put them down. Many Lucanians seemed sympathetic toward the brigands, praising them as defenders of local interests.

Writers from the south, especially Basilicata, tend to look more favorably on the brigands, viewing them as a product of their circumstances and acting out of necessity. The future Prime Minister Francesco Saverio Nitti, from Basilicata himself, wrote that brigandage resulted more from economic troubles than a political statement.[36] Nitti took a particular interest in the Southern Question, especially as it concerned Basilicata. Born in Melfi in 1868, he became a member of Parliament in 1904 and Prime Minister in 1919. During his time in Parliament, he dedicated much of his energy to apprising the government of conditions in the south and working to find ways to improve them. A contemporary historian of Basilicata, Monica Maggio, similarly argues that brigandage needs to be understood within a certain context and writes that "it was the logical consequence of a particular socio-political moment," largely shaped by the economic conditions in the region in the post-unification period.[37] Yet as scholars have noted, many observers both past and present, view widespread brigandage as proof of an uncivilized and backward society.[38]

Perceptions of Basilicata

Social scientists and anthropologists studying Basilicata in the twentieth century offered valuable firsthand information on their experiences examining economics and family structure in the region, but their observations largely fed into stereotypes of the south. Despite being written half a century after the time frame of this study, many of their observations still resonate. In the 1950s, political scientist Edward Banfield, who wrote about a two-year stay in an unidentified town, which he called Montegrano, postulated that poverty and backwardness persisted because people were so devoted to the good of their nuclear family, which led to the "inability of the villagers to act together for their common good."[39] This "amoral familism" as he called it, impeded their economic and other progress. Likewise, anthropologist John Davis spent time in the town of Pisticci in the 1960s. He stressed the importance of kin and family to its inhabitants, as well as the crucial role of honor in society, especially as it concerned women.[40] Overall, Davis portrayed the region as a grim and gloomy place, isolated, with customs that persisted from centuries past.

In another anthropological study of the region, Ann Cornelisen visited Basilicata in the 1970s and became one of the first scholars to consider gender in her observations. She lived among the women of the region, conversed with them, and got to know them, giving readers insight into their lives, problems, and thoughts. As she recounts, most of the men emigrated to the north or to other European countries for better-paid work, while the women were left to maintain the household. Cornelisen described Basilicata as a bleak region:

> bare and mountainous, with villages, some very large, perched precariously on high slopes or even cloudy little pinnacles, where, generations ago, it was

decided they could best defend themselves from the invaders and malaria of the valleys below . . . machinery is of little use and would only turn up more rocks than clay. Long since the topsoil has been washed out to sea by torrential rains, and that people still persist says much for the secret powers of optimism and more for the determination to live.[41]

Cornelisen showed that women of Basilicata lived difficult lives, and for many Lucanians, there was little hope of improvement or change. Yet, emigration, even in the 1970s, was still a way to improve their situation. Cornelisen wrote about one woman who finally decided to move to the north in search of work, who later told her "only the fools stay down there!"[42] As witnessed by the above accounts, many of the characteristics of the region highlighted in this book were still present decades later.

Life in Basilicata

It is a difficult task to recreate daily life in a region where few second-ary sources exist and firsthand accounts are scattered, usually written by outsiders, and largely biased. Parsing through the anthropological studies mentioned above can help depict life in the region. However, there are few historical accounts which focus specifically on Basilicata. Furthermore, archival sources rarely give agency to the common people. Women are even harder to locate in any of these sources. Despite these limitations, this study uses an array of sources to piece together aspects of life in the region.

In the nineteenth century, most of the inhabitants of Basilicata worked the land and were laborers dependent on daily wages. The most impor-tant crops were grains, fruits, and olives, and raising and herding cattle and sheep were also common. The olive oils, wines, cheeses, and wools produced were the main exports of the region. Most people were renters, and rents were paid largely in grain. Crop production often suffered due to the lack of agricultural technology, and the population lived at a level of subsistence that was difficult to break free of before large-scale emigration.

Because Basilicata was largely agricultural, the regional diet consisted of local products. Meat, a standard of class and wealth, was reserved for spe-cial occasions. François Lenormant, a French traveler in the region during the 1880s, described the general diet of the people he encountered as scarce and not very substantial. He noticed much of their diet consisted of cheese, chestnuts, legumes such as peas and beans, and fresh fruits and vegetables, such as cabbage and tomatoes. Lucanians ate little meat, but he noted, "the lack of meat is to some extent offset by a good dose of wine."[43] William Nelthorpe Beauclerk, a British aristocrat surveying the region also in the

1880s, observed that "bread, oil, and vegetables form the staple commodities of their diet, and wine is not wanting."[44]

Health reports submitted by the prefect in Potenza to the Ministry of the Interior (*Ministero dell'Interno*) in 1899 demonstrate a great deal about the social and health conditions of the region. Some of the most alarming health statistics cited in the reports were in regard to clean drinking water. A sampling of eighteen random towns from the health reports reveals that half lacked a source of fresh, running water in 1899, and of those only two had just received it in the past decade.[45] Conditions were slow to improve. In 1908, the town of Albano di Lucania still did not have a source of freshwater. Residents walked three kilometers for clean water, and carrying it back was difficult, usually requiring the help of a mule cart.[46] Even Carlo Levi, who lived in the region almost forty years after the health reports were compiled, spoke of how long it took for towns to gain access to freshwater. In Gagliano (Aliano), he described, "a small spring, which until a few years ago was the only resource in the countryside."[47] Thus, while the people of the region may have had a subsistence diet based on local products, many inhabitants lacked access to freshwater, which indubitably led to health issues.

Malaria was a major concern throughout Italy in the nineteenth and early twentieth centuries. In 1900, over 15,000 people died of the disease and thousands more were afflicted by it.[48] The Italian government devoted increased attention to eradicating malaria in the early 1900s, advocating health precautions and pushing for the distribution of quinine, a known remedy. Health surveyors in Basilicata reported that malaria was rare in most towns, but present in the countryside, and when the disease did occur, it tended to be in specific locations or at a specific time of year, particularly during the summer months.

When people did get sick, many towns had few resources to assist the ill. Health reports show the number of doctors and surgeons practicing in each town were few, if any existed at all. For example, the town of Picerno had a population of 4,401 in 1899, but only three doctors and two midwives. A town of similar size, Vietri di Potenza, had no doctors and no midwives. Spinoso, a town of 2,656, reported having no doctors and *una vecchia* (an old woman) as a midwife. Potenza, with a population of just over 16,000, only had twelve doctors and four midwives. The health reports also indicated that few towns had a dentist, and most only had one or two pharmacies.[49] These numbers show the decrepit state of healthcare in the region and give insight into why death and infant mortality rates were so high.

Other environmental factors, such as earthquakes and landslides, influenced the lives of the region's inhabitants. A number of recent studies have examined the effects of the environment on Italian history, showing how inhabitants were forced to contend with nature.[50] People of Basilicata experienced a number of environmental realities that shaped their history and even contributed to wide-scale emigration. Over the years, earthquakes and their aftermath have taken thousands of lives and have had disastrous effects on some towns. A major earthquake occurred in 1857, which destroyed a great deal of property and resulted in over 10,000 deaths in Basilicata and in neighboring Calabria. Many villages had to be completely rebuilt as a result, a process which was slow at best. Often, towns and buildings were left in ruins for decades because the inhabitants could not afford to rebuild.

Landslides were another common phenomenon in the area, partially due to earthquakes. Prime Minister Giuseppe Zanardelli made a special visit to the region in 1902, discussed below, and while there he noted that of the 124 municipalities in Basilicata, over half were prone to landslides.[51] These disasters also caused widespread loss of life and destruction to houses and buildings. In 1888, a landslide crushed a crowded train traveling from Naples to Potenza, killing nineteen people and injuring fifty-five.[52] Landslides also threatened the region's many hilltop towns. In 1901, an "immense rock" swept away part of the town of Acerenza, outside of Potenza, killing at least fifteen people.[53] In 1907, the people of Montemurro were "feeling in a panic" as a landslide threatened to wipe away a large section of the village.[54] According to reports "the roar of the avalanches was heard for a considerable distance." The whole town was devastated, leaving as many as 5,000 inhabitants without homes.[55] The town of Craco is one of the most striking examples of the effects of landslides. Largely built on top of a steep hill, the town was abandoned completely in 1963 because of earthquakes and the constant danger of landslides. Today, deserted streets and crumbling buildings serve as a reminder of the potential damage nature could cause. Threats of natural disaster were a constant cause of fear for the thousands of Lucanians who lived in the small hilltop towns.

Many villages were isolated and remote, especially because roads, if they even existed, were in deplorable condition. Highways began to be constructed by the eighteenth century, making parts of the region more accessible and connecting them with neighboring areas.[56] After traveling through Basilicata in 1902, Prime Minister Zanardelli noted that many villages still lacked roads on which mules could travel. Others were impassible during rain and storms, thus entirely cutting off some towns during inclement weather. According to a report to Parliament in 1902, thirteen villages were completely isolated and required the construction of roads in order to connect them to the main network.[57]

The lack of railroads also contributed to the region's remoteness. Until the 1880s, Basilicata was largely disconnected from the rail network of the rest of Italy. Between 1880 and 1900, over 1,250 miles of railroad were constructed in region, making it more accessible for travel and facilitating emigration.[58] Yet, the rail system did not (nor does it today) connect all parts of the region. Because of the mountainous terrain, building rail lines to certain towns and villages was difficult, leaving them inaccessible and isolated. The two main provincial capitals, Potenza and Matera, are not even connected by rail today.

Much of Carlo Levi's writing focuses on the fact that the people were insular and the region was out of touch with the rest of Italy. He wrote that "the peasant lives in misery and in the distance, his immobile civilization on barren soil, in the presence of death."[59] He also wrote of the disconnect between the people of Basilicata and the government in Rome: "for the peasants, the state is farther away than the sky."[60] Although Levi's trip to the region occurred in the 1930s, many of his comments portray the feeling of isolation in the region during the years of large-scale emigration decades before his arrival. Levi's words also give a sense of how people outside the region viewed it—as dark, unknown, and desolate. This study counters that narrative and argues there were indeed connections with the outside world, despite physical limitations. Levi even observed some of them when he discussed emigration and the connection many of the villagers had to America.

While descriptions of the harsh realities of the region abound from the few outsider accounts, some travelers or visitors found beauty in Basilicata. Crawford Tate Ramage, a Scottish traveler visiting the region in the 1820s, reflected on the countryside and observed a vista of a volcano which he described as more beautiful than that of Vesuvius.[61] Carl Wilhelm Schnars, a German traveler who visited the region a few decades later, made a similar observation about the beauty of the countryside, writing "landscape painters, several of whom one meets in Sorrento and Capri or those who are eternally painting Vesuvius, the Blue Grotto, and the house of Tasso, never came to this area that offers rich material for beautiful landscape paintings."[62] Another English traveler, Arthur John Strutt, compared the countryside and mountain vistas to the Italian north, saying "the scenery is not very different from that part of the Apennines that we both like, between Bologna and Florence: the same barren hills, the same valleys, and the same solitary aspect."[63]

Observers also commented about the inhabitants they encountered in their travels through Basilicata and expressed sympathy toward them. Schnars described the residents of Avigliano as "extremely kind and generous."[64] Maxime du Camp, a French writer, lamented on the condition of the people in Castelluccio and the desire by the ruling class to keep the masses ignorant. He observed that few children go to school, and education was looked down upon as if one was betraying the *paese*.[65] Traveling in the 1880s, François Lenormant wrote that the peasants work hard all day long for a low salary with little hope of ever being able to save enough money to better their lives or condition.[66] While these descriptions seem Orientalist and condescending in nature, they likely portray a semblance of the true conditions of the region.

In a survey of rural Italy published in 1888, the British traveler Beauclerk painted a picture of society in Basilicata. He noted the houses were poor and unsanitary, and children slept in the same beds as their parents. Yet, while surveying the regions of both Basilicata and Calabria, he noted "the peasants are less miserable than in the North of Italy, they are genial and kindly in disposition."[67] Nitti also recognized the difficulties that existed in the region, but wrote to his peers that "he who has not seen up close the condition of laborers of the provinces of southern Italy does not have an exact idea of the great poverty that forces them to leave their village."[68] In 1924, Nitti helped establish a magazine *La Basilicata nel Mondo*, which was an attempt to improve the image of the region and provide a more sympathetic view of it for outsiders.

The government focused its attention on Basilicata when Prime Minister Giuseppe Zanardelli visited and toured the region in 1902. Zanardelli, originally from Brescia, in the Lombardy region, and seventy-six years old at the time of his trip, was already an accomplished politician. He served as prime minister as part of the Historic Left from February 1901 to November 1903. This visit was the first time a prime minister not only brought attention to the region but also visited it personally. Before his trip, the south was relatively ignored by Rome, and the government did relatively little to address the region's various problems. Notable exceptions were Pasquale Villari, a politician who wrote about the realities of life in the south, and Leopoldo Franchetti and Sidney Sonnino, politicians who traveled to the south in the 1870s to perform an unofficial survey of the region. Reports of the horrible conditions and the large impact of emigration inspired these visits. The national government could no longer ignore the various problems and difficulties facing the region.

Zanardelli left Rome to tour Basilicata, along with reporters, deputies, and invited guests, in September 1902.[69] He traveled through the region in a horse-drawn carriage, and, where necessary, by mule, sometimes the only way to access the most isolated locations. During his visit to individual towns, the prime minister spoke to local inhabitants and took notes. Upon his arrival in each village, the people greeted him warmly, notably with a "rain of applause, with which the people of Lucania celebrate their champion."[70] Yet, despite having researched and read about the region prior to his visit, Zanardelli was surprised by the poor conditions he encountered and after his return to Rome pushed for legislation to improve them.[71] The Special Law for Basilicata, passed in 1904, would provide funds to assist and build up the region.

Basilicata has been one of the forgotten regions of Italy, both historically and historiographically. Because of its small population and lack of fertile land, the region tends to remain in the backdrop, both in histories of Italy as a whole and in regional histories. On the surface, based on the views of outsiders, Basilicata fit into the negative image of the south. Brigandage and other realities, such as difficult connectivity, poor agricultural output, landslides and lack of freshwater or healthcare, made life volatile, and for some, dangerous. The firsthand accounts of scholars, social scientists, and travelers, as well as official statistics, reflected a grim and often condescending indication of what life was like for ordinary people in the region. However, many of the difficulties that plagued the region were not the fault of the population, but a combination of unlucky natural circumstances, lack of concern by the local aristocracy, and little government attention or investment. Zanardelli's visit was an attempt to assist the region and provide funding for development, but many Lucanians still felt that emigrating was their best hope for survival. The fact that thousands of people decided to emigrate demonstrates that the people of Basilicata yearned to improve their lives.

Historiography

Migration from Basilicata was an important aspect of its history, and deeply impacted the lives of its inhabitants. Despite a recent plethora of migration studies, even some with a regional focus, little has been written about it from Basilicata. Perhaps this is because compared to other regions, the overall number of emigrants was rather small. Yet, the scope of emigration from the region was so great that the phenomenon and its consequences merit examination. The migrant experience, especially for the women of the region, helps us gain a more nuanced perspective of migration as a whole from Italy during this period.

Studies on migration in general have long focused on the migrants themselves and the impact they had on the place of arrival. More recently, rather than separately looking at migration in terms of the place left behind and the destination, scholars have begun to bridge this gap and apply a transnational approach to migration studies. These works recognize that migration was not simply linear and consider seasonal migrants, birds of passage, and the ideas that transcend national boundaries. Differing in methodology from previous studies, this new approach considers culture, place of origin, and connections and continuities among emigrating peoples.[72]

Transnational history examines events beyond the borders of the traditional nation-state. The term implies the circulation, interaction, and exchange of people, ideas, items, money, and institutions. Many historians argue that transnationalism is not a new approach, but a new set of questions applied to the same areas of study. Its usefulness lies in the fact that it reconceptualizes historical events in a new way, not just in terms of the nation-state but also in broader historical perspective. This approach is particularly valuable when considering the women who remained behind.

Scholars in many areas of Italian history have begun to apply a transnational lens to their work. Some of the most common trends involve reconceptualizing the Risorgimento, the fascist period, and the mafia using a transnational frame.[73] In employing transnationalism, scholars have shown broader historical implications for seemingly "national" events, and that global influences can affect local attitudes and actions. Migration history is inherently transnational, as the people involved in emigration existed in two worlds. Italian migration was especially so due to the back-and-forth nature of movement. Those who remained behind were influenced by ideas and people from abroad, gained increased access to money, and lived in a society where people had traveled all over the world, even if seemingly isolated in a small village. They had family abroad, sometimes in multiple locations, heard returning migrants speak in foreign languages, and communicated across borders through letters and other messages. Their world was increasingly transnational, and their actions when left behind reflect a changing society. The women who remained behind in Basilicata were part of a larger network of Italian migration and must be viewed through a transnational lens. The people who took part in emigration were not closed off from the rest of the world. Even though many women were immobile, global connections were present in their lives and influenced their thoughts and actions.

Historians of Italy have been slow to integrate migration into the national history, but this study argues that emigration cannot be disconnected from it. Until the 1970s, emigration from Italy was still ongoing, so many scholars did not incorporate the phenomenon into national histories. In the past thirty years, as the flux of immigrants to Italy has increased and Italians have begun to reflect on their emigrant past, migration studies has become a flourishing field. Now, scholars place more focus on emigration, its impact, and the experience of migrants, as well as the recognition that migration was not new and is an integral and ongoing part of Italian history.[74] Many aspects of emigration deal directly with the nation, nation building, the economy, laws, civics, and government agencies. So while there are benefits of taking the borders of the nation-state out of migration studies and simply using a transnational focus to understand social dynamics, one cannot ignore the crucial role of the Italian state in this narrative.

Sources and Methodology

Constructing a narrative about the region and its inhabitants in the era of mass migration has required the piecing together of an array of primary and secondary sources. It is not uncommon to find gaps in archival material, complete lack of archival material, or archivists in the Central Archives of Rome asking why one would study Basilicata. Additionally, because this study focuses on rural, illiterate, and married women who were left behind, sources directly from them are rare. Most emigrants, male or female, did not leave behind written records. They relied on word of mouth, and consequently the thoughts and actions of most migrants have been lost. Various types of records and documents have helped bring to light these seemingly invisible women, revealing what they were saying, doing, and thinking when their husbands were absent.

Archival sources, particularly requests women sent through their local mayors' offices, were some of the most valuable sources consulted for this study. Requests were of two kinds: passport applications and petitions to find relatives abroad. Both required that women go to the mayor and send a petition to the prefect. The sources, although not written by the women themselves, do contain their voices. With the assistance of the mayor, their desires, emotions, fears, and requests come to light, and some reveal the circumstances in which women were living. In other words, these various petitions give women a voice and offer a unique glance into their world, one that is difficult to find in official statistics, and show some of the emotions that accompanied emigration. The personal stories that come through in these documents reflect the realities faced by many women in similar circumstances. Although each family may have experienced emigration differently, both positively and negatively, these exchanges are some of the most direct extant sources from women of the period.

Court records from the *Corte d'Assise* (Court of Assizes or High Court) are another major archival source consulted for this study, especially cases involving women and the crimes they committed while their husbands were away. These case files include witness accounts with testimonies given by women and show what life was like in towns where men emigrated and women were left behind. Various cases give a glimpse into how the community functioned and how close neighbors were and provide information about town networks of gossip and commentary. Neighbors knew who had emigrated and what was going on in the lives of their fellow villagers. Case testimonies demonstrate what was important to the local inhabitants: family, children, honor, economy, and community.

Other primary sources used in this study include government bulletins, statistics, and national and local newspapers, as well as local correspondence, and reports specific to Basilicata. As the reading public overall in Italy was largely urban, until the late nineteenth century, the region was not a center for journalism or newspapers. Some of the first newspapers published in the region were political, mainly in the years after unification. At the turn of the century, as literacy rates were slowly rising, journalism began to diversify and papers began to reflect the various interests and political opinions of the population. Additional sources, such as passport applications, ship manifests, and government statistics, provide concrete and reliable information and allow a glimpse into the emigrant experience. Despite neither telling personal stories nor shedding light on the emigrants' feelings or intentions, these sources offer insight into general trends and practices. Few contemporary sources document women's lives when on their own, and even fewer recognize their contributions to society and the economy. For example, in the countless newspaper reports on emigration, few discuss the major impact the phenomenon had on women, save a line or two about how they suffered in the absence of their husbands.

Due to the nature of the sources, many of the stories presented here focus on abandonment, poverty, and despair, but such cases might not have been the most common. Those in dire circumstances were more likely to petition for help, and thus their voices exist in the historical record. Wives who received remittances and whose husbands returned were more numerous than those whose husbands abandoned them. Yet, the stories discussed here highlight the array of scenarios that resulted from emigration. While each story is unique, each contributes to our larger understanding of how women experienced migration. Their circumstances and actions can be used to highlight the overall role of women in the region, even if they did not emigrate. Their stories can also add to a larger narrative about the changes Italian women experienced in the Liberal Period.

One final note on periodization—this study covers the time frame between 1876 and 1914, during the great wave of Italian emigration. Migration picked up beginning about a decade after unification, and in 1876, the Italian government first began keeping statistics on the growing phenomenon. The study ends at the start of World War I due to the fact that the war disrupted transatlantic migration, although travel did not completely cease during the war. (Italy did not enter the war until 1915) Furthermore, the character of migration changed in the post–World War I period with the rise of Fascism in Italy combined with severe restrictions on immigration in the United States. Large-scale Italian emigration did not pick up again until after World War II, but that phenomenon falls outside of the scope of this study.

Each chapter of this study begins with a story demonstrating how migration affected specific women, and then covers a different aspect of life for the women who remained behind. Chapter 1 begins by offering context on the role of women in Italy during the Liberal Period. The chapter specifically looks at marriage and how mass emigration impacted and transformed the institution. Requests for information about their husbands reveal the emotional impact of emigration and how women perceived their marriages. The chapter also discusses abandoned women and how they dealt with the loss of their husbands, despite continued legal restrictions. The second chapter focuses on motherhood and migration, and how emigration and absence transformed a

woman's primary role as a mother. Women were often left to raise a number
of young children on their own and were responsible for their education and
well-being. In this period, women also coped with emigrating children, both
young kids traveling with their fathers, or even older ones migrating on their
own. Some families even signed contracts allowing for their young children
to emigrate with *padroni* to earn money on the streets of major international
cities. The era of mass emigration changed the relationship between mothers
and their children, and introduced a type of transnational motherhood.

Chapter 3 focuses on the economic changes both the region and the
inhabitants experienced as a result of large-scale emigration. While women
already generally practiced some economic responsibility and managed
household finances, emigration gave them an even greater role. Many of the
women who remained behind received remittances which enabled them to
become independent consumers. The chapter examines how women spent
the money they received, whether to buy necessities, pay for a daughter's
dowry, buy tickets to emigrate, or pay off their husband's debts, and demonstrates that emigration allowed women an increased economic role outside
of the private sphere. Chapter 4 examines the relationship between women
and the Italian state. Since national unification in 1861, contemporaries
and historians have argued that the state apparatus in Italy forgot about the
southern regions and was primarily concerned with the more industrialized
north. This chapter counters that narrative by showing that not only was
the state present in Basilicata but also that women came in contact with
and turned to state officials when in need. As migration increased over the
course of the Liberal Period, not only did the state become more heavily
involved in protecting migrants but also the women who remained behind.
The chapter documents how women petitioned the state, specifically by
requesting passports and information to search for husbands and relatives
abroad, in order to show that women trusted the state to help them when in
need. Mayors, prefects, and even consulate workers abroad not only aided
but also protected wives who remained behind. Such interactions helped to
forge a new relationship between southern Italian women and the modern
state.

Chapter 5 examines the role of the family, community, and the church in
the migration process and how each assisted and supported women and children who remained behind. Many residents feared emigration drained small
towns of all able-bodied young workers and threatened the future of their
small villages. These largely unfounded fears demonstrate the scale of emigration in some localities and foreshadowed what might occur if unrelenting
emigration continued. This chapter shows how not only women but also the
community as a whole coped with large-scale emigration. Chapter 6 discusses

those women who turned to criminal or dishonorable behavior when left on their own. There was an ever-present anxiety among officials that the absence of men in towns would be dangerous for women, who might turn to criminal behavior. The chapter discusses the various criminal activities to which some women turned, especially if abandoned. Other women turned to what many deemed as dishonorable or sinful behavior, having affairs while their husbands were absent. If these encounters led to pregnancy, women would have to make a difficult decision, one that might lead to abortion, infant abandonment, or infanticide. While not the case for an overwhelming number of women, it was an unfortunate reality for a small minority who turned to a disreputable life for survival, demonstrating that emigration left some in dire circumstances.

In contrast to the focus on women who remained behind, the final chapter discusses women who emigrated. It begins with the possible impact of male migrants returning home. Some returnees remained in Italy and retired, while others would migrate again. Whether migrating with their husbands or called to join them, women were often required to obtain passports, buy tickets, sell property, and travel abroad. Others who did not have proper authorization or who perhaps wanted to leave the village, tried to emigrate illegally. The circumstances discussed in this chapter give another glimpse into the resilience and determination of southern Italian women. The book ends with some concluding remarks about emigration from Basilicata and the overall impact it had on the women who remained behind.

The stereotypes of an uncivilized and backward south imply the Mezzogiorno, or Italian south, was not modern. For many intellectuals at the time and even scholars today, modernity is associated with enlightened ideas, democracy, capitalism, and industrial progress. Emigration, among its many effects, introduced new ideas, led to increased circulation of money and consumerism, gave people incentive to learn to read and write, and brought them into a national community by compelling them to take advantage of state bureaucracy. In other words, emigration brought typical aspects of modernity to places largely considered unmodern, and migration created a population of transnational people in the hills of Basilicata's small towns. While the Lucanians may have been living in poverty by outside standards, they had formed their own sense of modernity and many experienced improved standards of living. Emigration was a factor that led to change in the region and its impacts help disprove inaccurate stereotypes about the south and the women living in it. Migration thus affected all involved, not just individuals who left, but also wives, mothers, children, and even the community who remained behind.

NOTES

1. First names and last initials are used to protect the privacy of the individuals mentioned in this book.

2. Stato Civile, Potenza, Atti di Matrimonio 1871, Atti di Nascita 1872, 1875, 1877.

3. Archivio di Stato di Potenza (ASP), Atti di Pubblica Sicurezza, Cat. 6. Busta 41.

4. ASP, Atti di Pubblica Sicurezza, Cat. 6. Busta 41.

5. ASP, Atti di Pubblica Sicurezza, Cat. 6. Busta 41.

6. ASP, Atti di Pubblica Sicurezza, Cat. 6. Busta 42.

7. ASP, Atti di Pubblica Sicurezza, Cat. 6. Busta 43.

8. See: Linda Reeder, *Widows in White: Migration and the Transformation of Rural Italian Women, Sicily 1880–1920* (Toronto: University of Toronto Press, 2003).

9. Jonathan Dunnage, *Twentieth Century Italy: A Social History* (New York: Pearson, 2002), 5.

10. Dunnage, *Twentieth Century Italy*, 4.

11. Christopher Duggan, *The Force of Destiny: A History of Italy since 1796* (New York: Houghton Mifflin Company, 2007), 265.

12. See: Jane Schneider, ed., *Italy's 'Southern Question:' Orientalism in One Country* (New York: Berg, 2001); Marta Petrusewicz, *Latifundium: Moral Economy and Material Life in a European Periphery* (Ann Arbor, MI: University of Michigan Press, 1996); John A. Davis, *Naples and Napoleon: Southern Italy and the European Revolution 1780–1860* (Oxford: Oxford University Press, 2006).

13. Maria Sophia Quine, *Italy's Social Revolution: Charity and Welfare from Liberalism to Fascism* (London: Palgrave Macmillan, 2002), 41.

14. Adrian Lyttelton, "Introduction," in *Liberal and Fascist Italy: 1900–1945*, ed. Adrian Lyttelton (New York: Oxford University Press, 2002), 3.

15. Salvatore di Maria, *Towards a Unified Italy: Historical, Cultural, and Literary Perspectives on the Southern Question* (New York: Palgrave Macmillan, 2018), 19.

16. See: Angiolina Arru and Franco Ramella, *L'Italia delle migrazioni interne: Donne, uomini, mobilità in età moderna e contemporanea* (Rome: Donzelli, 2003).

17. Dunnage, *Twentieth Century Italy*, 14.

18. Direzione Generale della Statistica, *Statistica della emigrazione italiana per l'estero negli anni 1904 e 1905* (Rome: G. Bertero E.C., 1906), xii.

19. Donna Gabaccia, *Italy's Many Diasporas* (Seattle, WA: University of Washington Press, 2000), 72; Mark Choate, *Emigrant Nation: The Making of Italy Abroad* (Cambridge, MA: Harvard University Press, 2008), 8.

20. *Statistica della emigrazione italiana per l'estero negli anni 1904 e 1905*, xiii.

21. *Statistica della emigrazione italiana per l'estero negli anni 1904 e 1905*, viii.

22. Francesco Campolongo, *La delinquenza in Basilicata* (Rome: Unione Cooperativa Editrice, 1904), 16.

23. Matteo Sanfilippo, ed., *Emigrazione e Storia d'Italia* (Cosenza: Pelligrini, 2003).

24. Paola Corti and Maddalena Tirabassi, "Introduction," in *Racconti dal mondo: narrazioni, memorie e saggi delle migrazioni*, eds. Paola Corti and Maddalena Tirabassi (Torino: Fondazione Agnelli, 2007), 1–8.

25. Choate, *Emigrant Nation*, 4.

26. Adolfo Rossi, "Vantaggi e danni dell'emigrazione nel mezzogiorno d'Italia (Note di un viaggio fatto in Basilicata e in Calabria dal R. Commissario dell'Emigrazione)" *Bollettino dell'Emigrazione* 13 (1908): 1572.

27. Dino Cinel, *The National Integration of Italian Return Migration, 1870–1929* (New York: Cambridge University Press, 1991), 190.

28. Carlo Levi, *Christ Stopped at Eboli* (Turin: Einaudi, 1945), 1.

29. Cited in: Campolongo, *La Delinquenza in Basilicata*, 16.

30. Archivio Centrale dello Stato (ACS): Archivio Crispi-Roma, Fasc 749-Emigrazione.

31. Cited in Pietro Lacava, "Sulle condizione economico-sociali della Basilicata," *Nuova Antologia* (March–April 1907), 111.

32. Pantaleone Sergi, *Storia del giornalismo in Basilicata: per passione e per potere* (Rome: Laterza, 2009), 43.

33. Pietro Dalena, "Quadri ambientali, viabilità e popolamento," in *Storia della Basilicata*, eds. Gabriele de Rosa and Antonio Cestaro, Vol. 2 (Rome: Laterza, 1999), 45–48.

34. Carmine Crocco (1830–1905) was born in Rionero in Vulture (Basilicata) and became one of the most well-recognized brigands, known for his guerilla-like tactics. While many of his activities disturbed law and order in the newly unified Italian state, many locals consider him a folk hero.

35. See: John A. Davis, *Conflict and Control: Law and Order in Nineteenth Century Italy* (Atlantic Highlands, NJ: Humanities International Press, 1988).

36. Francesco Saverio Nitti, "L'emigrazione italiana e i suoi avversari," in *Scritti Sulla Questione Meridionale*, Vol. 1 (Bari: Editori Laterza, 1958), 358.

37. Monica Maggio, "Banditi lucani: antropologia storica della dissidenza," *Basilicata Regione Notizie* 101 (2002): 87.

38. John Dickie, *Darkest Italy: The Nation and Stereotypes of the Mezzogiorno, 1860–1900* (New York: St. Martin's Press, 1999), 35; See also John A. Davis, *Conflict and Control.*

39. Edward C. Banfield, *The Moral Basis of a Backwards Society* (New York: Free Press, 1958), 10, 155.

40. John Davis, *Land and Family in Pisticci* (New York: Humanities Press, 1973), 22.

41. Ann Cornelisen, *Women of the Shadows: Wives and Mothers of Southern Italy* (South Royalton, VT: Steerforth Press, 1976), 20.

42. Cornelisen, *Women of the Shadows*, 77.

43. Lenormant, "Caveant Consules!" in *Viaggiatori stranieri in terra di Lucania Basilicata*, ed. Giovanni Caserta (Venosa: Osanna Edizioni, 2005), 148–149.

44. William Nelthorpe Beauclerk, *Rural Italy: An Account of the Present Agricultural Condition of the Kingdom* (London: Richard Bentley and Son, 1888), 35.

45. ACS, Direzione Generale Sanità, Busta 344, 1899 Basilicata (Potenza).

46. Rossi, "Vantaggi e danni dell'emigrazione nel mezzogiorno d'Italia," 1552.

47. Levi, *Christ Stopped at Eboli*, 68.

48. Frank Snowden, *The Conquest of Malaria in Italy, 1900–1962* (New Haven, CT: Yale University Press, 2006), 89.

49. ACS, Direzione Generale Sanità, Busta 344, 1899 Basilicata (Potenza).

50. See: Marco Armiero and Marcus Hall, eds., *Nature and History in Modern Italy* (Athens: Ohio University Press, 2010); Vito Teti, *Il senso dei luoghi: Memoria e storia dei paesi abbandonati* (Rome: Donzelli, 2014).

51. Atti Parlamentari, Camera dei Deputati, XXI Legislatura, II Sessione, Disegno di Legge, seduta del 27 giugno 1903, 9.

52. "An Italian Railway Disaster," *The New York Times*, October 22, 1888; "Current Foreign Topics," *The New York Times*, October 24, 1888.

53. "Italian Village Destroyed," *The New York Times*, May 16, 1901.

54. "Entire Mountain Falling," *The New York Times*, March 3, 1907.

55. "Havoc by Falling Mountain," *The New York Times*, March 4, 1907.

56. Antonio Capano, "La lunga storia della viabilità del potentino nord occidentale: La strada Tito-Atena nell'800," *Basilicata Regione Notizie* 119–120 (2008): 120.

57. Atti Parlamentari, Camera dei deputati, XXI Legislatura, II Sessione, Relazione della commissione, seduta del 2 febbraio 1904, 2, 67.

58. Roy Palmer Domenico, *The Regions of Italy: A Reference Guide to History and Culture* (Westport, CT: Greenwood, 2002), 34.

59. Levi, *Christ Stopped at Eboli*, 1.

60. Levi, *Christ Stopped at Eboli*, 70.

61. Crawford Tait Ramage, "A dorso di mulo, tra il canto delle allodole, nell'area del Vulture," in *Viaggiatori stranieri in terra di Lucania Basilicata*, ed. Giovanni Caserta (Venosa: Osanna Edizioni, 2005), 49.

62. Karl Wilhelm Schnars, "A Vietri, nelle osterie, regnava un gran chiasso," in *Viaggiatori stranieri in terra di Lucania Basilicata*, ed. Giovanni Caserta (Venosa: Osanna Edizioni, 2005), 109.

63. Arthur John Strutt, "A Lauria, una vecchia acida e grossa," in *Viaggiatori stranieri in terra di Lucania Basilicata*, ed. Giovanni Caserta (Venosa: Osanna Edizioni, 2005), 54.

64. Schnars, "A Vietri, nelle osterie, regnava un gran chiasso," 96.

65. Maxime du Camp, "A Castelluccio, la scrittura era un'invenzione del diavolo," in *Viaggiatori stranieri in terra di Lucania Basilicata*, ed. Giovanni Caserta (Venosa: Osanna Edizioni, 2005), 122–123.

66. Lenormant, "Caveant Consules!" 150.

67. Beauclerk, *Rural Italy*, 24, 35.

68. Nitti, "Scritti sulla questione meridionale," 359.

69. Giampaolo D'Andrea, "Tra ordinarietà e straordinarietà: l'intervento nel mezzogiorno nel primo novecento," in *La Scoperta del Mezzogiorno: Zanardelli e la questione meridionale*, eds. Giampaolo D'Andrea and Francesco Giasi (Rome: Edizioni Stadium, 2015), 46.

70. Giuseppe Lupo, "La Carovana Zanardelli," in *La scoperta del mezzogiorno: Zanardelli e la questione meridionale*, eds. Giampaolo D'Andrea and Francesco Giasi (Rome: Edizioni Stadium, 2015), 98.

71. Francesco Giasi, "Rileggere Zanadrelli," in *La scoperta del mezzogiorno: Zanardelli e la questione meridionale*, eds. Giampaolo D'Andrea and Francesco Giasi (Rome: Edizioni Stadium, 2015), 33.

72. Loretta Baldassar and Donna Gabaccia, eds., *Intimacy and Italian Migration: Gender and Domestic Lives in a Mobile World* (New York: Fordham University Press, 2010); Mark Choate, *Emigrant Nation*; Donna Gabaccia and Franca Iacovetta, eds., *Women, Gender and Transnational Lives* (Toronto: University of Toronto Press, 2002); Stefano Luconi, "Emigration and Italians' Transnational Radical Politicization," *Forum Italicum* 47, no. 1 (May 2013): 96.

73. See: Maurizio Isabella, *Risorgimento in Exile: Italian Emigres and the Liberal International in the Post-Napoleonic Era* (New York: Oxford University Press, 2009); Salvatore Lupo, *The Two Mafias: A Transatlantic History, 1888–2008* (New York: Palgrave Macmillan, 2013).

74. A key group of scholars have led Italian migration studies, including Emilio Franzina, Piero Bevilacqua, Matteo Sanfilippo, Donna Gabaccia, Michele Collucci, Paola Corti, Mark Choate, Maddalena Tirabassi, and Andreina DeClemente.

Chapter 1

Marriage, Tradition, and Emigration

Rosa Maria C. married Giovanni C. in 1896 in the small town of Picerno, just outside of Potenza. Like a typical late-nineteenth-century Italian married couple, they immediately began having children. A first son, Rocco, was born in 1897 but died the following year, and a daughter, Lucia, was born in 1899. At that time, the family made a decision: Giovanni would emigrate. In 1903, he traveled to Naples, likely on the rail line connecting Potenza to the port city, and boarded a steamship for America. Rosa Maria, left on her own, gave birth to their third child, Maria Giuseppa, while her husband was in New York. Giovanni returned later in the year, only to depart again in December 1904. He had returned by late 1907, and a son, Donato, was born in June 1908. Giovanni left the family again in 1909, and returned by late 1911, nine months before the next child, Antonietta, was born in July 1912. The following year, he emigrated to New York for a fourth and final time. Eventually, he returned to his family in Picerno and lived the rest of his life in Italy. During each of these trips, Giovanni's wife Rosa Maria remained in her home village with her children. There is evidence that she may have temporarily emigrated with her two daughters in 1905, but if so she returned home within a few years.

This family's story is a typical account of the experiences of wives and mothers in Basilicata during this period of emigration. Rosa Maria married Giovanni at about age twenty, but unlike her mother or women in earlier generations, her marriage was characterized by her husband emigrating for months at a time. He was a "bird of passage," traveling back and forth between New York and Basilicata, working to save money and provide for his family while abroad, and then continuing to build that family each time he returned. Like many others, Giovanni eventually settled in his home village to retire. His wife had to adapt to living, raising her children, and managing the household and family finances on her own with her husband away for extended periods of time. Her situation provides the perfect example of what life was like for married women who remained behind and how emigration impacted traditional marriage.

The basic foundation of life in Basilicata, indeed in all of Italy, was the family, and some of the most important social effects of emigration were on marriage and gender roles. Whereas earlier, women might have lived a more traditional life in a nuclear family setting, emigration resulted in women being left on their own, taking on a number of additional responsibilities in the household. This is not to say that the extended family and community did not play a crucial role in the lives of women who remained behind. Yet, emigration impacted how both men and women viewed their marriage and their responsibilities within the union. Absence challenged the traditional roles of both husband and wife. For most couples, separation was only temporary, and birds of passage eventually returned and settled home, like Giovanni in the opening of this chapter. For others, the circumstances may have been different; perhaps husbands never returned, either because they died or decided to remain abroad, abandoning their wives and family. Emigration thus shifted traditional spousal duties and altered women's everyday position in the home and as parents. As a result, some men temporarily overlooked certain social and economic restrictions on married women, as wives took on a greater burden to compensate for the loss of the head of household. Examining requests and petitions made by women of Basilicata after their husbands migrated provides a sense of the overall expectations and duties within marriage, particularly financial, and what occurred if men did not comply. While no single or unique narrative exists, there is no doubt that emigration impacted the institution of marriage for those involved, and even for those who did not migrate. The meaning of marriage from both a practical and an emotional perspective was transformed due in part to large-scale emigration. Historian Christiane Klapisch-Zuber has argued that marriage is a useful vehicle to understand the workings of a society.[1] Thus, by looking at marriage during the period of mass emigration, one can better comprehend how the women who remained behind lived.

ROLE OF WOMEN IN ITALY

In the late nineteenth and early twentieth centuries, women held a subordinate position in Italy as in most other European nations. They were considered weak and inferior, in need of the protection and guidance of male family members, and even the state. Social customs, political structures, and legislation centered around the patriarchal idea of women in the private sphere as mothers in the home, and women were denied many of the same rights that men enjoyed. According to the Civil Code of 1865, discussed in more detail later in this chapter, a husband was the father and head of the household, a wife and all the children were subordinate to him, and he was responsible for their care and protection. The sections below examine the typical phases of women's lives with an emphasis on how emigration allowed women to act above and beyond their designated position.

Childhood and Youth

In Basilicata, married couples generally lived in a nuclear family, rather than in a larger family group, as was more common in northern Italy. Peasant families, whether large or small, lived in modest houses with little furniture and few modern comforts. British diplomat William Beauclerk, traveling through Basilicata in the 1880s, noted that the houses were poor and that infants and even older children often slept with their parents in the same beds.[2] His observations reveal that children who grew up in poor peasant households shared limited space with siblings, parents, and even livestock.

Infant mortality was high in Basilicata, both after the first month and after the first year of life.[3] According to Anna Maria Gatti, 24% of children in Basilicata between 1863 and 1870 died before the age of one. The number for Italy as a whole in that same period was 22%. That figure decreased to 15% in Basilicata and 12% for Italy by 1921.[4] The lack of medical professionals and facilities in the region left most without proper medical care, contributing to high mortality rates well into the early twentieth century. It was not uncommon for women to give birth to upward of five to ten children, and yet for only two or three to survive to adulthood. Rosa's family, discussed at the start of this chapter, fits this pattern.

A young girl growing up in Basilicata would typically be one of a number of children, educated to work in the home in order to help her family, and to one day have a family of her own. Few children experienced a childhood as one would recognize today. Children in the nineteenth century were treated like small adults, with the expectation of helping out around the house and contributing to the family economy. Although the prevailing image of children was beginning to change by the late nineteenth century as more attention was given to their care and upbringing, this new mentality was slow to arrive in the Italian south, especially among poor rural families who benefited from their children's assistance.[5]

Despite compulsory education laws (further discussed in the next chapter), if children survived infancy, they were not generally sent to school, but to work. Many families were even resistant to education, especially for girls. An 1887 report on Basilicata in the national newspaper *La Stampa* stated that a local prejudice against educating women existed among traditionalists. The article described the general notion that "education makes women become mischievous" and the popular belief was that girls did not need to attend school.[6] Young women learned at home from their mothers, grandmothers, and other female relatives the tasks needed to be performed in and around the household. Women in the agricultural classes worked for their families and then for their husbands. Education was simply not necessary.

Young unmarried daughters played a key domestic and social role. As soon as girls were old enough, they helped out around the household, often taking care of younger siblings. During this period, they learned many of the skills and tasks needed to one day run their own household. Outside the home, communities were tight-knit, and neighbors were usually well aware of what was going on around town. Because men commonly left the village daily for agricultural work or for longer periods to emigrate, women both young and old generally interacted in and around the house and town center. They performed household tasks, went to the market, and met with friends and socialized. During these activities they would gossip, perhaps learn of local or national news, and maybe even hear about members of the village who had emigrated or returned. Thus, within the town itself, women were part of a network of information about activities going on both locally and around the world. Young girls were part of this community and grew up in this atmosphere.

The role of young women took on a greater significance if their fathers and other male relatives had emigrated. By the turn of the century, children in Basilicata were used to their fathers being away for extended periods of time. They would view him as a provider and one to support the family economically through his labor. They saw him when he returned from abroad, or they might be called with the rest of their family to emigrate and join their fathers. Teenage girls in Basilicata considering marriage would also know that if they wed, their husband might emigrate, leaving them in the same position as their mothers, or perhaps taking them to live abroad.

Other Single Women: Unmarried Women, Nuns, and Widows

While the path for most women was to marry, not all did. Single women, or women who never married, were a very small percentage of the population in Basilicata. According to statistics, in 1861 the percentage of women between the ages of fifty to fifty-four who never married was 13.5%, a number that dropped to 10% in 1881, and fell to 7.4% in 1911. These percentages are a bit smaller than the overall numbers for Italy during those same years: 12.3% in

1861, 12.1% in 1881, and 10.6% in 1911.[7] Thus, about 10% of Italian women during this period never married.

While the law limited married women, single women had more autonomy once they reached adulthood. Unmarried women could own property, make wills and participate in legal transactions on their own, and were not tied to the permissions of a husband. Single women who owned property were free to do with it as they wished, without the need for a man to oversee their possessions. Notary records show the freedoms single women had. For example, in a will filed in 1881 in Matera with the notary Vincenzo T., Anna Teresa A. named her nephew Emmanuele her universal heir, showing women could choose whom they wished to inherit their property.[8] No authorization of any kind was needed for her to file this will.

Despite more legal freedoms, single women still encountered many restrictions, largely a result of unwritten social norms. As gender historian Perry Willson points out, single women were seldom alone and rarely lived alone. Most remained with their parents, siblings, or other family members. Willson cites statistics for all of Italy, saying that overall only 4.9% of women lived alone, demonstrating that even as adults, single women were still very much surrounded by family members.[9]

In terms of emigration, single women had fewer passport restrictions, as married women required the authorization of their husbands. Nonetheless, unmarried women rarely emigrated on their own. Receiving countries were also hesitant to admit single women. For example, women were denied entry into the United States if they arrived at Ellis Island alone, and U.S. authorities detained them until a male relative picked them up. Single women nonetheless were also affected by the emigration of their family and friends in the community, especially if they were left behind.

Joining a religious order was another option for single women. Despite the apparent pervasiveness of religion in southern Italy, joining a convent was not a popular option for many women in the Liberal Period, unlike earlier centuries where it was a much more common path. In fact, very little has been written on nuns in the modern era, as opposed to medieval and early modern Italy. According to census numbers, there were 335 nuns in Basilicata in 1881, 302 in 1901, and 294 in 1911.[10] These figures show the decrease in the number of women in Basilicata joining religious orders in the early twentieth century, in contrast to the numbers in Italy as a whole, which increased during that same period. The change might be due to population decline as a result of emigration, or because unmarried women played an important role in households where the head had emigrated.

Nuns were an important part of the community and did a great deal to support the local population. They worked as teachers at local schools and acted as nurses and caretakers for the sick, notably in rural areas of the region where few hospitals or even a sufficient number of doctors were present. They also managed orphanages and took care of foundlings, especially in areas of the south that experienced high rates of infant abandonment.[11] Nuns also cared for women in need, many of whom were affected by emigration.

Widows were another group of single women in Basilicata. These women could be young or old and had a great deal of autonomy, as they were released from the need for marital authorization, and could even authorize activities of their children, such as marriage. To again refer to the notary records, widows did not need marital permission or authorization from a son or male family member when completing transactions. For example, a widow and property owner from Ferrandina, Maria F., drew up documents with a notary to sell her vineyard.[12] She was free to do with her property as she wished and did not need the authorization of a male relative.

However, because the burden of having small children was heavy for some young widows, they often remarried. According to statistics cited by Massimo Livi-Bacci, 49% of widows under the age of fifty remarried in the south, as opposed to 28% from central Italy.[13] He attributes this difference to the dominant pattern of nuclear families in the south, which meant less of an extended family in the home to care for widows and their children, as was more common in the north. Although it meant a loss of certain rights, remarriage allowed widows the financial support needed to raise their children.

Widows could also choose to emigrate, especially if their children or other relatives lived abroad and invited them to migrate. Officials were cautious about issuing passports to widows. Although these women did not need consent, they did need a document issued by the mayor called a *nulla osta* stating that there were no impediments to migration. Officials were very careful about making sure women were truly free of any impediments. In one instance a widow, Girolama L. was denied a *nulla osta* because she did not live in the town where she made the request, and the mayor could not verify for certain that her husband was deceased.[14] Widows, like other women, were permitted to migrate only if they had correct documentation. Officials still frowned upon women traveling alone or with young children, even if widowed and legally permitted to do so.

Marriage

Marriage was the most common path for young women, and between 1900 and 1915, approximately 85% of adults in Italy were married.[15] Young girls in rural Basilicata were under the constant care of their families, a role that passed to their husbands after marriage. Parents often arranged matches based on economic considerations or family connections. Marriage age in Italy varied according to the year and region. In general, women married younger in the south, especially in Sicily and in Basilicata. According to the Parliamentary Inquest of 1910, women in Basilicata married on average between sixteen and twenty-one, and men between twenty-four and twenty-five.[16] In all of Italy, the mean age for first marriage was 24 for women and 27.5 for men.[17] Thus, women in Basilicata generally wed young and most couples began having children shortly after marriage.

Married women were legally inferior to men and had very few legal options without the permission of their spouses. The Civil Code of 1865, also called the Pisanelli Code, upheld the tradition of patriarchy and clearly spelled out subordinate gender roles. The law included a section on marriage, which reiterated that the husband and father was head of the household. It stated, "The husband is the head of the family, the wife follows his civil condition, assumes his surname, and is obliged to accompany him wherever he sees fit to establish residence."[18] Moreover, under the law women were limited in making financial and legal transactions, such as taking out a loan or giving consent to a child's marriage, without the authorization of their husbands.[19] The law also required that a husband, no matter where he was located, had the responsibility to support his wife and children. A section of the law stated, "The husband has the duty to protect his wife, to keep her near him, and to provide her with the necessities of life in proportion to his means. The wife should contribute to the maintenance of the household if her husband does not have sufficient means."[20] Thus, at marriage, women lost many of the legal rights they had as single women and became legally and financially dependent on their spouses.

Finally, in terms of custody of the children, the law clearly stated that *patria potestà,* or custody, was in the hands of the father. Unless others could present sufficient evidence that he could not exercise it, then it would be given to the mother.[21] So even while a father was abroad, he still had legal custody over the children and was responsible for their upbringing and well-being. He would also be required to give his consent if they were to eventually marry. A married woman received custody of her children only when their father died or in rare instances if it was granted to her by a court.

The legal limitations within which married women were required to operate were present whether their husbands were home in Italy or abroad. The Civil Code was written prior to large-scale emigration, so it did not address circumstances that would arise with large numbers of absent men. The husband's duty was to support his wife and children, but it is unclear what should happen if the husband did not have the necessary means to support his family or if he simply refused. The wife must contribute if need be, but it is not clear to what extent. While the law does allow for some exceptions, uncertainties would have to be settled locally in the courts. There is little evidence women resorted to these judicial means in Basilicata. During the time period covered in this study, women frequently acted well beyond their limitations, often without turning to the courts to make it "legal."

Exceptions to the patriarchal system did exist, which were enumerated in the law, and could justify a man not supporting his wife while abroad. The law stated that "the obligations of the husband to support his wife cease when the wife abandons her home without just cause."[22] If a husband could prove his wife was unfaithful or she had strayed from the household, he had the right to stop supporting her. However, this law did not mean he was free from providing for his children.

Another exception to a married woman's limitations was the dowry, the property a woman brought to marriage and an important social custom. For wealthy families, a dowry (*dote*) could include land, precious jewels, or even cash. For poorer families, dowries usually consisted of "moveable goods," such as cloths, sheets, linens, dishes, and utensils.[23] The dowry tied brides to their natal families, and upon death was to be passed directly to her children, not her spouse. These possessions would remain important in this period of large-scale emigration and allow wives some independence. Thus, the traditional dowry system in southern Italy gave married women some economic power in marriage, but was usually not worth enough for a wife to survive on her own for an extended period of time without remittances.

Notary records show the power of (mostly upper class) women and their legal capabilities in the Liberal Period. Married women made wills and left their possessions to the person they wished (usually their husband). Although many of the individuals writing wills were upper class (*gentildonna*) and/ or landowners, all married women needed their husband's authorization when using any service provided by the notary, whether it be a sale, lease, will, deposit, or any other legal transaction. For example, each entry made in the notary records by a married woman contained the words "authorized by her husband," who was usually present at the time the act was drawn up. However, if a woman was unmarried or widowed, no such authorization was needed or stated in the document.[24] Some men were generous to their wives, leaving them in control of their possessions after death. A survey of wills from the town of Ferrandina between 1900 and 1909 shows that most married men who made a will left everything to their wives, if living.[25] While women did take part in some notarial transactions, a large majority of them took place by men and between men. In these records, it is clear that husbands did deem their wives capable of managing their money and property once they passed on. Emigrating men, although generally not of the same economic means, placed this same trust in women. Many husbands depended on their wives to manage their house and finances while they were away. This confidence allowed men to leave, knowing they could rely on their wives to look after their interests. While the Civil Code and other laws may have been restrictive for women, in practice men trusted women, and often gave their wives appropriate authorizations when necessary.

Although paid employment was rare for women in Italy, they were legally permitted to work outside the home with marital authorization. Industrial production grew in the decades after unification, especially in the 1880s, which attracted rural workers to industrial centers. Both men and women found work in these factories, especially in northern Italy with the availability of nearby industrial centers, such as Milan, Turin, and Genoa. Working women were excluded from most professions and could only select from a small number of jobs, like teaching, childcare, secretarial positions, and factory work. By the late nineteenth and early twentieth centuries, legislation began to place protective restrictions on certain aspects of women's employment. For example, a 1907 law limited women and children's work to no more than twelve hours a day, and prohibited women from working night shifts. Until the aftermath of World War I in 1919, women were banned from holding specific positions, such as jobs in public office, even if authorized to work.

Fewer women worked outside the home for a salary in the south. If they did, women's wages were lower than those of men. They were by no means idle, however, and in fact probably performed a great deal of physical labor in the home and in the fields. They could also find work outside the home if needed. If their husbands were not present to authorize their employment, women could earn money selling food, in cleaning and domestic service, or as agricultural workers. Even those who received remittances might have worked on the side for extra income. Women's work was largely outside the public sector, yet it made an enormous contribution to the local economy and often ensured family survival.

Marriage was for life and divorce was not a legal option in Italy until the 1970s. After unification in 1861, the new Italian state only recognized civil marriage, not religious marriages performed in church. Despite legitimizing civil union, the state would not allow that union to be dissolved. In the Liberal Period, between 1873 and 1920, Parliament considered a dozen proposed laws on divorce[26] Yet despite many attempts at legislation and heated debates on the issue, Parliament never passed a law favoring it. Historian Mark Seymour argues the opposition to divorce was mostly based on the fact that only a small percentage of people actually wanted it.[27] Although pertaining to a relatively a small group, not having the option of divorce particularly limited women whose husbands had emigrated and abandoned them, also likely a small group. Because they had little legal autonomy and were not permitted to remarry until there was absolute proof of a husband's death, in many instances, women were trapped without the option of divorce and limited in what they could do without court intervention.

Without the option of divorce, married women whose husbands emigrated were still subject to the same binding laws, even if their husbands were abroad for years, or had completely lost contact. For example, a living father was needed to give consent to his child's marriage, even if he was not present. Even if he emigrated and no longer communicated with his family, he was still assumed to be alive. Children may have had to delay marriage while an emigrant father was located abroad. This predicament was only remedied if a wife, along with male relatives, went to court and declared him absent. Then, the mother would have the right to give her consent to legal acts involving the children, including marriage. The mother's consent was enough if it could be proven that her spouse was in fact deceased. Another complication was the clause that stated a wife was required to live where her husband chose. If he decided to emigrate and move the family abroad, she would have little legal recourse to prevent it.

Couples wanting to separate could file for a personal separation (*separazione personale*) in certain cases, such as adultery, abandonment, abuse, or mutual consent. Persons granted a legal separation were permitted to live separately but could not remarry. The option seems to have been used rarely at most, and according to Seymour, more often in the north.[28] Living apart was an option for troubled couples, although women were still legally bound to their husbands. Court records show a number of living situations within the small communities of Basilicata. For example, after four years of marriage, Annantonia T. left home in 1901 to stay with a neighbor, leaving her husband and daughter.[29] The specific circumstances are unclear, except that there was evidence of physical abuse. This is an extreme example, however, but it shows that women did take steps to leave their homes, even if it meant abandoning their children. Her husband disagreed with her decision and tried to convince her to return home, but she refused, eventually leading to her death at his hands.

Emigration was another option for couples wanting to separate, and as long as the husband sent money and completed his obligations as head of the family, he could remain abroad, even though neither could legally remarry. Yet, those situations did not usually benefit women who were still bound by the need for marital authorization.

The legal role of women did not change a great deal between 1876 and 1914, despite the attempts of various women's groups. The global first wave feminist movement, which began in the late nineteenth century, pushed to enfranchise women, among other aims. After unification in 1861, only a small number of wealthy men in Italy could vote. In 1882, the education and wealth requirements were lowered, thus expanding the electorate to include more men. Between 1861 and 1888, major debates in Parliament over the issue of women's suffrage were spurred by the growing international feminist movement. As the women's movement gained more momentum, in 1908 the National Council of Italian Women (*Consiglio Nazionale delle Donne Italiane*) met in Rome. The organization aimed to generate attention for the plight of women in Italy and addressed a number of issues concerning Italian women, one of which was emigration. While the conference did not lead directly to political change, news organizations covered the event, which gave it publicity throughout the country. The debate for the vote intensified in 1912, when under Prime Minister Giovanni Giolitti, Parliament passed a bill authorizing universal suffrage for men over the age of thirty. Although the feminist movement strengthened in the years prior to World War I, the outbreak of war in 1914 forced it to an abrupt halt. After the Great War, women in some belligerent countries were granted more legal rights, in part because of the important role they played in the war effort on the home front. While women in Italy did not gain the right to vote like their counterparts in Britain, Weimar Germany, or the United States, the government passed favorable legal changes in the years after the war. The July 1919 law, entitled *Norme circa la capacità giuridica della donna*, meant emancipation in many respects for women. This legislation abolished marital authorization and gave women the freedom to practice (almost) any profession, except judicial and military positions.[30] In a major change for the status of Italian women, the legislation freed wives from relying on their husbands and gave them independence to pursue professions that had been previously forbidden. While much of the permissions required of married women were lifted, they still had little legal power within the family and were still denied the right to vote. The Fascist regime came to power by 1922, and with its emphasis on traditional gender roles, all hopes of female suffrage were lost. It was only in 1945, after World War II, that women in Italy won the right to vote, and not until 1974 that family law was reformed. While overall the position of Italian women by the end of World War I had shifted, on the surface large-scale emigration influenced few of these changes. However, legal changes coincided with social and cultural transitions happening on a local level, many a result of emigration.

CHANGING GENDER ROLES IN MARRIAGE

In Basilicata, it was common for men to be away from home. Traveling locally to other villages or regions for work, local patterns of labor migration were usually seasonal and could last up to a few months. However, during the age of mass migration, men left Italy in greater numbers and traveled to other European countries or across the ocean. This new migration pattern not only meant a larger distance existed between families but also communication and travel back and forth was more difficult and took a great deal longer. The possibility of earning higher wages and being able to save money to improve their standard of living persuaded men, and sometimes whole families, to migrate. Husbands were described in the sources as leaving for America where they could earn money to provide bread for their wives and children. In fact, providing bread for the family or having enough of it to eat were phrases that appeared many times in women's petitions. As the most basic form of sustenance, not having bread was a symbol of dire poverty. The women at home would often feel the repercussions of lacking these basic necessities, especially if on their own. Husbands thus migrated to be able to provide for their families, and in their absence, wives took on an extended role within the home, shifting traditional gender roles within the marriage.

Emigration changed marriage patterns and influenced choices concerning the decision to wed. A young man might marry right before emigrating and not consummate the marriage, as he would be able to ensure the "purity" of his wife and honor of his family upon return. Another option was to marry before emigrating so that a man could send remittances to his wife, rather than to his parents. Thus, he would be working toward building his own home and family and not having to give up his wages to his parents. In some circumstances, young husbands emigrated, leaving wives who were perhaps pregnant or already had young children. As cited earlier, men in Basilicata generally married in their early twenties, an age when they often wanted to start a new family, establish their own household, emigrate, and make their own money.[31] Many young and newly married women must have known that their husbands were thinking about or wanted to emigrate. Husbands may have even asked their young spouses to emigrate with them. If women remained behind, they would have more responsibilities in or around the home with their husbands gone. Emigration thus altered the position of women both before and after marriage, making them the de facto heads of household and the primary parental figure with their husbands gone.

When a head of household was absent, his responsibility toward his wife and family remained. There is no way to calculate the percentage of men who complied with their marital duty and supported their family from abroad, but the majority likely did. Even those who lapsed, or went months or even years without sending any money back home, often resumed doing so with a little nudge. These husbands were well aware that it was their duty to care for their wives. Even if they were not present or did not return home, husbands sent money to their families. Records largely exist for those who did not. While the cases cited here might have been exceptional, they demonstrate the interactions between spouses and how they viewed their role in the marriage. It is important to remember that each family circumstance differed and not all fathers or husbands abroad were neglectful.

In the case of a woman who wrote in search of news from her long absent husband, the nature of the spousal relationship, or lack of one, is apparent. This woman wrote that her husband, Rocco L. emigrated and had not sent word in twelve years. Her request stated that "he has not given any thought to his wife and five children who are living in the most squalid misery."[32] She explained that she wanted him to return, or to at least send some aid to her and her children. He responded three years later excusing himself for not writing sooner and promising to send money, but it is unknown if he ever made good on his word. This is a glimpse into the relationship between husband and wife—she wanted him to return, but it was more important that he send money. A situation like this could provide insight into their marriage: a husband gone for twelve years, a wife desperately waiting for any type of support. Was there any emotional bond? Surely the couple was together for fewer than twelve years before the husband decided to emigrate. What kind of relationship would they have been able to build in this short time together? Their marriage was likely based more on a mutual sense of cooperation rather than on a shared emotional bond.

The case above demonstrates how duty tied couples together, even if some might have barely known their spouse. Marriage for love was rare in this period, as social restrictions on women prevented them from socializing and meeting potential matches. Parents often arranged marriages for their children. It was also important not to wait too long to marry off daughters, or they would be in danger of remaining single, a fate young girls wished to avoid. Thus for many women, husbands may have seemed like strangers. This is not to say that married couples did not love or care for one another, just that the emotional bond between them may not have been strong or have had time to grow if a husband emigrated soon after marriage. Emigration highlights the nature of marriage in the late nineteenth and early twentieth centuries—it was a partnership where each spouse had their obligations, regardless of emotional connection. Men were working for wages whether nearby or across the ocean, and women remained at home and worked for the household.

Most men complied with their duty, sending money home to support their wives and children. As will be seen in this and the chapters to come, if husbands did not support their families, women could petition the mayor (*sindaco*), who forwarded their requests to the prefect of the province and then to Italian consulates abroad. In those requests, some women simply asked for news of husbands, relatives, or friends abroad who they had not heard from. Many petitions were straightforward and did not include overly sentimental language. Others relate heartbreaking stories and state the emotions and hardships women experienced as they waited for a response.

It was also possible that as husbands spent an extended period of time abroad without returning home, they lapsed into sending money to their wives. This situation seemed quite common for husbands who had been gone for years at a time, many of whom had no immediate intentions of returning home. Some sent money when prompted, maybe because their wives had gone to the mayor to urge their compliance. For other wives, it was not easy to get in touch with their spouse or obtain a response from him. For example, a request made by the wife of Pasquale C. claimed he left her and five children under the age of ten for Buenos Aires, Argentina. In the two years he had been away, he did send money, but her request stated that it was not enough. The wife and children claimed to be living in "grave pains for the lack of news and in financial anguish."[33] The family was pleading for more. Yet, Pasquale had not responded to letters and could not be located, and the family was beginning to worry due to the lack of news. In circumstances like this, families ran out of options. They could continue to search for the person in the last known location, but if he had moved or attempted to conceal his identity, finding him abroad would be nearly impossible. The above wife wrote on behalf of her children, all seemingly in distress. The children would have been too young to earn wages to support the family, so they were left to the charity of other family members, the community, or the church. The economic and emotional impact of migration and noncommunicative husbands was significant.

Other husbands may have outright refused to support their families. Such circumstances were likely rare, and often came with justification on the part of the husband. As per the law code, husbands did have a right to cease support for wives in extreme circumstances. However, they still had an obligation toward their children. Social pressure, family honor, and image in society might have also been strong factors in how an absent husband treated his wife at home. For example, one such husband told the consulate he had "grave reservations" that prevented him from replying to his wife's requests and sending her money.[34] Another husband, Nicola F., located in Paraguay, responded to a request stating he refused to support his wife Giuseppa B., "accusing her of reprehensible conduct."[35] These women might have had recourse in the courts, but in the present were left without spousal support.

Despite the impact of emigration on society, the law remained constant. If a husband stopped sending remittances to his family, the most state officials could do was intervene and urge that he complied with his duty. In 1881, Celestina T. from San Costantino Albanese went to the mayor's office to inform him that her husband had emigrated to Argentina nine years prior, but had not fulfilled his promise of sending money. She explained in her petition that the family waited year after year, but received nothing from him. Now, various issues required his presence at home. He had to pay back debts he incurred before emigrating, and he was needed to give his consent for the marriage of two of his children. After relating the story of Celestina T., the mayor pleaded with the prefect to contact the consulate in Rio de Janeiro and "compel the aforementioned to repatriate or to send aid, or in the worst case sign a power of attorney for his wife, authorizing her to do any act that which he feels is needed to repair the different family situations."[36] The consulate was not able to respond because more information was needed as to the whereabouts of the spouse. Since this particular emigrant could not be located, it was impossible to compel him to respond. Officials would have to keep searching for him in his last known location. In other circumstances, the husband could respond with a number of legal options: he could return, send money, or sign a power of attorney giving his wife the ability to authorize documents. Wives only gained legal authority with a power of attorney, an *atto di procura*, or a court order.

While some men abandoned wives, others denied their existence. When these men were the subject of a search abroad, they stated their reasoning to officials. For example, the wife of Giuseppe F. of Trecchina requested information about her husband in Brazil. The official who located him abroad wrote that he promised to send money to his wife at home, "but it seems that he does not really intend to, because he is telling friends that he does not care about his family at all."[37] The letter further stated that he lived with a woman but could not marry her because it was locally known that he had a wife in Italy. The church in Brazil would not perform a marriage for an Italian without a certificate stating he was free to marry. So Giuseppe denied and abandoned his wife at home and began a new life in Brazil, despite not being legally permitted to remarry. In a similar situation, the wife of another man, Vincenzo F., received news of his whereabouts via the consulate in Argentina. The report stated that at first, he denied having a wife, but then later gave his promise to help her or send money so she could join him in Argentina. The official composing the letter included his opinion about the matter, stating "the whole of his conduct seems that he has no intention of doing either."[38] Consular officials did not sugarcoat the information or give false hope to wives.

Sometimes, women learned that their husbands were not living the most respectable or honorable lives abroad, like Arcangela in the Introduction. In another instance, the wife of Pasquale M, an emigrant living in Brazil, received word from the consulate that her husband was the proprietor of a hotel for women of questionable morals, likely a brothel.[39] Such news would have been a terrible blow for many women, whose husbands not only neglected and denied them but also lived immoral and dishonorable lives abroad. The women who remained behind in these circumstances would have had to emotionally disconnect from their husbands in order to endure infidelity and denial.

In general, it was common for wives to deal with marital infidelity, even if their husbands did not migrate. While society deemed it important for women to remain chaste, a double standard existed regarding the behavior of men. It was socially acceptable for men to engage in premarital sex and to be unfaithful to wives. According to Perry Willson, casual sex for a married man was deemed "irrelevant."[40] As stated in the legal code, unless a husband "flagrantly kept a concubine in the marital home or elsewhere,"[41] women had no recourse and had to accept the behavior of their husbands. This is not to say that all husbands were unfaithful, just that it was not out of the norm for such conduct to occur in Italy, or among Italians abroad.

Legalized prostitution existed in Liberal Italy and state-regulated brothels registered prostitutes and tested women for venereal disease. Parliamentary debates and law codes grappled with the extent to which brothels and legalized prostitution should be controlled and regulated, whether by police or doctors or some combination of both. This situation was largely the case in urban areas of Italy. In rural Basilicata, there were far fewer prostitutes and much less government regulation, given the remote location.[42] In general, there was little stigma attached to men frequenting such establishments or hiring prostitutes. As historian Mary Gibson explains, men visiting prostitutes was deemed acceptable because of the "strong and uncontrollable nature of male sexuality." Prostitutes, and even other "dishonored women," acted as an outlet for the male sex drive and protected wives and other "pure" women.[43] It is not surprising that the same mindset existed among emigrants and this same behavior continued abroad.

The story of Francesco L. in the Introduction to this book shows how adultery impacted the women who remained behind. In that specific case, the blatant infidelity of her husband did not seem to bother Arcangela, although there was little she could have done about it. For Arcangela, the financial security of her family seemed more important. The return of her husband was secondary, and since he had been gone for years, any emotional bond or love that existed between the two seemed to have been long broken.

A woman in a similar situation petitioned officials because she worried her husband had remarried and would not return home. Isabella D. requested news of her husband after he emigrated, leaving her with three children living in poverty. She told the mayor that he wrote letters promising to send money, but never did. The request stated that her husband had not given any signs of life in two years. The children asked her for bread, and she feared that soon she would not be able to feed them. She received a response from the consulate in Montevideo five months later, saying her husband had not remarried like she had suspected. He promised that he would soon write to his family to send them some aid.[44] Perhaps she sent this request out of jealousy, wondering if her husband had found another woman. She had also heard similar promises before from him, so she likely was not very hopeful of receiving a remittance, even if her husband did not have a mistress abroad.

Women might even receive news that their husbands had been arrested or were imprisoned abroad and were required to deal with the emotional and economic consequences of having criminal spouses. In May 1880, Rosa N. of Spinoso sent a letter entitled "prayer" (*preghiera*) to ask officials to search for her husband, Luigi A., who was imprisoned in Cartagena, Colombia, for petty crimes. His wife knew that he had served his time, but "he still has not repatriated, or sent any letter, and thus she had reason to believe he was deceased."[45] With no response to the initial letter, five months later she wrote again, inquiring about the whereabouts of her husband. In November 1880, she received a response in which the Foreign Ministry reported that her husband and fifteen-year-old son were in prison in Cartagena for killing a man, slicing his neck with a sabre during an attempted robbery. Authorities charged her husband with theft and murder and sentenced him to ten years in prison. However, while in prison, he committed another crime, wounding another prisoner with intent to kill, for which he received a year and a half added to his prison sentence. Her son, Vincenzo, was released after five years in prison and was believed to be living in Barranquilla, Colombia.

Rosa's story was a peculiar and somewhat unique case. First, it shows some of the suffering women endured, not knowing where their husbands and children were located when abroad. The wife was also well aware of her husband's illegal activities in Cartagena. She knew he was in prison, and was probably waiting for him to be released so he could return to Italy, or send remittances for economic assistance, for while he was in jail, he would not earn wages or be able to send remittances home. This woman was not passively waiting for her husband to return, but actively sought out information about his whereabouts. Her initial letter also implied that she was interested in whether or not her husband was still alive, which would have implications on her legal status. It is also interesting to note that her initial petition did not reference the son, and she only sought the whereabouts of her husband. It is a shame there is no follow up from Rosa. What would her reaction have been when she discovered her husband committed yet another crime and was in prison again? The title of her letter "*preghiera*," or prayer, indicated a desperate petition or plea for assistance. Surely, the answer to her inquiry was not well received as she realized her husband would not return and due to his circumstances could no longer support the family.

Other women wrote for information out of curiosity and did not express a dire financial need, even though it may well have been present. In 1879, a woman from the town of Stigliano petitioned the Foreign Ministry for information on her husband who emigrated thirteen years prior. This request does not demonstrate much of an emotional marital bond, and simply stated that the woman wanted to know "her own civil position" as she was "abandoned and is without any means."[46] The mayor asked the prefect to do all he could to find out if her husband was alive. Three months later, she received a response, informing her that her husband was alive and last known to be working a few months earlier in Uruguay. With this petition, there was not a request for money, a plea that the woman and her children were suffering, or a request for the husband to comply with his duty. She simply wanted to know what her civil status was and whether or not she was free to remarry. A similar request sent by a woman from Lagonegro in 1880 simply asked for news of her husband. She did not plead her case, did not beg for assistance, and did not express suffering.[47] These women may have been surviving on their own or with the support of family and/or the community. Perhaps they wanted to remarry, or simply wanted to gain legal rights as a widow. It is also possible they just wanted to know for sure the fate of their husbands. Most women seemed concerned about their husbands insomuch as it related to their rights, legal position, or economic well-being.

Wives may have gotten used to husbands being absent for months and even years at a time. But eventually, it became clear that some of their husbands would not return and that they must adjust to surviving on their own. The requests of these women surprisingly do not indicate resignation, but include a sense of hope that their husband might be found abroad and send money home, or even return. It is not uncommon to read requests of women whose husbands were gone for five, ten, or even fifteen years. Even if women wanted to migrate to go searching for their spouse, they were not permitted to obtain a passport without their husband's consent. It was also difficult for the consulates to locate these men, especially if women had outdated or inaccurate addresses. The consulate conducted searches for people through local newspapers, priests, and other contacts, but if migrants moved to a new area, say from Argentina to Brazil, then it would have been even harder to locate them.

It often took months to receive an answer to a request, so women frequently waited in suspense or despair. Maria Gerarda S. of Potenza wrote asking for news of her husband, who emigrated over eleven years prior and whom she believed was in Montevideo. She did not know his exact location, or if he was dead or alive, and asked the prefect to contact the consulate to give her news of him. Without getting a response, she sent another request almost ten months later. Another eight months passed before she received a response stating that the consulate abroad had not been able to locate her husband.[48] So after eleven years of absence, Maria Gerarda got a reply from authorities almost eighteen months after her initial query into her husband's whereabouts. It is impossible to gauge how typical this situation was or the emotional impact it had on women, but in general women waited months for official responses.

During Prime Minister Zanardelli's special visit to Basilicata in 1902, he experienced firsthand stories of women abandoned by their emigrant husbands. Ausonio Franzoni, a man working with Zanardelli, told him about a woman in Latronico, recalling, "a forty-year-old woman with superb features, but with wrinkled skin, welcomes us as enemies . . . her husband has been in America for ten years, he left her with two small children, he sent money the first five years; now, though she knows where he is, she no longer gets any aid. She is forced to work in the field."[49] This anecdote demonstrates that abandonment was a serious issue for some women in Basilicata, and there was an awareness of its pervasiveness among the highest government officials.

The stories in this chapter demonstrate how emigration created new realities and relationships between spouses. Every family experienced emigration differently. Married couples were able to communicate not only through family members, friends, and possibly letters but also through mayors, prefects, and consulates if necessary. The increased intervention of the state in marriages and in ensuring spouses complied with their duty was also evident at the time. With few firsthand accounts, it is challenging to reconstruct what the majority of women experienced. Letters and petitions give a sense of the complicated relationships which existed between husbands and wives. Some women may not have been concerned for their husbands out of love, but for other motives, especially financial. Other wives expressed simple interest in their husband's well-being—where he was, was he even alive, did he forget about his family at home. Petitions to the mayor's office might have been embellished, fabricated, or even held back information due to shame or embarrassment. These might have been people in atypical situations, so it is difficult to gauge how representative they are.

Many women wrote requests because they wanted their husbands to send money from abroad or to return home, *rimpatriare*. Either way, the petitions reveal the nature of marriage and the bond, or lack of one, between spouses. In a time when few rural, lower-class couples married for love, some women did not seem concerned about the behavior of their husbands while abroad. They could have lovers, commit crimes, or lead immoral lives. Some women were simply interested in the remittances their husbands would send home. Others perhaps were more heartbroken about the news they received from spouses. In the case of prolonged absence or even abandonment, the wife and mother would have to take charge in order to earn money and procure food for her family. Women could not just wait for husbands to return or rely on the foreign consulates to locate and demand that they send money back home. As will be discussed in Chapter 3, wives might even turn to work to earn some money by sewing, cleaning, selling bread, or more extreme acts such as begging for money on the streets or turning to prostitution. However women chose to maintain their families, they were acting above and beyond their designated legal roles.

The women of Basilicata in the Liberal Period were familiar with the Civil Code and used it to their advantage when petitioning the mayor and prefect. As seen in their requests, women were well informed of their rights and the obligations of their husbands. These requests demonstrate a great deal about how women suffered, but survived, with husbands away. One can also get a sense of the nature of marriage and marital duty, as understood by these women, whether husbands complied with their obligations or not. Emigration complicated traditional marriage roles, and some wives had to demand what was rightfully theirs. Women took on increased responsibility in their marriages, crucial to the survival of the home and family. While these changes gave women a lot more freedom, they often led to many new challenges.

Yet despite the changes women experienced, there were some constants in their lives. Legally, gender roles remained the same, and married women had a number of limitations placed on their activities. Marriage was forever, despite mistreatment, neglect, or abandonment by migrant (or non-migrant) husbands. The sexual double standard also persisted. However, if left on their own for months or years at a time, the role of women as a wife and, as shown in Chapter 2, a mother, was greatly altered.

NOTES

1. Christiane Klapisch-Zuber, "Introduzione," in *Storia del Matrimonio*, eds. Michele de Giorgio and Christiane Klapisch-Zuber (Rome: Laterza, 1996), ix.

2. William Nelthorpe Beauclerk, *Rural Italy: An Account of the Present Agricultural Condition of the Kingdom* (London: Richard Bentley and Son, 1888), 35.

3. Lorenzo Del Panta, "Infant and Child Mortality in Italy," in *Infant and Child Mortality in the Past*, eds. Alain Bideau, Bertrand Desjardins, and Hector Perez Brignoli (New York: Oxford University Press, 1997), 13.

4. Anna Maria Gatti, "La mortalità infantile tra ottocento e novecento. La Sardegna nel panorama Italiano," (2002) http://veprints.unica.it/445/1/q2_02.pdf, 9.

5. See: Carl Ipsen, *Italy in the Age of Pinocchio: Children and Danger in the Liberal Era* (New York: Palgrave Macmillan, 2006).

6. "L'istruzione fa divenire la donna maliziosa." "Un lembo ignorato d'Italia: La Basilicata, VIII" *La Stampa*, October 7, 1887.

7. Massimo Livi-Bacci, *A History of Italian Fertility during the Last Two Centuries* (Princeton, NJ: Princeton University Press, 1977), 106.

8. Archivio di Stato di Matera (ASM), Atti Notarili, Matera, 1881, notaio Vincenzo T.

9. Perry Willson, *Women in Twentieth Century Italy* (New York: Palgrave Macmillan, 2010), 11.

10. Giancarlo Rocca, "Congregazioni religiose femminili e la chiesa in Italia," Dizionario Storico Tematico La Chiesa in Italia, Vol II-Dopo l'unità nazionale. http://www.storiadellachiesa.it/glossary/congregazioni-religiose-femminili-e-la-chiesa-in-italia-2/.

11. Willson, *Women in Twentieth Century Italy*, 12.

12. ASM, Atti Notarili, Ferrandina, vol. 15, 1888, notaio Tommaso M.

13. Livi-Bacci, *A History of Italian Fertility during the Last Two Centuries*, 357.

14. ASP, Atti di Pubblica Sicurezza, Cat 6, Busta 42.

15. Livi-Bacci, *A History of Italian Fertility during the Last Two Centuries*, 101–102.

16. Cited in Marzio Barbagli, "Marriage and the Family in Italy," in *Society and Politics in the Age of the Risorgimento: Essays in Honour of Denis Mack Smith*, eds. John A. Davis and Paul Ginsborg (New York: Cambridge University Press, 1991), 108.

17. Livi-Bacci, *A History of Italian Fertility during the Last Two Centuries*, 99–101.

18. Codice Civile 1865, Title V, Article 131.

19. Codice Civile 1865, Title V, Article 134.

20. Codice Civile 1865, Title V, Article 132.

21. Codice Civile 1865, Title VIII, Article 220.

22. Codice Civile 1865, Title V, Article 133.

23. Caroline Brettell, "Property, Kinship, and Gender: A Mediterranean Perspective," in *The Family in Italy from Antiquity to the Present*, eds. David Kertzer and Richard Saller (New Haven, CT: Yale University Press, 1991), 340–343.

24. ASM, Atti Notarili, Ferrandina vol 15 1888 January–December 31 notaio Tommaso M.

25. ASM, Atti Notarili, Ferrandina vol 23 1900–1909 notaio Tommaso M.

26. Michela de Giorgio, "Racontare un matrimonio moderno," in *Storia del Matrimonio*, eds. Michela de Giorgio and Christiane Klapisch-Zuber (Rome: Laterza, 1996), 343.

27. Mark Seymour, *Debating Divorce in Italy: Marriage and the Making of Modern Italians 1860–1974* (New York: Palgrave Macmillan, 2006), 59.

28. Seymour, *Debating Divorce in Italy*, 19, 65.

29. ASM, Corte d'Assise, Busta 194, n. 1198.

30. July 17, 1919, n. 1776, Article 1 and Article 7.

31. Maura Palazzi, *Donne sole: storia dell'altra faccia dell'Italia tra antico regime e società contemporanea* (Milan: Bruno Mondadori, 1997), 371.

32. ASP, Atti di Pubblica Sicurezza, Cat. 6. Busta 42.

33. ASP, Atti di Pubblica Sicurezza, Cat. 6. Busta 42.

34. ASP, Atti di Pubblica Sicurezza, Cat. 6. Busta 41.

35. ASP, Atti di Pubblica Sicurezza, Cat. 6. Busta 41.

36. ASP, Atti di Pubblica Sicurezza, Cat. 6. Busta 42.

37. ASP, Atti di Pubblica Sicurezza, Cat. 6. Busta 41.

38. ASP, Atti di Pubblica Sicurezza, Cat. 6. Busta 41.

39. ASP, Atti di Pubblica Sicurezza, Cat. 6. Busta 41.

40. Willson, *Women in Twentieth Century Italy*, 7.

41. Willson, *Women in Twentieth Century Italy*, 7.

42. Mary Gibson, *Prostitution and the State in Italy, 1860–1915* (New Brunswick, NJ: Rutgers University Press, 1986), 86–87.

43. Gibson, *Prostitution and the State in Italy,* 5.

44. ASP, Atti di Pubblica Sicurezza, Cat. 6. Busta 42.

45. ASP, Atti di Pubblica Sicurezza, Cat. 6. Busta 41.

46. ASP, Atti di Pubblica Sicurezza, Cat. 6. Busta 41.

47. ASP, Atti di Pubblica Sicurezza, Cat. 6. Busta 41.

48. ASP, Atti di Pubblica Sicurezza, Cat. 6. Busta 42.

49. Maria Schirone, "Le donne e l'emigrazione," *Basilicata Regione Notizie* (1998): 111.

Chapter 2

Motherhood and Migration

Nicola, the son of Antonia L. emigrated in 1874, leaving his family in search of work in Algeria. While he may have left promising to take care of his wife, daughter, and widowed mother, years passed and he lapsed in his duty. Without sending any money home, his wife and mother would have been forced to survive on their own, finding some source of income or way to procure food for the family. Concerned and with no other way to contact Nicola, the women made the decision to turn to authorities to assist them. The emigrant's mother made the initial request, arriving at the mayor's office and writing on behalf and her son's wife and daughter. The mayor, who described her as a "a derelict widow," would help her compose her petition and forward it to the prefect. Antonia begged for sympathy. Her petition explained that her son left eight years prior, leaving his wife and a small child, and presently they were living in "desolate misery." The family believed Nicola was in Africa working as a coppersmith, but he did not respond to any of the letters the family directed to him. Antonia put her faith in the prefect and asked him to compel her son to return home or send some correspondence to his "old" mother, who lived with his wife, or to send money so they could at least buy bread.

Three months after the mayor forwarded their request, the women received a response from the consulate which began with a warning: "The consulate has received bad news."[1] It learned that Nicola was still in Algeria and although others described him as a hard worker, he exhibited terrible conduct (*pessima condotta*) and spent all his earnings. He did not seem to care about the appeals made to him by the family, and the consulate wrote that he was unlikely to send them help. The women could try to write again, but the result was not likely to differ.

These two mothers were in a difficult and unique situation, desperate in their search for news and aid from their son/husband. They had not heard from him in years, despite various attempts at contacting him. After waiting three months for a response, they received disheartening, yet probably not surprising, news. They knew his personality and maybe they already thought his return was doubtful. Maybe they turned to the mayor after sending multiple private letters unsuccessfully thinking the officials or public pressure would coerce him into returning or sending money, especially if others knew he was neglecting to care for his mother, wife, and child. Nonetheless, the story demonstrates the emigration of children, young and old, whether they kept in touch with home or not, was another anguishing aspect of migration for the women who remained behind.

Motherhood was one of the most important roles for women in Liberal Italy. The image of the nurturing Italian mother, protective of her children, particularly her sons, is arguably a stereotype that developed in the twentieth century. Nonetheless, there is little doubt mothers in this period cared for their children. During the age of mass migration, mothering would take on new meaning. Married mothers did not have legal custody of their children, but they were largely responsible for them while their fathers were away. With absent spouses, however, women took on a greater role within their families and made the everyday decisions that their husbands could not make from abroad. As historian of emigration Casimira Grandi writes, this was a complete "rethinking of the traditional model of wife and mother."[2] This chapter will consider two facets of motherhood during this period: mothering with an absent husband and coping with emigrating children.

Mothers became the primary parental figures when their spouses emigrated. Not only would they be in charge of economics and family finances, mothers also became responsible for making sure the children were fed, attending school, and helping around the household. They became the primary decision-makers. Opportunities for schooling and literacy grew in Basilicata as emigration rates continued to rise and parents began to see the value of education not just for their children but also for themselves as well. Women benefited from the opportunity to learn to read and write, which gave them greater control and privacy over interactions with relatives abroad. With remittances, families were more economically secure, and mothers could decide to send children to school rather than work or perform tasks in the home. In sending children to school, a novel practice in Basilicata in the late nineteenth century, women helped shape their children's lives and future opportunities. Thus, wives no longer held a subordinate position in their own homes, but were in charge as head of household, even in the eyes of their children. This new role signaled a major shift in the position of women and in the role of the mother.

Women were also faced with other consequences of emigration not only on themselves but also on their children. With emigration increasing from Basilicata, mothers knew that there was a good possibility that their children, both young and old, would eventually leave the village and emigrate abroad. Parents might have even pushed their children to migrate, as it offered them opportunities not otherwise available at home. Some fathers took young children, especially sons, with them when emigrating. Other young men or women might migrate, leaving mothers in Italy. In extreme circumstances, some migrating children might emigrate on their own, or with a *padrone*, to work abroad and earn money for the family. Whether young kids, teenagers, or adult children migrated, mothers felt the emotional impact of their departure. In the opening story of this chapter, the emigrant's mother and wife, also a mother, were concerned with his well-being and requested information on his whereabouts. His long absence caused them great suffering. This chapter examines the complexities of motherhood during this period of emigration when mothers from Basilicata had children all over the world, and motherhood became transnational.

MOTHERHOOD

Having children was the societal expectation for married women. Fertility rates were high in the south, with women averaging between four to six children in the late nineteenth century, a number that did not decline until after World War I. Basilicata had the second highest birth rate among married women in all of Italy in the last decades of the nineteenth century, with 6.35 children per woman. The lowest birth rate was in Liguria with 5.12 children and the highest was in Puglia with 6.74 children per woman. With little birth control available for women, couples used natural methods, such as *coitus interruptus*, and women frequently breastfed babies for up to two years, which often delayed pregnancy.[3] Nonetheless, women generally gave birth every eighteen to twenty-four months.

Most women gave birth at home, some with a midwife present. Poor medical care in the region meant that few women received prenatal care or even had access to a medical facility. Records from Potenza show the lack of trained medical professionals in many small towns and villages of Basilicata, albeit the professionalization of doctors in the late nineteenth century was relatively new. In one particular town in 1903, local officials advertised a job for a "midwife for the poor." In 1907, another notice went out, calling for a midwife who could assist poor families free of charge.[4] This ad indicates that pregnant women were not left to give birth on their own, but received assistance from professional midwives. Although they were not medical doctors, midwives were well-trained to assist women in giving birth. The call for a qualified midwife also indicates that local authorities took interest in the well-being of women giving birth.

While both spouses had the obligation to raise and educate the children, men possessed *patria potestà,* or custody, of their children and it legally passed to the mother only in circumstances in which the father could not exercise it.[5] The law also stipulated that the father must give his consent to all legal acts regarding his children, such as requesting a passport or consenting to a marriage.[6] One of the possible reasons a father could not exercise his right was if a court declared him absent (*assente*). According to the law, after three years without news from someone, a court could pronounce that person absent. If that individual had children who were still minors, the mother would assume custody and could take possession of any property.[7] Thus, women with emigrant husbands had little power to authorize legal acts for their children unless the husband was deceased, or they went to the courts. In circumstances where the father was unknown or not recognized, or unmarried mothers gave birth, mothers possessed *patria potestà*. These children might be raised by single mothers, despite the enormous social stigma of being a "dishonored" woman with an illegitimate child. The impact this had on women and migration will be discussed in depth in Chapter 6.

Emigration impacted fertility, childbearing, and motherhood. Caroline Brettell was one of the first to identify the relationship between emigration and demographic phenomena in her study of Portugal. She demonstrated that couples married later and bore fewer children as a result of migration.[8] After her study, various scholars have looked at changes in marriage and childbearing brought about by emigration, posing questions like: did the marriage age change, what happened to the marriage market as a result of emigration, and did men return to marry?[9] In his study of Italian demographics, Massimo Livi-Bacci has also argued that emigration impacted the net increase in population, as well as structures of family and fertility of couples.[10] While anthropologists have shown that fertility decline did not reach southern Italy until World War II, Livi-Bacci argues that emigration contributed to the decline because it reduced population pressure.[11] Furthermore, while traditional values were less likely to shift, emigration may have carried away young people most open to change. Thus, migration may have perpetuated traditional patterns of having more children at home, while those who emigrated had fewer children.[12] Jane and Peter Schneider's study of Villamaura, Sicily, showed that emigration led to a falling birthrate, yet many men who emigrated returned to marry and have children.[13] This was true of Giovanni and Rosa Maria, the couple introduced at the beginning of Chapter 1. Birds of passage frequently returned home to conceive children before emigrating again. It was also common for young emigrants to leave pregnant wives or women with a number of young children. Therefore, a number of factors, including emigration, led to shifts in fertility rates in Basilicata.

MOTHERING ALONE

One of the greatest impacts of emigration was the absence of a father for many young children. As mentioned prior, this was not necessarily a new circumstance, as husbands and fathers in Basilicata, especially of the poorer agricultural classes, generally spent a great deal of time away from home working. The absence might not have been new, but the duration of it was. Thus, women took on a more important role than ever before, especially with their children. Mothering alone was a key aspect of family life during the age of mass migration, but husbands and fathers were not always completely absent. Most fathers continued to care for their children, both financially and emotionally, while abroad.

Education

Whether alone or with a husband present, mothers began to realize the importance of education for their children, as well as for themselves. Emigration sparked rising literacy rates and the increasing desire to send children to school, despite prior prejudices. It may have also been more economically feasible to send children to school rather than having them work, especially if the husband was dutifully sending remittances from abroad. Historian Linda Reeder has shown that emigration from Sicily forced inhabitants to see the benefits of literacy and the value of an education, more so than they might have previously when poor peasant and agricultural families never saw the need to read or write.[14] A similar phenomenon occurred in Basilicata. Whereas prior rural women had little need for literacy and education was frowned upon because some feared it would lead to immoral behavior, it became necessary for communication once relatives traveled abroad. The practicality of knowing at least how to read and write overcame many of the negative preconceived notions about the dangers of educating women. With men away, women took care of paperwork at home, paying bills, and receiving remittances, so the need to be literate greatly increased. When men started emigrating and sending letters home, women began to see a realistic need to learn to read and write, and the benefits of literacy became more apparent. Women wanted to be able to read in private what their relatives wrote from abroad, and not have to bring letters, which might have contained sensitive matters, to others to read for them.[15] In addition, if an illiterate woman wanted to send a letter to her husband, she would have to rely on someone else to transcribe it for her. In many of the documents analyzed for this study, women depended on the mayor to write their requests. It might have been humiliating for some to reveal private details of their marriage to him, as others might discover the intimate details of their lives. Women likely preferred to contact their husbands privately, and they could only do this if literate. Although progress in combating illiteracy was slow, these circumstances served as a catalyst for learning to read or write.

Since the mid-nineteenth century, laws in some Italian states and then in the unified Italy required schooling for all children. In the years leading up to unification, the state of Piedmont began to take control of schooling from the church, which was traditionally responsible for education. The Casati Law, passed in 1859, made primary school compulsory, and required local towns to be responsible for education. This law was extended to all of Italy after unification, although illiteracy continued in many areas. In 1877, the Coppino Law required that children receive schooling up to the age of nine. Both laws also allowed for adult education classes. Much of the impetus behind these laws was to combat widespread illiteracy throughout the country. Despite mandated schooling, literacy rates continued to be low in Basilicata, especially among women. Perhaps one reason was because before mass emigration, literacy did not impact daily life, especially in a largely agricultural society where reading and writing was not part of or needed in daily activity and young children were more useful working in or around the house. Impoverished families saw little value in education when mere survival was their main objective. Politician, writer, and philanthropist Umberto Zanotti-Bianco perfectly captured the prevalent sentiment: "Children are good for farm work and to guard the livestock."[16] An article from the Turin-based newspaper *La Stampa* also reported education was worse for girls, and many parents from agricultural or poor families did not educate their daughters because of the belief that women were destined to work in the home, first for their families and then for their husbands. Beyond elementary education, by 1887, there were *licei* (high schools) in both Potenza and Matera, technical schools in Matera, Melfi, and Marsico Nuovo, and an art school in Potenza.[17] Education more often than not depended on economic status. Upper-class families sent children, both boys and girls, to school outside of the region, in Naples or other major cities. Poorer families were left to attend the schools in the region.

Illiteracy was a major problem in all of Italy after unification, but was far worse in the Mezzogiorno. Much of what outsiders saw as backward about the south was the lack of education and the high illiteracy rates. According to the 1881 census, 87.3% of the population of Basilicata was illiterate, a number that only improved to 79.2% by the 1901 census.[18] In a 1907 article written by Pietro Lacava of the Ministry of Finance, he explained the *vergogna* or disgrace of the state of education in the region. Lacava referred to the 1877 law requiring mandatory education as a complete failure. He cited that thirty years after the implementation of the law, illiteracy was still at about 80% in Basilicata.[19] Because few children went to school, illiteracy rates were slow to decrease. According to the 1901 census, 74.6% of the population of the province of Potenza was illiterate, with higher rates only in Catanzaro, Cosenza, Reggio Calabria, and Teramo.[20] By 1911, half of the overall population of the south was still illiterate, while the national illiteracy rate was down to 38% (in Calabria it was 70%, Basilicata 65%, Apulia 60%, and Sicily/Sardinia 58%).[21] Despite mandatory education laws, there was little enforcement and few results.

In 1888, Rionero in Vulture, a town in the province of Potenza, held a conference entitled *Educhiamo la Donna*, or Let's Educate Women. The bulletin for the conference gives insight into the state of education for girls in the region at the time. While the education of boys was becoming more common, that was not so for girls. The goal of the conference was to eradicate some of the outdated thinking about women and education. An excerpt from the report summarized the predominant mentality of the time, "if she has a dowry, whether educated or ignorant, she will always find a husband."[22] The conference tried to counter these ideas, in part by arguing that an educated mother was a better one because she could educate her children, teach them good manners, keep them clean, and instruct them to have good behavior and morals.

Attitudes about education began to change by the early twentieth century when school attendance began to rise, especially for girls. In Basilicata, female school attendance went from 32 per 1,000 in 1883–1884, to 39.7 in 1901–1902. Literacy rates at marriage show the effects of an increase in education. In 1872, 96.1% of women contracting marriage in Basilicata were illiterate, compared to 85.9% of men. The average in Italy for this period was 75.3% illiteracy for brides and 56.2% for grooms. By 1905, the illiteracy rate in Basilicata dropped to 77.6% for women and 61.4% for men. The average rate in all of Italy that same year was 43.5% for females and 30.3% for males.[23] While these numbers might not be an indication of true literacy, and in fact just proof that they could write or sign their name, at minimum they demonstrate a changing mindset toward more education and increased literacy for both men and women in Basilicata.

The burden for providing education fell on the localities, a major reason for high illiteracy rates and poor schooling. Reports from the newspaper *La Stampa* stated that although the government advocated for education and even sent teachers to some areas, no town built adequate school buildings, the location of schools often changed from year to year, and parents simply did not send their children. Perhaps lack of enthusiasm was matched by the absence of qualified teachers in the region. A 1905 article from a local paper, *La Vita Lucana*, reported "perennial absences of teachers in our schools."[24] In another article summarizing statistics in elementary schools during the 1892–1893 school year, Basilicata (along with Puglia) had the worst ratio of teachers to students, with less than one per thousand inhabitants (most other regions had two or more per thousand) and one school for every 837 inhabitants (other regions had one for every 400–500).[25] An article in the same paper lamented how the population in the region was uneducated and illiterate, arguing this led to mental depression, and people who turn to wine, rather than a book.[26]

Sending children to school was not always easy or convenient despite growing interest. Elementary schools were funded locally but were not always well-maintained. Even state-funded schools were not without problems. Local newspapers demonstrate some of the deplorable conditions of many schools in the region. A 1905 article from *La Vita Lucana* described the situation at one school in Potenza, citing the lack of qualified teachers at the institution, and that the school building itself was in bad condition. The institution was an all-girls high school and thus aimed at more advanced students beyond elementary education. While the number of students had doubled in recent years, the lodgings for the students lacked air and light, and were cold and unhygienic. The report noted, "When the sky is cloudy, one cannot do anything, not read, not write, nor do work of any kind, because it is dark like a cellar."[27] While the article painted a grim picture of the conditions at a particular school, there were some positive points to note. First, attendance at the school, which was specifically for girls, had doubled, indicating a growing interest not just in education in general, but also in educating young girls in Potenza. The article also called for funding and assistance from the Ministry of Education. Workers at the school and members of the community recognized the importance of education and wanted to improve the conditions of the school for its students. They petitioned the government to help maintain the school, hoping to be able to accept more students, increasing education opportunities even more.

Prefects even advocated for schools in their provinces. In a specific example from 1884, the prefect of Potenza wrote a letter to the Ministry of Education in Rome, requesting funds for an all-girls high school in Lagonegro. The school seemed to be in danger of closing because of lack of funding and poor results. In his letter, the prefect asked for the school to remain open, writing, "Lagonegro (capital of the district) is a small municipality with few resources, no trade, and has no secondary school other than the school in question." He explained that if the school closed, the workers would have no place to send their children, and parents "who, by losing school, would lose the hope of giving an education, and a position to their daughters."[28] Schooling meant not only basic literacy, but for some it also led to hopes of social advancement.

Despite the poor conditions of some institutions, there were positive signs that education was improving. In 1907, the newspaper *Primavera Lucana* reported on an initiative to open schools for adult education in Potenza. Funded by the Ministry of Education, these schools provided evening and weekend hours for adults, showing there must have been a demand for adult learning.[29] The Ministry of Education not only had an interest in combating illiteracy in children but also in adults. While there are no statistics on the number of pupils in the institutions, it is likely that many of those interested in education were impacted or influenced by emigration.

In thirty years, the compulsory education law did little to combat illiteracy in the region. However, the increasing rate of emigration, especially after 1900, amplified the need for literacy, especially among women. The changing attitude meant more parents sent children, both boys and girls, to school and more mothers with husbands abroad made sure their children were educated. Linda Reeder has shown that attendance at schoolhouses in Sicily peaked in the years of heavy emigration, arguing a correlation between emigration and the desire to become literate. Upward social mobility was also a motivating factor behind the increased desire for education. If a husband had emigrated and sent remittances home to his wife and children, families could aspire to a better social position. Children of these families had the prospect for a better future if educated.

Providing for Children

Besides educating children, another major aspect of mothering alone was ensuring children were well provided for financially. One of the ways women did this was by using remittances sent by their husbands abroad for family expenses. This money sent to women could be used for basic needs, like food and clothing. Most wives with emigrant husbands relied on remittances for family survival.

Yet not all wives received money from their husbands abroad. In these cases, women saw it as their duty to ensure their husbands took care of and provided for their children. Some wives not receiving anything might obtain assistance from family or friends in the community. Other women would be compelled to contact authorities for assistance to ensure their husbands sent money home. When women petitioned the mayor, they often referred to the children, and made sure to point out that not only they were suffering but also the rest of the family as well. Perhaps the women (or the mayors who helped them compose their letters) knew that requests were more likely to be successful if they mentioned the suffering children. It is through these requests that one can observe how fathers perceived their duty and how mothers advocated for their children's rights.

In a letter to the prefect in 1881, the mayor on behalf of an "unhappy woman" from Potenza wrote that her husband emigrated twelve years prior, leaving behind two daughters. They helped their mother all they could, but despite their efforts she said they lived "in a deep and abject poverty" without even a "donation" sent back from their father. She explained that she was writing this letter, pleading to the prefect, because she had no other recourse. She asked for her husband to carry out his marital obligations and duties, since the desolate family found itself in deplorable living conditions. In a response, the husband refused to send money because of rumors of illicit behavior on the part of the wife.[30] By claiming that his wife was misbehaving, the husband would have reason to cut off her support. However, the obligation toward his children remained. It is unclear if the husband's accusations were true, but the mayor, unable to verify the veracity of the allegations, nonetheless advocated for the woman.

As seen in Chapter 1, husbands could refuse to support their wives, especially if they accused them of shameful conduct. In some instances, a husband might have abandoned his wife, but still took care of his children. The request of a woman from Potenza, Giovanna L., demonstrated that fathers continued to care for their children even if they no longer wished to support their wives. In the letter, Giovanna not only claimed that she was abandoned and left in poverty because her husband did not send money, she also wrote because her eldest daughter planned on getting married and needed her father's consent. The husband, Alessandro, responded, stating that he did not wish to have any type of relationship with his wife. However, he asked that the family send him the name of the daughter's fiancé so he could sign an act of consent to the marriage, as well as send a 2,000 lire dowry. He also promised he would do the same when his second daughter was ready to marry. The letter ended with the reiteration that Alessandro would not send his wife money, as he claimed she owned a small store and from that made enough to maintain herself and their children.[31] While this man cared about the well-being of his children and was quick to take action to respond to their needs, including preparing dowries for their upcoming marriages, that concern did not extend to his wife. Nonetheless, this mother advocated for the children in her petition, perhaps in an attempt to receive a response, but also to ensure their well-being.

Mothers often had to prompt their husbands to care for their children, and many fathers subsequently showed concern for the families they left behind. In a case discussed in Chapter 1, Rocco L., after an absence of twelve years, promised to send aid to his family back home. Yet part of the initial request for information about Rocco included a plea for him to return because his daughter was of age and ready to marry. The father had to either give his consent from abroad or return to Italy and do so. Rocco's response to the consulate stated that he did not want to give his consent to his daughter's marriage without meeting the intended husband.[32] In this case, the father showed interest in the well-being and future of his daughter. On the other hand, his words seem quite strange, since he had been away for so long and probably did not even know his own children very well. Rather than just giving his blind consent for her to marry (and be less of a financial charge for him), he wanted to first meet her prospective husband, get to know him, and see if the family was a good match. His letter shows that many of the emigrants who went abroad had the interests of their families in mind, even if their actions did not seem to demonstrate that. Sense of duty was stronger than an emotional bond—a father's role was to ensure his daughter married well. The subsequent correspondence from Rocco arrived almost three years later in 1884. In it, he excused himself for not writing sooner.[33] There is no way of knowing if this was the first time he contacted home after the initial request, or if letters had been exchanged in the interim. However, this case shows the importance of family, and the concern for the well-being of the children on the part of some emigrating fathers. Emigration did not always break family ties and men did not simply see it as an escape from family and duty. Rather, they saw it as fulfilling an economic responsibility toward their family.

As these cases show, not all fathers took care of children from abroad, and mothers were forced to advocate not only for themselves but also for their children as well. Women's petitions show the selfless nature of some, who ask their husbands to take care of their children, even if they themselves were denied assistance. Unfortunately, children were often a casualty of marital abandonment and neglect. Whether in contact with husbands or not, women would not necessarily be mothering alone, especially if they had older children or other close family nearby. In many circumstances, children were forced to take on an increased role with their fathers away. They helped their mothers and, if old enough, even worked for wages to support the family, especially if the father was not sending money from abroad. So both the wife and the children took on more responsibilities when the head of the household was absent.

Emigrating Children

Emigrating children was another likelihood that deeply impacted mothers in Basilicata in this period. General emigration statistics from the years between 1876 and 1920 indicate that 11.5% of migrants were under the age of fifteen.[34] However, the percentage of child migrants was higher from Basilicata, about 20% in the same period, perhaps because more parents sent or took their

children abroad to offer them better opportunities.[35] Children typically emigrated with one or both of their parents, who were responsible for requesting
their passports through the mayor's office. Once issued, a child's passport
was usually tied to that of their father, the head of the family. It did not matter
if the parent was bringing the child abroad to work, which was quite common,
even for children under fifteen. As long as a parent accompanied the child, no
reason for emigration was required. Single mothers could request passports,
even for illegitimate children, and they were granted. Children could also
migrate with other family members, including siblings, aunts and uncles, or
cousins.

Laws regarding the migration of minors shifted as the Italian government
and receiving countries passed legislation regarding emigration. For example,
a sixteen-year-old boy from Craco was given a passport in 1881 after he
told officials he had family in New York. The passport was issued with the
rationale that the boy had family in America and he would surely find work.[36]
The 1901 emigration law increased state intervention to protect minors, and
following its passing, children under the age of fifteen could no longer travel
abroad without their parents. When a fifteen-year-old girl requested a passport to travel to the United States alone to join her sister, the mayor denied
her request, citing U.S. law that prohibited the entry of minors under the age
of sixteen alone, unless their parents called for them.[37]

In many cases, children traveled abroad with their fathers. Mothers might
take comfort in knowing their husbands would care for the children, but still
likely worried, especially if the children were young. This was the case of
Giuseppa B., who had two children living abroad with her husband. Her situation was exceptional, because her husband refused to send any money home,
accusing her of reprehensible conduct. Nonetheless, he remained abroad with
the children. The paper trail for this couple ends here, but their situation intro-
duces a number of difficulties for this woman who was left behind. Would
she see her children again? Her husband had the authority to keep his children
with him abroad, and even force his wife to move to South America with him,
although in this case it does not seem likely he wanted her to emigrate.[38]

Some children migrated on their own, without their family or a guardian,
especially in the years prior to 1901 when there were fewer legal restrictions.
When migrating themselves was not an option, some parents decided to send
their children abroad as contracted workers in an attempt to earn wages.
Again, duty and economic necessity dominated parental decisions. In a
period where children working in the household or in the fields was common,
emigration was also an option for families hoping to make money from their
child's labor. Historian David Kertzer has argued that parents sometimes sent
children away from home to work as laborers or apprentices, which would
mean separation from the family. Thus, he argues, allowing a child to travel

abroad with a recruiter was not much of a change for parents.[39] As a result, many children from Basilicata emigrated on their own, as parents contracted them to work as part of a group of traveling musicians.

Fanciulli Girovaghi

Wandering children (*fanciulli girovaghi*) or street musicians (*suonatori ambulanti*) were the most well-known examples of the recruiting and exploitation of children in order to send them abroad. Agents sought out children from all over Italy, but Basilicata became infamous for the number of child musicians originating from the region. Recruiting agents came to the various towns of Basilicata and offered contracts to parents. In some cases, these men were from southern Italy and may have even been locals, which gave parents a greater sense of trust in them. They promised to care for the children and teach them to play an instrument. In return for cash, either a lump sum or an annual payment, agents signed contracts with parents for a set period of time, generally one to three years. They brought the children to a port city and from there transported them abroad, where they would most likely become street performers or musicians in major cities, such as London, Paris, New York, and Buenos Aires. The agents then returned to Italy to search for new "merchandise."[40]

It is not wrong to label these agents as traffickers. Prior to the passing of the major laws regulating emigration in 1888 and 1901, and in the chaos of the south in the decade after unification in 1861, many of these traffickers had free reign and very few restrictions placed upon them. Most of the children, both boys and girls, were between ten and fifteen years old, but some were as young as six or seven. In fact, the younger children were more desirable to the traffickers because they attracted more sympathy from passersby and were likely to collect more money.[41] Without any form of identification, many children were given false names, and sometimes boys were disguised as girls and vice versa.

Traffickers played off the desperation of some of the poorest and neediest people in Italy. Parents knew that it would be difficult for their children to earn high wages in agriculture, and saw migration as an opportunity for their children to earn more money and perhaps learn a new skill, similar to an apprenticeship. Many parents were also still illiterate and uneducated, and unable to read or understand the stipulations of the agreement they were signing. Those who could not write signed their name with an X on official documents.

From the mid-nineteenth century on, the agents brought hundreds of children from Basilicata all over Europe and the Americas to work. Writing on the phenomenon for a regional magazine, Michele Strazza notes that "many

English and French cities were overrun by an army of *fanciulli girovaghi*, from the towns of Viggiano, Marsicovetere, Corleto Perticara, Laurenzana, Tramutola, Calvello, Picerno [. . .] all of whom walked the streets playing the harp or the violin."[42] In fact, the famous child harpists from the town of Viggiano performed on the streets of Paris and Marseilles until the last decades of the nineteenth century.[43] Others were taught to play the organetto, flute, guitar, or were even trained to juggle or perform gymnastics.

Caretakers of the children abroad were known as *padroni*, and more often than not treated the children terribly. *Padroni* did not care about the well-being of the children as long as they were able to earn their quota by the end of the day. Children lived in terrible conditions and were not monitored. Every morning they set out in the city to play music, perform, and collect donations. The *padroni* had promised they would watch the children, but most spent the day in the tavern or were nowhere to be found. Children roamed the streets well past dark, in all corners of major cities. An interview with a Neapolitan doctor revealed that out of 100 children who were sent abroad, only about twenty return home, while around thirty remain in another country, and fifty succumb to illness, privation, or poor treatment.[44]

Some children managed to escape or run away. They were then left to beg for food or money in the streets, hoping their *padrone* would not discover them. A nine-year-old boy working in Barcelona fled his *padrone* and police found him wandering the streets. Officials eventually brought him to the Italian consulate, which sent communication to local authorities in Basilicata, including the family, stating the boy was found. The report mentioned the boy's condition and stated that the "*padrone* mistreated him in a barbaric manner."[45] Sometimes the children ended up in prison abroad, arrested for vagrancy. In August 1867, the prefect of Potenza received a report that seventy-two children from Basilicata were arrested in Paris and would be returned to their homes.

In a disturbing letter to the mayor of the town of Corleto Perticara, the prefect of Potenza related the fate of four children from Basilicata, all victims of a particular trafficker who was known to take children abroad to Europe. Two of the boys were treated poorly and escaped. Another boy was abandoned abroad. His exact location was unknown, but he may have been in France. The fourth child, a twelve-year-old boy, died in Switzerland, a victim of "torture and mistreatment" at the hands of the trafficker. The prefect ended his letter by asking how he could help to stop "the shame of our nation." [46]

At times, children were abandoned along the journey or escaped from the traders before even arriving at their destination. When this occurred, it was nearly impossible for them to find their way home, especially if they were very young. Often, strangers found them abandoned and the police helped return them to their parents. The police in the town of Picerno found a young girl abandoned in the train station. The report stated she was left on her own and in a condition of complete misery. Officials took steps to return her home to the nearby town of Baragiano.[47] Another police report from Tito concerned a seven-year-old girl who was found completely abandoned, claiming she was an orphan. Police also facilitated her return home.[48] Although many of the children were young, there is no direct evidence among official correspondence of sexual exploitation, but the possibility cannot be ruled out.

Traffickers most often got caught because of incorrect or missing paperwork, such as traveling without passports. If traders abandoned the children or were arrested and the children were still in Italy, the government took steps to return them to their homes. This was the case with a sixteen-year-old girl from Laurenzana. Her mother signed a contract for six years and in return she was to be taught to play the piano and other instruments. However, the agent was arrested in Naples because he did not have correct documentation. Neapolitan authorities then saw to it that the girl be returned to her hometown.[49] In another case, a letter from the Questura in Naples informed the prefect of Potenza that two sisters, ages fifteen and six, from the town of Salandra were found abandoned in Naples and picked up by the authorities because they did not have money to sustain themselves.[50] The girls were then accompanied back to their village.

Parents who signed contracts or whose children were swindled from them had few options if trouble arose or they wanted to locate their children. Most likely, the child was taken out of the village, and probably even the country. Parents had difficulty getting their children to return or receiving news of them. The situation might be worse if husbands had emigrated and a mother was alone searching for her missing child. One recourse similar to searching for missing husbands was petitioning the prefect for information, who would forward the request to the Foreign Ministry and from there to foreign consulates to locate the missing child. This was often futile.

Government officials opposed allowing children to emigrate with *padroni* as early as the 1860s. Correspondence among various agencies demonstrates that these officials were very much averse to the practice and said so explicitly. One official described the practice as "a vile market of children practiced in this province." The Questura of Naples hoped to put a stop to "the greed of these human traffickers" and expressed his hope that the practice could be eliminated.[51] Even the prefect of Potenza, who witnessed firsthand the desperate requests from parents and often the sad news from officials in Italy and abroad, wrote that societies such as the *Società Italiana* in Paris, which was key in aiding lost child emigrants return home, should find a way to put an end to the "sad business of the emigration of travelling child musicians."[52] A witness to the practice himself spoke of the traffickers, who "are an embarrassment to the country." He explained that the traffickers keep children working on the streets all day while they pass the day drinking, and when the children arrive in the evening, they only find small morsels of food. The witness goes so far as to say the children are treated like slaves.[53]

Even the Minister of Interior critiqued the practice of issuing passports to young children who leave with speculators, because it was "painful" to see Italian boys and girls in these circumstances.[54] Perhaps the practice was best summed up in a piece from the Italian Charitable Society of Paris (*Società Italiana di Beneficenza di Parigi*), which reported on the issue of *fanciulli girovaghi* in 1868, noting "several hundred young people of all ages, of all sexes, depart from their villages, in groups of three to ten, under the care of individuals who say they are their relatives or their masters. But in reality, these men are true masters of slaves, because these children are rented, sold, or confided to them, by virtue of contracts signed on both sides, and which the two parties probably assume are regular."[55]

The Italian government began to address the issue of child trafficking in the 1870s. An 1873 law prohibited the trafficking of children for wandering professions (*professioni girovaghe*).[56] Yet, the law itself did not stop the practice. Restrictions on issuing passports to minors suspected of emigrating for this purpose eventually reduced the trade. The practice also slowed when countries such as France and Britain passed legislation prohibiting child musicians from working in the streets.[57] Another Italian law passed in December 1888 warned that any agent allowing a minor to emigrate for *mestieri girovaghi* would lose his license.[58] The 1901 emigration law further upheld these restrictions on child workers, forbidding the emigration of minors under the age of fifteen from emigrating for the purpose of work. Despite this legislation, an article from *La Stampa* demonstrated illegal child migration continued to be a problem well after the turn of the century. A 1909 article reported many Italian children still worked on the streets of Paris, and the paper called for the creation of societies abroad to assist children and remove them from the *padroni*.[59] Clearly, the issue was still a concern to officials. A 1911 law prohibited the issuing of a passport to minors under the age of twelve unless they were traveling with a parent or guardian, or going to meet a parent or guardian. Thus, it took years of legislation from Italy and other countries to slow the practice. This instance of state intervention, where laws were put in place and enforced, indicates that the state did not completely turn a blind eye to troubles in the south.

Because of reforms, the practice mostly disappeared by the 1880s, as more oversight and awareness on the part of the government prevented child emigration without proper consent and documentation. Yet, the topic came up in a 1913 article in the *Bollettino dell'Emigrazione*. The article stated that "when one goes in the little villages, where people are more ignorant and more credulous, boys, lured by the promise of a salary of about 200 pounds per year, enticed by the overtures of very good treatment and loving care, by the desire to travel, to see the big cities, are themselves pushing families to let them go."[60] The article insinuated that some of the older children might want to emigrate, lured by the stories of big cities and riches abroad, and escape the pressures and isolation of their small village. The article warned that parents rarely receive news of their children once they left.

The topic of *fanciulli girovaghi* was a phenomenon that touched the lives of many families in Basilicata. Historian John Zucchi contends that at the height of the trade in the 1860s and 1870s, between 3,000 and 6,000 Italian children were performing in various cities around the world, playing their instruments and peddling for money.[61] Mothers and families in desperate situations turned to this practice to relieve them of some of their hardships. Perhaps the practice was more prominent in Basilicata because of the poverty and desperation of many families living there. Nevertheless, this phenomenon demonstrates another aspect of emigration. Women, thus, not only took part in the decision of their husbands to migrate but also had to agree to the contracting of their children. They not only dealt with their husbands leaving but also their children as well, adding to the emotional strain and possible stress of being left on their own, with little, if any, information from family who had emigrated.

Deciding to sign their children off to work abroad must have been a difficult decision for parents, and one made purely out of desperation. The family made money from the agreement and probably hoped their child would have a better life. Some argued that parents who sent their children with strangers should be denounced to the authorities. Yet others saw it as a necessity, especially if mothers were alone and hoped for a better future for their children. Parents were persuaded by the money and likely believed they were giving their child a chance at a better life. However, these mothers did not have the comfort of knowing their child had emigrated with their father or other trusted relatives, and surely felt uncertainty, panic, longing, and desperation.

Searching for Missing Children

Not all children migrated as a result of these contracts. In fact, the majority did so with their parents. Emigrating children may have returned to Italy, either with their fathers, siblings, other relatives, or as adults. Yet, this was not always the case. While younger children had less control over where they were taken and whether or not they could return home, older children sometimes disappeared or willingly did not respond to requests from family and friends at home. These stories add another dimension to the image of the suffering Italian mother, one whose child was missing abroad.

Women had a number of options when attempting to search for emigrant children. If literate, women could directly write to family members abroad, including children. This direct communication between mother and child was rare for emigrants from Basilicata in the late nineteenth and early twentieth centuries, considering the low literacy rates. Yet letters or messages could be sent through other family and friends, or through official means.

As seen in Chapter 1, women made requests to search for missing husbands, asking them to return or to comply with their spousal duties. Women also requested information about their children who had emigrated. In fact, requests made by mothers inquiring about missing children were much more emotional than those regarding husbands, and although some asked for money and aid, most were concerned with the well-being of their children and when they might return home. Unfortunately, their searches were not always fruitful. For example, Giuseppa S. wrote "begging" for information about her son in Paraguay. There was no response.[62] The mother of Fernando G. who emigrated to Marseilles a few months prior was missing and she requested information on his whereabouts. The petition indicated the father was deceased, and so "the unfortunate mother" contacted authorities for information about her son.[63] The consulate in Marseilles was not able to locate the young boy.

Once children were gone from the village, it was very difficult to locate them. In one instance, parents from the town of Genzano di Lucania were searching for their twelve-year-old son after he seemingly disappeared without a trace. The request gave a physical description of the boy. Replies from various nearby provinces such as Foggia and Bari were in vain. The paper trail ended at this point, but the parents kept searching for their son, although they had no idea where he was located.[64] Chances are their son was never located.

The nature of motherhood changed significantly during the age of mass migration. Many women confronted mothering alone, without their husbands present. These mothers did not always receive financial support, and older children would be required to help them in and around the house, perhaps even finding a job to assist financially. Receiving remittances may have allowed families more financial stability, allowing mothers to send their children to school. Despite laws mandating elementary education, emigration perhaps pushed families to educate their children, even girls, as many Lucanians began to believe schooling to be beneficial to their future.

Along with emigrating husbands, mothers of the time also dealt with emigrating children. Some may have been adults themselves, making their own decision to migrate. Others may have been minors, too young to make the decision on their own and thus migrating with parents or other relatives. Yet circumstances pushed some parents to send children abroad on their own, often with dire consequences. The *fanciulli girovaghi* examined in this chapter demonstrate some of the most heartbreaking circumstances of emigrating children, a reality for the inhabitants in Basilicata. No matter the circumstances, mothers at home were concerned about their children abroad. For them, mothering became transnational, as many had children living across the globe.

NOTES

1. ASP, Atti di Pubblica Sicurezza, Cat. 6. Busta 42.

2. Casimira Grandi, *Donne fuori posto: L'emigrazione femminile rurale d'Italia postunitaria* (Ann Arbor, MI: University of Michigan Press, 2008), 44.

3. Massimo Livi-Bacci, *A History of Italian Fertility during the Last Two Centuries* (Princeton, NJ: Princeton University Press, 1977), 47, 61, 88–89, 285.

4. ASP, Atti di Pubblica Sicurezza, Cat. 6. Busta 42.

5. Civil Code of 1865, Title V, Article 138; Civil Code of 1865, Title VIII, Article 220.

6. Civil Code of 1865, Title VIII, Article 224.

7. Civil Code of 1865, Title III, Article 46.

8. Caroline Brettell, *Men Who Migrate, Women who Wait: Population and History in a Portuguese Parish* (Princeton, NJ: Princeton University Press, 1986), 5, 164.

9. See: Carl Ipsen, *Italy in the Age of Pinocchio: Children and Danger in the Liberal Era* (New York: Palgrave Macmillan, 2006); David Kertzer and Richard P. Saller, eds., *The Family in Italy from Antiquity to the Present* (New Haven: Yale University Press, 1991); Perry Willson, *Gender, Family, and Sexuality: The Private Sphere in Italy, 1860–1945* (New York: Palgrave Macmillan, 2004); John Zucchi, *Little Slaves of the Harp* (Quebec: McGill-Queens University, 1992); Jane Schneider and Peter Schneider, *Festival of the Poor: Fertility Decline and the Ideology of Class in Sicily* (Tucson, AZ: University of Arizona Press, 1996).

10. Livi-Bacci, *A History of Italian Fertility during the Last Two Centuries*, 53.

11. See: Schneider and Schneider, *Festival of the Poor*.

12. Livi-Bacci, *A History of Italian Fertility during the Last Two Centuries*, 271.

13. Schneider and Schneider, *Festival of the Poor*, 131–133.

14. See: Linda Reeder, "Women in the Classroom: Mass Migration, Literacy, and the Nationalization of Sicilian Women at the Turn of the Century," *Journal of Social History* 32, no. 1 (Autumn 1998): 101–124; Donna Gabaccia, *Italy's Many Diasporas* (Seattle, WA: University of Washington Press, 2000), 90.

15. Reeder, "Women in the Classroom," 109.

16. Umberto Zanotti-Bianco, *La Basilicata: Storia di una regione del mezzogiorno dal 1861 ai primi decenni del 1900* (Venosa: Edizioni Osanna, 2000), 14.

17. "Un lembo ignorato d'Italia: La Basilicata, VIII," *La Stampa*, October 7, 1887.

18. Cited in Pietro Lacava, "Sulle condizione economico-sociali della Basilicata," *Nuova Antologia* (March–April 1907).

19. Pietro Lacava, "L'analfabetismo in Basilicata," *Primavera Lucana*, May 7, 1907.

20. "Tutela degli emigranti in patria e durante il viaggio transatlantico," *Bollettino dell'Emigrazione* 14 (1905).

21. Paul Corner, "State and Society, 1901–1922," in *Liberal and Fascist Italy: 1900–1945*, ed. Adrian Lyttelton (New York: Oxford University Press, 2002), 21.

22. Vincenzo Solimena, *Educhiamo la donna: Conferenza letta al circolo degli artigiani* (Rionero in Vulture: Tipografia di Torquato Ercolani, 1888), 5, 13.

23. The Immigration Commission, "Emigration Conditions in Europe," (Washington, DC: Government Printing Office, 1911), 187, 190.

24. "I locali della scuola normale," *La Vita Lucana*, December 23, 1905.

25. "Rassegna di Statistica, Le Scuole," *La Vedetta*, November 1895.

26. "Istruzione Popolare in Basilicata," *La Vedetta*, November 1895.

27. "I locali della scuola normale," *La Vita Lucana*, December 23, 1905.

28. Prefettura Gabbinetto Io Versamento 1861–1934, Cat XIX Ministro della Pubblica Istruzione, B. 366, #14.

29. "Contro l'analfabetismo," *Primavera Lucana*, September 30, 1907.

30. ASP, Atti di Pubblica Sicurezza, Cat. 6. Busta 42.

31. ASP, Atti di Pubblica Sicurezza, Cat. 6. Busta 43.

32. ASP, Atti di Pubblica Sicurezza, Cat. 6. Busta 42.

33. ASP, Atti di Pubblica Sicurezza, Cat. 6. Busta 43.

34. Maria Rosa Protasi, *I fanciulli nell'emigrazione italiana: una storia minore, 1861–1920* (Isernia: C. Iannone, 2010), 27.

35. Felice Lafranceschina, "I lucani in Argentina, Brasile e Cile," *Basilicata Regione Notizie* 94 (2000): 73.

36. ASP, Atti di Pubblica Sicurezza, Cat. 6. Busta 40.

37. ASP, Pubblica Sicurezza di Lagonegro, anni 1915–1924 #42.

38. ASP, Atti di Pubblica Sicurezza, Cat. 6. Busta 41.

39. See: David Kertzer and Marzio Barbagli, eds., *The History of the European Family: Family Life in the Long Nineteenth Century* (New Haven: Yale University Press, 2002).

40. Michele Strazza, "I piccoli 'desaparecidos' Lucani dell'800," *Basilicata Regione Notizie* 117 (2008): 65.

41. ASP, Atti di Pubblica Sicurezza, 1868, Cat 13, Fasc 2, Sottofasc 1: Rapporto sull'emigrazione all'estero di fanciulli italiani come suonatori ambulanti.

42. Strazza, "I piccoli 'desaparecidos' Lucani dell'800," 63.

43. John E. Zucchi, *The Little Slaves of the Harp: Italian Child Street Musicians in Nineteenth Century Paris, London and New York* (Quebec: McGill-Queens University Press, 1998), 19, 32.

44. ASP, Atti di Pubblica Sicurezza, 1868, Cat 13, Fasc 2, Sottofasc 1: Rapporto sull'emigrazione all'estero di fanciulli italiani come suonatori ambulanti.

45. ASP, Atti di Pubblica Sicurezza, 1867, Cat 13, Fasc 2, Sottofasc 4: Rimpatrio di Fanciullo Giacomo Antonio Salero di Laurenzana.

46. ASP, Atti di Pubblica Sicurezza, 1867, Cat 13, Fasc 2, Sottofasc 22: Richiesta sul suonatori ambulanti Egidio Romano Di Laurenzana ed in particolare su Ragazzi che aveva condotto con se all'estero.

47. ASP, Atti di Pubblica Sicurezza, Cat. 3. Busta 31.

48. ASP, Atti di Pubblica Sicurezza, Cat. 3. Busta 31.

49. ASP, Atti di Pubblica Sicurezza, Cat. 3. Busta 31.

50. ASP, Atti di Pubblica Sicurezza, Cat. 3. Busta 31.

51. ASP, Atti di Pubblica Sicurezza, 1867, Cat 13, Busta 14, Fasc 2, Sottofasc 1-Rimpatrio di Andrea di Marco e Pasquale Pavliello (December 10, 1867).

52. ASP, Atti di Pubblica Sicurezza, 1867, Cat 13, Busta 14, Fasc 2, Sottofasc 3: Notizie sul fenomeno dell'emigrazione all'estero dei fanciulii suonambulanti.

53. ASP, Atti di Pubblica Sicurezza, 1867, Cat 13, Busta 14, Fasc 2, Sottofasc 9: Denuncia di Maltrattamento

54. ASP, Atti di Pubblica Sicurezza, 1867, Cat 13, Busta 14, Fasc 2, Sottofasc 27: Informazioni su Donato Toci di Corletto e sui 6 Fanciulli che ha condotto con se in Francia.

55. ASP, Atti di Pubblica Sicurezza, 1868, Cat 13, Busta 14, Fasc 2, Sottofasc 1: Rapporto sull'emigrazione all'estero di fanciulli italiani come suonatori ambulanti.

56. Strazza, "I piccoli 'desaparecidos' Lucani dell'800," 66.

57. Strazza, "I piccoli 'desaparecidos' Lucani dell'800," 66.

58. Legge 30 dicembre 1888, n. 5866.

59. "L'emigrazione dei fanciulli," *La Stampa*, August 13, 1909.

60. "L'emigrazione delle donne e dei fanciulli dalla provincia di Caserta," *Bollettino dell'Emigrazione* 13 (1913): 3.

61. Zucchi, *The Little Slaves of the Harp*, 39.

62. ASP, Atti di Pubblica Sicurezza, Cat. 6. Busta 43.

63. ASP, Atti di Pubblica Sicurezza, Cat. 6. Busta 41.

64. ASP, Atti di Pubblica Sicurezza, Cat. 3. Busta 31.

Chapter 3

Women and Economic Change in an Era of Mass Migration

In December 1883, Lucrezia A., a woman from the town of Viggiano asked the mayor to issue her a passport for America. She told him that her husband had emigrated to South America eight years prior, and she had not heard from him in five years. He left promising to continue to provide for the family in his absence, as was his marital duty, but he had not kept his word, which Lucrezia said saddened her. She explained to the mayor that she was a struggling mother with three young children and because her husband did not send money to support the family, she was forced to work as a servant. However, she often did not find steady employment and on some days the family went without eating. Legally, Lucrezia was not permitted to work without her husband's authorization, and as a woman there would be few opportunities for her to earn enough to care for her family. Lucrezia went to the mayor to request a passport so she could travel to America in search of her husband. Without his authorization, her request was denied; she would not be permitted to emigrate. The mayor urged her instead to write to the Foreign Ministry (*Ministero degli Affari Esteri*) with a petition to locate her husband and ask him to send money home.[1] The archival documents do not indicate whether or not Lucrezia did in fact make that suggested request. Either way, she would not receive a response or any financial assistance from her husband for months.

Most of the emigrants who left Basilicata, and indeed all of Italy, did so to earn higher wages abroad. Lucrezia, like most wives in Italy, was completely economically dependent on her husband. Without him present and without financial support, she was in a desperate situation. Many wives remained behind believing husbands would send money home in the form of remittances, and most wives did in fact receive them. Others, like Lucrezia, did not. Not all emigrants were successful abroad, so for some, sending money home was difficult to afford. For individuals who did earn enough to save and send remittances, life for the family would change significantly. Some successful migrants chose to remain abroad and build new lives there, perhaps eventually calling their wives, children, or other family members to join them. Others might have hoped to eventually return home, and thus sent money back to Italy in anticipation. This money, like that of emigrants from other regions, poured into the local banks and entered the pockets of those who remained behind, eventually entering the local economy. A host of new economic opportunities became available to women as a result of both emigration and remittances.

This chapter uses an array of primary sources to piece together information about economic life in Basilicata and to reconstruct how these changes impacted the role of women during the age of mass emigration. The economic situation in Basilicata during the late nineteenth and early twentieth centuries was not optimal, and there was little opportunity for growth or social mobility. Emigration and remittances changed the fundamental socioeconomic structure of the region. Women were able to partake in financial activity if given permission by an absent husband, receive and withdraw remittances from banks, and spend money with a number of new consumer opportunities open to them. The newly acquired access to cash that many Lucanians now possessed, especially women, was used to pay off debts, purchase consumer goods, pay dowries, buy and sell property, and acquire a number of items that were not within reach prior to migration. With more cash circulating, wages increased, and a largely barter economy shifted to one relying on cash, making the region more capitalistic. While not uncommon for peasant women to manage household funds previously, in many cases, they were handling larger sums and spending it in the absence of their husbands. This influx of money as a result of emigration created new opportunities for women, altered the social status of some families in small villages, and transformed the region's economy.

LAND AND ECONOMY

As noted in the introduction, by the turn of the twentieth century Basilicata was a rural, mountainous region, dependent on subsistence agriculture. Yet, it had not always been one of the poorest regions in Italy. During Roman times, the land was covered in thick forests and used for animal pasture. Over the centuries, forests were cut down to clear lands for grain production and farming. Some of the major crops of the region were food items, such as wheat, oats, barley, lemons, almonds, figs, and olives. Vineyards were also widespread, and an array of grapes helped produce unique wines in each area. Because of the forests and rugged terrain, large areas of the region, especially in the West, could not be cultivated at all. Peasants generally used these lands for pasture for cattle, sheep, and pigs, although pasturage had decreased by the 1860s and 1870s due to brigandage and the dangers it posed.[2]

The use of common lands, many church-owned, was a key component of the economic well-being of peasant families in the region over the centuries. In the post-unification years, the new state sold church lands in Basilicata to private owners, and as a result, peasants lost access to them. The sale of church property interfered with the use of common lands for *usi civici*, a practice with feudal origins that continued in Basilicata. These lands were communal areas which peasants could use for grazing, growing, gathering, and collecting wood. The use of communal property was still common in the region in the late nineteenth century, and many peasants relied on it for survival. Loss of access to some of these lands in the 1860s may have been a factor in deciding to emigrate. The new landowners were usually wealthy aristocrats, often absent, who closed off their lands to communal use. The exchange of ownership thus caused a building resentment for the church, the aristocracy, and the new state.[3]

Landholding patterns and land ownership varied throughout the region. Many outsiders associate the south with *latifondi* or large estates that employed much of the local population. *Latifondi*, however, generally did not exist in Basilicata, in contrast to areas of Sicily and Calabria.[4] Small landholders owned most of the land in the region, especially in the mountainous and hilly areas of Potenza and Lagonegro, many of which employed day laborers.[5] These workers were paid a daily salary of lire, and often received wine as part of their compensation. Only a small number of large landowners lived in the region. The local aristocracy was mostly absentee, whether to escape malaria in the summer, to avoid harsh winters, to educate their children elsewhere, or to escape the isolation of the region.[6] The inhabitants of Basilicata criticized the aristocracy for not showing interest in investing in new agricultural tools and techniques, which impeded development and production. Farmers used old tools, had outdated plows, lacked fertilizers, did not practice crop rotation, and were in need of modern machinery.[7] For the most part, the region survived on subsistence agriculture, and as a result, very little cash circulated.[8]

Outside observers even noted that the local aristocracy was absent and did not seem interested in the land. A French traveler in Basilicata in the 1880s, François Lenormant remarked that disinterested landowners did not care to improve the conditions or invest money in their land. He wrote that "in no other region do we feel the results of the total disinterest of the landed aristocracy, who live in the big cities of Naples and Rome, where they own impressive palazzos, lavish villas with all the sophistication of refined luxury, and who, instead of dealing with their vast landholdings, avoid visiting them and entrust them to the care of administrators. . . . They avoid any cost of improving the property, in which, as has been said, they are completely disinterested."[9] William Beauclerk, a British diplomat traveling in the region, also observed the lack of investment in new technology, writing that "the earth is almost entirely left to work its natural resources, artificial manures and scientific farming not having been hitherto introduced."[10] Thus at the turn of the century, the region, still largely agricultural, relied on outdated farming techniques, lacked any form of industry, and had a largely disinterested local aristocracy.

The people of Basilicata lived in small towns, and agricultural laborers generally walked to work, waking up each morning before dawn and carrying their tools to the fields.[11] A typical workday generally lasted ten to twelve hours, with workers making around 1.60 to 1.70 lire in the 1890s, in addition to occasional allowances such as food, drink, and produce.[12] Generally, day laborers did not own land, and often migrated to nearby towns and regions searching for seasonal work. Thus, in Basilicata, male laborers commonly traveled to other villages or were away from their families for an extended period. In this sense, migration was not new, but the destination and the earnings changed. Although compared to other regions, wages were relatively higher due to scarcity of labor, individuals from Basilicata still emigrated. In fact, emigration was higher from regions with small landowners who relied on wage laborers (*braccianti*) rather than those areas with large estates or *latifondi*, where work was more secure and landowners provided protections and a system of social welfare for the family.[13]

According to an 1899 report from the prefect of Potenza to the Ministry of Health in Rome, the state of the countryside (*stato della campagna*) was reported as "good" in most towns. Some villages were worse off than others, but for the most part farming was mediocre to good at best. Emigration made the situation worse, as the few areas that were able to produce crops were often abandoned as farm laborers migrated, leaving the fields uncultivated because landowners could not find sufficient workers. The town of Montemurro reported that farming was "in decay due to the great emigration." Trivigno also similarly reported having a "barren countryside" and that the town had been abandoned by heavy emigration. Thus, emigration made a bad agricultural situation worse.[14]

Much of the country's industrial development was concentrated in the north, with little to none present in Basilicata. According to the statistics from 1905 to 1907, 1,917 industrial establishments existed in the region, with a total of 4,834 workers. These numbers were very low compared to neighboring regions and the rest of Italy. For example, in Calabria there were 6,749 industrial establishments with over 31,000 workers, and similarly in Puglia 6,310 establishments with over 37,000 workers.[15]

Travelers to the region also observed the absence of industry. François Lenormant, traveling in Melfi, observed that very little industry existed in the area and most people dedicated themselves to farming and agriculture.[16] Francesco Saverio Nitti, a native to the region, wrote in 1910 that "our immense region does not have one single industry, not a single office, not a single industrial company, not even a motor in a factory however modest with fifty to one hundred workers. Machines are unknown."[17] Little industrial activity in the region also meant fewer worker organizations. In 1907, there were three labor unions with only 242 members. In contrast, Calabria had fifteen unions with over 4,000 members, and Puglia had fifty-nine unions with over 37,000 members.[18] Even in the early decades of the twentieth century when the Industrial Revolution had been long underway in areas of Northern Europe, Basilicata was still largely agricultural.

Emigration challenged the traditional economic situation in Basilicata, especially because the youngest, ablest workers were the ones who decided to leave and look for fortune abroad, leading to a shortage of labor in the region. This pattern concerned officials, as it left jobs unfulfilled and hurt the state of agriculture in the already impoverished region. As stated in a report on the conditions at the time, many of the region's inhabitants viewed emigration as "a peaceful but continuous strike." Furthermore, because there were fewer workers to fill certain roles in agriculture, salaries rose. In the early 1900s, harvesters (*mietitori*) made 2.00–2.50 lire a day plus wine (women made 1 lira for harvest work) and construction workers (*muratori*) made 3.50–4.00 lire per day.[19] These salaries were significantly higher than those in the years prior to mass migration. However, despite the availability of better salaries, emigration still occurred. These higher wages improved the quality of life for wage laborers who did not want to emigrate, giving them access to new foods and better goods. Yet, labor shortage was still a concern in many towns.

One solution to the scarcity of workers in the region was to invite in laborers from other areas of Italy. At first this initiative was seasonal, coinciding with key cultivating seasons, and workers came from neighboring regions, such as Puglia. After 1904 and the introduction of funds following the visit of Prime Minister Zanardelli and the passing of the special law for Basilicata, workers were recruited from northern regions of Italy, such as the Romagna. These workers were meant to move permanently to Basilicata, as they generally signed labor contracts for two years, bought houses, and brought their families.[20] Agricultural societies issued a number of pamphlets aimed at explaining life in Basilicata, differences from northern regions, and possible difficulties in moving there. The information in the pamphlets did not hide the fact that life in Basilicata would be different than that in the north, yet migration offered an opportunity to laborers who had difficulty finding work. This immigration seems to be purely for economic purpose and was meant to assuage the large absence of the native workers in Basilicata.

The arrival of immigrants in Basilicata impacted the women who remained behind. Towns that seemed to be emptying were now likely growing again, with new residents from the north. Women interacted not only with migrants returning from abroad but also with individuals from other regions of Italy, who spoke Italian and not the local dialect. Immigrants would be strangers, who perhaps made better wages and lived in nicer houses. They would also be a disruption to local life and the informal networks that existed in small villages. In a culture where knowing someone and his or her family was crucial, strangers might not be accepted initially in close-knit communities. Newcomers might also be a source of anxiety, especially in towns with a large number of women on their own.

While government agencies worked on plans to assist families migrating to Basilicata to fill the great need for labor, women were not considered as possible substitutes. Women were never asked to "fill in" for men or to replace them in these agricultural jobs. There could be a number of reasons for this. While women could perform some agricultural work, they would not be able to complete more labor-intensive and time-consuming tasks. They also would not be able to leave home for extended periods of time and travel to find work, in the case of the olive harvest for example. Women could not physically perform certain types of jobs, such as construction. One of the prevailing narratives during World War I was that women replaced men in the workforce when they went off to war, performing tasks previously deemed inappropriate for women. This mindset did not appear to exist by the early 1900s in Basilicata. While women might have taken over for their husbands in certain jobs, such as a shopkeeper or a postman, women in fact did not simply step in and replace men in their agricultural jobs when they emigrated. Employing females did not even appear to be a feasible option when labor was scarce. Despite emigration, the role of women was clearly defined. "Officially" married women were forbidden from completing certain tasks, despite their expanded role in other areas. Unfortunately, most of their activities are unknown and the lack of sources or records makes it difficult to gauge the unofficial economic activity of women.

Out of necessity, many rural women did in fact take on a greater, more demanding role in agriculture with the departure of their husbands. Married women worked on the lands they owned or rented, and single women worked as day laborers, a characteristic unique to Basilicata.[21] An article in *La Stampa* noted it was common to see women laboring in the fields in the region. The article contended they worked like beasts, lost their femininity, and "aged before their time."[22] Because *La Stampa* was a national publication from Turin, the viewpoint was likely biased, but other accounts from outsiders also describe the women of Basilicata using these same depictions and stereotypes. As mentioned earlier, many areas of Basilicata lacked modern farm tools and machines, making work in the fields even more grueling. Performing more backbreaking work to make up for the absence of men, women who were only thirty appeared to be forty-five or fifty years old.[23] An article from the *Bollettino dell'Emigrazione* elaborated on some of the effects of emigration in this respect, stating, "The women, left alone, to the harsh work in the fields, quickly lose the freshness of youth, and generate weak sons, who, when grown up, are no longer tall, robust, and flourishing."[24] The observer pointed out that the effects of physical labor were taking a toll on women and affecting the strength of the children they produced. Outsiders and officials observing the effects of emigration were concerned about its impact on local women.

Some women might have been able to work in other areas, performing small tasks such as selling bread or knitting items of clothing to sell. With these small jobs, women made their own money and that put them in charge of their own earnings. They could spend the money as they deemed fit. Even if they did not have surplus or disposable income, women did have to make decisions about how to spend their little earnings. Abandoned women often relied on this type of work to earn money to feed their families. For them, these small earnings were key to their survival.

Atto di Procura

Despite limitations, women did in fact have an increased economic role during this period of mass emigration, especially when left on their own. As explained in Chapter 1, married women did not have much legal or economic power and could not make official decisions about finances without the consent of their husbands. While these limitations may not have been a problem when married couples were in the same location, emigration complicated these restrictions, especially if husbands could not be found or contacted abroad. Although the law requiring marital authorization did not change in the years prior to World War I, everyday practices did, and within the boundaries permitted, women took on a greater legal and economic role. One such way was through the *atto di procura*, or a power of attorney, which in this context gave women limited authorization to perform certain activities for which marital authorization was required. These acts had to be legalized/notarized with witnesses either in Italy or abroad, and were required if married women were to take part in legal activity without their husbands present. While not absolute, the act gave women agency and economic power as never before. It does not seem out of the ordinary for men who had emigrated to sign an *atto di procura* for a wife still in Italy, or for married couples to sign one together before a husband migrated. This was a method for married male emigrants to provide their authorization and consent for any legal activity involving their wives, children, or other physical property.[25]

An *atto di procura* was not just utilized by wealthy families or large land-owners, but by people of all social positions. One man, Antonio S., a farmer from Brienza who emigrated to Montevideo, Uruguay, signed an act which gave his wife permission to sell their furniture and their property. He also authorized his wife to spend the money from the sales on tickets to emigrate, as well as on all the necessary purchases that needed to be done beforehand.[26] In this case, a husband abroad permitted and authorized his wife to complete the sale of their property, an act she could not have done without his permission. In the same act, he gave her very specific instructions, along with his authorization, on how to spend the money from the sale. Thus, once given authorization, the wife could legally act according to the terms of the *atto di procura*. These documents demonstrate that men trusted their wives to act in their best interests and handle their legal and economic affairs. In these circumstances, women had some freedom to act, but did not have complete discretion and were still limited in their activities by the stipulations outlined in the power of attorney.

On the other hand, some men distrusted their wives and did not want to give them the power to handle the family's finances. Giacomina G. of Lauria requested information in June 1879 about her husband who emigrated to Brazil. She received a response almost a year later, in May 1880, stating the local consulate could not find her husband because the address where she believed he was located did not exist. However, a little over three months later, she received word that her husband worked as a traveling merchant and was currently away on business. Two months later, another letter arrived with word from her husband. He informed officials that he had sent money home with others who were returning to Italy in order to pay off a debt, but his wife did not use the money for that purpose because of her desperate economic situation. In his letter home, he was sure to indicate he complied with his duties and sent money, but his wife did not follow his instructions about how to spend the money. Officials would see he sent assistance home, but his wife did not manage it well, according to his claim. It appeared she used the money to buy food. The husband expressed that he did not trust his wife and wrote that the only way to prevent her from spending all the money he sent back was by calling her to join him in Brazil. This would give him more control over his own affairs and how his wife spent his money.[27] While the veracity of these claims is unclear, both men and women used manipulative language to accomplish an objective, especially when their disagreements were public. Some men were not completely trusting of their wives, especially relating to money, if they were not nearby and could not monitor their activity. Perhaps husbands tried to avoid sending home remittances by manipulating authorities to support their claims. It is difficult to determine who to believe. Nonetheless, Giacomina would have limited economic power without her husband's consent.

Husbands granted authorization to their wives on a case-by-case basis. While some may have trusted their wives to conduct business for the family, others, such as the man above, did not. These men could have signed an *atto di procura* allowing someone else, perhaps a male friend or relative, to complete these transactions instead of their wives, especially if they did not want to return home. Others may have trusted their wives more than their own brothers or male relatives. However, once this legal act was signed, married women obtained financial capabilities that they would not have otherwise legally had if their husbands had not emigrated.

REMITTANCES

Whether legally authorized or not, women took on an important economic role after their husbands emigrated. Not only were they responsible for the management of the home and children, but they were also responsible for handling remittances, or money a husband sent back home from abroad. This was perhaps one of the greatest economic changes for women and opened up a world of new opportunities for them. They received remittances and then handled cash and spent money as they deemed appropriate: buying land, building houses, fixing the house, paying off debts, buying consumer goods, and more. Some may have had to learn to manage a larger budget than ever before on their own.

Officially, if an emigrant wanted to send money home, he would send it in the form of a remittance. The emigration law of 1901 stipulated that the *Banco di Napoli*, or Bank of Naples, would become the official means for emigrants to send remittances to Italy from abroad. The emigrant wanting to send money home would go to a Bank of Naples, or an affiliated bank, in their location overseas. The emigrant deposited a sum of money and then once the exchange rate and commission were calculated, he received a special money order from the bank. The emigrant then sent that money order directly to a family member, such as his wife, in Italy. Once she received it, she took the money order to the local post office or a branch of the Bank of Naples (or one of its affiliates), where it could either be redeemed for cash or deposited in a *Cassa di Risparmio*, or savings account. While this process was the official means of sending remittances home, migrants had other options, such as obtaining an international money order, using private banks other than the

Bank of Naples, or simply sending banknotes in the mail or with another individual.[28]

Because only the remittances sent through official means can be calculated, it is difficult to know for sure exactly how much money emigrants sent home to Italy. The official numbers for Basilicata were significant. In 1896, 7,319,530 lire were deposited. This number almost doubled by 1905 to 13,802,018 lire.[29] Statistics gathered between 1902 and 1913 show the average remittance amount for Italy as a whole was 290,224,278 lire a year.[30] While official records for remittances provide an idea of the amount of money transferred and sent home, many others carried cash themselves or sent it home with a trusted friend or relative. This was probably more common, especially if people distrusted banks and preferred to send money directly through family or acquaintances. Thus, the actual amount of remittances was likely much higher than official statistics indicate. The influx of cash added to the economy was no doubt positive for all of Italy, but especially for poorer regions of the south, like Basilicata. Historian Richard Bosworth even goes so far as to say that remittances prevented the south from going bankrupt.[31] Remittances aided the local economy, despite the fact that at the same time, economic loss from emigrating laborers was hurting the region. Nonetheless, remittances helped some of the poorest regions of Italy and provided the money and aid that the government did not in a time when assistance was desperately needed.

Often when men sent back remittances, they directed the money orders to women, who went to the local bank or post office to redeem them. According to an economist cited by historian Andreina De Clementi, a majority of the money orders for remittances were deposited in the name of women.[32] Men trusted their wives to collect the remittances and use the money not only to manage the household but also to pay off debts, arrange dowries for their daughters, make purchases, and complete sales. With remittances, women possessed more money to spend than ever before. Depending on any specific instructions the emigrant stipulated, women then had the option to manage and spend the funds as they saw fit.

In addition to sending money to maintain and support their families, men sent remittances for a number of other purposes, and all required that women take responsibility for the money. Men commonly sent remittances to pay off debts at home. Many times, an emigrant would be indebted to another who had lent him money to pay for his initial ticket to emigrate. Money could also be sent home to buy land or new property. Families used the money to build new, better houses, or to improve or redesign their current homes.[33] With the handling of remittances and managing of money, women became consumers, buying better clothing, new furniture for their homes, and different types and varieties of food. If men were able to and were responsible enough to send remittances home regularly, those who remained behind were better off economically, and experienced improved living conditions.

For some women, remittances completely changed their lives. Not only did the money relieve them from poverty, but even allowed some to move up socially, especially if they were able to buy property. Most emigrants were farmers or *contadini*, so their wives were generally of the same social status. With remittances, these women may have seen their position differently. Not only wives, but husbands also may have seen themselves in a new light, and if men returned to the village after earning and saving money, few wanted to go back to the difficult life of an agricultural worker.

Remittances had more than simply individual benefits. Local accounts demonstrate how remittances helped whole villages. Journalist Adolfo Rossi, surveying the region in 1908, noted that "the post offices of poor villages, of 2,000–3,000 inhabitants, had movement of hundreds of thousands of lire a year, a result of the savings of laborers." Rossi interviewed a politician from the town of Corleto Perticara, who claimed that without emigration the amount of poverty in the town would increase. A doctor in agrarian sciences interviewed in Viggiano commented that emigration benefited the town and millions of lire had come in through remittances, resulting in many people opening savings accounts.[34] For most in small towns, the benefits of emigration gave them more financial support and opportunities than ever before. As one author wrote, it was *una fantastica pioggia d'oro* or a fantastic golden shower.[35] So while some officials feared too much emigration and depleting populations in many villages, others saw the benefits of remittances and the boost they gave to the local economy. An article in the *Bollettino dell'Emigrazione* best sums up the economic impact of emigration, both directly and indirectly, on the small towns of Basilicata: directly the money emigrants sent and brought home led to improvements to their land, houses, and way of life, and indirectly it stimulated landowners to modernize and improve technology, actions they had previously avoided, which would lead to improved output.[36]

This money came at a cost. Millions of families were separated, men traveled and lived in uncomfortable circumstances, and laborers worked hard, sacrificing home, time with family, and the comforts of what was familiar. A 1907 article in the *Bollettino dell'Emigrazione* reminded readers that "millions in savings came sent to Italy: but they represent a number of great pains."[37] So while some families may have reaped the rewards of success abroad, others may not have been so lucky or may have had to deal with insufferable pains in order to earn that money.

Not all men sent remittances home, and sometimes women left on their own were economically abandoned by their husbands, as seen in many instances in this book. If married men did not send remittances to wives and children, families were left in a difficult situation. A wife from Pignola wrote in search of her husband and her two sons who were living in Paraguay. The letter from the mayor stated that "in two years he has not sent any news of himself or his children, having left his wife in the most squalid misery." The consulate wrote back to say that the family members were alive, but her husband refused to send money to her, stating "he has decidedly declined sending any aid to his wife, accusing her of reprehensible conduct."[38] The file ends here and the fate of this family is unclear. One can only imagine how a wife would have taken this type of news. Her husband was abroad, and she remained behind, forced to fend for herself and not able to work without her husband's consent. Thus, while some women benefited greatly from remittances, others suffered immensely if their husbands did not send any home.

SPENDING MONEY

In a largely agricultural economy where bartering was still common and records for everyday transactions do not exist, it is difficult to gauge how women spent remittances. Although wives could not buy property without marital authorization, they were permitted to take part in certain other economic activities. Unlike women living in larger towns or even cities where there were different types of shops, women in Basilicata were in a largely rural setting and did not have access to a variety of stores. Unless they lived in or near Potenza, Matera, Melfi, or other larger towns, there would not be many purchasing options open to them, and they would be limited to what was available in their village.

Examining advertisements printed in newspapers and journals from Basilicata and directed toward women is one way to gauge their economic activity. While a majority of women may not have been able to read or might not have had access to a newspaper if it was printed in Potenza, they might have seen advertisements or posters with pictures, drawings, and visuals. Although many prospective consumers might not have been literate enough to read an article on the front page of a newspaper, they could still look at the back page (where most advertisements were listed in this period) and get a general idea of what it was selling. Overall, advertisements give a sense of how stores and companies tried to sell their products to female consumers. In general, ads were likely not aimed at the poorest classes, but that was not always the case, considering the variety of ads. Despite their socioeconomic status, the large number of remittances increased the number of female consumers in the region, and advertisers consequently targeted them.

One of the more common ads was for items of clothing. There were many ads for emporia, or general shops, selling clothes for both men and women.

These ads included sketches of some of the products they sold, which contained articles of clothing of all price ranges. Ads would sometimes list the prices or mention that certain pieces were imported. One entitled "Parigi a Potenza" announced new arrivals for women: cloaks, scarves, shawls, gloves, and skirts.[39] The ad implied that this store brought in the latest styles from Paris, a center of fashion, to Italy, perhaps targeting women with more disposable income.

Stores also advertised to women as sewers and seamstresses, and there were several ads for textiles and fabrics. A store in Potenza sold Italian and imported textiles, claiming to have new selections available every season.[40] Singer sewing machines were also advertised in a number of different publications throughout the years. The company even offered to send potential customers an illustrated catalog for free. Singer products were sold not only in Potenza, but in Melfi and Matera as well.[41] An ad for a London-based company selling sewing machines claimed their machine was "the most welcoming holiday gift: excellent for mothers, brides, sisters, and lovers."[42] Although the sewing machine was a product mainly used by women, the advertisement seemed to be aimed at men who bought them for women as gifts. Most women in this period likely still made clothes for themselves and their children. These ads focused primarily on women's tasks in the home and were aimed at bringing them affordable machines and supplies to make their domestic work easier.

Domestic goods, products, and other appliances were also advertised in the newspapers of Basilicata during this period. A company in Bari advertised electric lighting, telephones, and other electrical appliances.[43] By 1909, a shop in Potenza offered electric lighting. The ad included a chart comparing the costs of lighting a home by candlelight to that of electric light.[44] In an ad perhaps aimed at a larger portion of the population, the "Grande Emporio Macchine Agricole" piece included photos of agricultural tools and machines.[45] The incentive for small landowners to buy newer tools and improve the output on their farms meant they could expect an increased standard of living. Advertisements for other goods such as silverware, irons, spring water, even foods and meats were present in many newspapers throughout the time period. A seasonal ad in a December 1911 issue promoted a store that sold Christmas cards and other types of paper to send holiday greetings.[46]

Magazzini Michele Marino was a large store in Potenza that sold all types of products, including imports, and this business frequently advertised in various newspapers. In 1892, it claimed to exclusively sell certain American brands, perhaps a draw for recently returned migrants.[47] The store took out a half-page ad in 1909 and included drawings of some popular products: hand bags, pocket watches, trunks, and more.[48] His ad in the same paper a few months later contained pictures of different items, new arrivals which included cloaks, hats, and shoes.[49] In the following March, the store promoted furniture and home goods and included pictures of bedframes, cribs, and chairs.[50] All of these products would appeal to women as housewives and consumers, and women of various social classes could afford these items.

Medicines and medical remedies were another interesting subject of advertisements aimed at both male and female readers. One store from Naples advertised "miraculous injections" to cure venereal diseases and syphilis.[51] Another from 1900 promised a remedy for anemia, cloro-anemia, and the aftereffects of malaria.[52] An ad from 1905 claimed to cure the symptoms of malaria in six days for only six lire.[53] Doctor Bandiera in Palermo offered remedies for tuberculosis, bronchitis, and other pulmonary diseases. The ad asked potential clients to write clearly and to send their address along with postage to his office in Palermo.[54] Numerous other doctors or pharmacies advertised miraculous cures or pills for all types of conditions. Some of the most common were pills or injections to cure stomach pain, as well as pills for urinary tract health. Bayer Aspirin was also promoted in newspapers as a tried and true remedy for certain types of ailments.

Other ads focused on their readers as emigrants or as individuals with family or friends abroad. Some papers contained ads for postal service to the Americas, with weekly service to New York, Montevideo, Buenos Aires, and other major cities.[55] Ads for emigration agencies also appeared, as well as others for navigation companies. One such ad in 1912 demonstrated how comfortable, relatively speaking, the transatlantic journey had become. This company's ships provided "tables for emigrants, rooms with windows, electric lighting, irreproachable treatment and service."[56] Prospective migrants might be convinced to emigrate when reading about the new accommodations on steamships.

As a whole, these advertisements demonstrate a number of important points about consumerism and economic life in Basilicata. Ads for clothing, remedies, or home goods could appeal to both male and female consumers, which must indicate a market. While some stores were located in Naples, Rome, or other Italian cities, most ads were for establishments within Basilicata. The ads confirm that as capital, Potenza was a major commercial center of the region. Retailers in Potenza also offered to ship products directly to individuals living outside of the city, expanding their consumer reach. Inhabitants of smaller towns relied on these shipments, as well as local shops or various markets that came to the village. These advertisements also targeted women by appealing to a more "feminine" consumer with ads for clothing, sewing machines, and other household appliances. Advertisers knew that while many women did not have complete economic freedom or much disposable income, they could still be influenced as consumers through advertisements.

As observers began to realize the importance of remittances and the impact of women as consumers on the local economy, calls grew for a change in how women were educated. Connected to a greater financial role, by the early 1900s, education for young girls became more popular. A report relating information from the conference entitled *Educhiamo la Donna* discussed reasons why daughters, not just sons, should be educated. While several important arguments were stated, including the importance of developing more capable wives and mothers, as examined in Chapter 2, one argument regarded economy. An educated woman would be able to make more with less; she "knows how to make a better soup with less spending, she knows when spending is necessary and she knows when instead to save."[57] Thus, education made women more economical and better able to spend and save money.

The report also argued that some men believed it was useful for women to be able to read and write and to know rudimentary math. This knowledge might provide women the opportunity to work as a shopkeeper, deemed an acceptable profession. The report relayed the story of a man looking for a wife who would help him run his business, even when he was not present. He stated: "I need my wife to know how to manage the games in my shop, which I cannot always attend."[58] This example also demonstrates men accepted educated women, and that schooling was not a detriment to a woman's character or marriage prospects. On the contrary, trust existed between married couples, especially regarding financial matters, and some men considered an educated wife an asset.

Men who emigrated also left their business in the hands of their wives. For example, Giovanna L.'s husband emigrated to Buenos Aires, leaving her in charge of his small shop. In fact, it seems that he let his wife manage the store and keep the earnings so he did not have to send back remittances.[59] Thus, women were given responsibilities and in some cases left to care for their husband's business or even replace them in their profession, especially if their spouse was absent from the village. In this case, the income was not enough for Giovanna, and she wrote requesting her husband send additional money from abroad.

Sometimes women themselves lifted the family out of poverty or found ways to make money or provide food for their children. The report from the conference gave another reason why education was important for women: it allowed some the opportunity to use those skills to earn money. The conference report told the story of a young woman in Forenza, the wife of a cobbler (*ciabattino*) who made little money. Knowing how to read and write, she used these skills to help others in the town. The report explained that "the wife was able to sustain the family by reading and writing letters for everyone in the village." In return for her assistance, villagers brought her potatoes, fruit, flour, and firewood.[60] So while not working or earning wages, by helping others in the town she was able to barter her skills for necessary everyday items.

Most women faithfully handled remittances and used the money to care for themselves and their families, or conduct business mandated by their husbands. However, not all women did as instructed. Some were deceitful and even found themselves in financial trouble. They might disobey their husbands and spend money on other purchases, or they might attempt to take initiative and make economic decisions on their own. For instance, a widow, Annarosa P., owed thousands of lire to a number of people. It is unclear if she borrowed this money out of greed or necessity. The men she was indebted to accused her of trying to leave the country illegally without repaying her debts.[61] This example is likely an exceptional case, but does show that not all women left behind carried out their end of the agreement.

During the age of mass migration, towns and villages of Basilicata lost a large percentage of their population, especially young males who performed agricultural labor and key economic tasks. At the same time, these emigrants sent millions of lire back home to Italy in the form of remittances. Women who remained behind were likely to receive this money if their husbands sent it from abroad. The large influx of cash to the region had a number of effects. While the women who received remittances often did not have complete economic freedom and were limited in how they could spend the money, they nonetheless had access to cash, a rare occurrence in rural Basilicata, which gave them economic power. With their husband's permission they could perform certain economic transactions, but often they could also spend money as they deemed fit. Officials began to realize that educated women would be more economical wives and would make better financial decisions, and advertisers increasingly began to target women as consumers. There was a growing consumer culture in Basilicata in the years of mass migration due in great part to women having more access to cash. Despite limited sources recording their economic activity, it is clear that women took on a greater economic role within the family and within society during this period of mass emigration.

NOTES

1. ASP, Atti di Pubblica Sicurezza, Cat 6, Busta 43.
2. William Nelthorpe Beauclerk, *Rural Italy: An Account of the Present Agricultural Condition of the Kingdom* (London: Richard Bentley and Son, 1888), 33.

3. Antonio Lerra, *Chiesa e società nel mezzogiorno: dalla "ricettizia" del secolo XVI alla liquidazione dell'asse ecclesiastico in Basilicata* (Venosa: Edizioni Osanna, 1996).

4. Pietro Lacava, "Sulle condizione economico-sociali della Basilicata," *Nuova Antologia* (March–April 1907): 120–121.

5. Cesare Cagli, "L'emigrazione e l'agricolutra in Basilicata," *Nuova Antologia* CXLVIII (July–August 1910): 135.

6. Pietro Lacava, "Sulle Condizione economico-sociali della Basilicata," 121.

7. The Immigration Commission, "Emigration Conditions in Europe," (Washington, DC: Government Printing Office, 1911), 162.

8. Andreina De Clementi, "Gender Relations and Migration Strategies in the Rural Italian South: Land, Inheritance, and the Marriage Market," in *Women, Gender and Transnational Lives: Italian Workers of the World*, eds. Donna Gabaccia and Franca Iacovetta (Toronto: University of Toronto Press, 2002), 81.

9. François Lenormant, "Caveant Consules!," in *Viaggiatori stranieri in terra di Lucania Basilicata*, ed. Giovanni Caserta (Venosa: Osanna Edizioni, 2005), 151–152.

10. Beauclerk, *Rural Italy*, 26.

11. "Tornando dalla Basilicata," *La Stampa*, October 26, 1890.

12. "Un lembo ignorato d'Italia: La Basilicata, VI," *La Stampa*, October 3, 1887.

13. De Clementi, "Gender Relations and Migration Strategies in the Rural Italian South," 83. Also see Marta Petrusewicz, *Latifondium: Moral Economy and Material Life in a European Periphery* (Ann Arbor, MI: University of Michigan Press, 1996).

14. ACS, Direzione Generale Sanità, Busta 344, 1899 Basilicata (Potenza).

15. Annuario Statistico 1905–1907, cited in The Immigration Commission, "Emigration Conditions in Europe," (Washington, DC: Government Printing Office, 1911), 166.

16. François Lenormant, "A Melfi, percorrendo l'Ofanto," in *Viaggiatori stranieri in terra di Lucania Basilicata*, ed. Giovanni Caserta (Venosa: Osanna Edizioni, 2005), 132.

17. Francesco Saverio Nitti, "Sui provvedimenti per la Calabria e la Basilicata," in *Scritti sulla questione meridionale* (Bari: Editori Laterza, 1958), 538.

18. Annuario Statistico 1905–1907, cited in The Immigration Commission, "Emigration Conditions in Europe," 161.

19. Dott. Ilario Zannoni, *Per la immigrazione di contadini settentrionali nella Basilicata* (Milan: Ufficio Agrario della Societa' Umanitaria, 1906), 12–13.

20. Cagli, "L'emigrazione e l'agricolutra in Basilicata," 137–138, 145.

21. Maura Palazzi, *Donne sole: Storia dell'altra faccia dell'Italia tra antico regime a società contemporanea* (Turin: B. Mondadori, 1997), 382.

22. "Un lembo ignorato d'Italia: La Basilicata, VIII," *La Stampa*, October 7, 1887.

23. "Mali e dolori dell'emigrazione," *La Stampa*, January 5, 1907.

24. "Le ombre nel quadro della nostra emigrazione," *Bollettino dell'Emigrazione* 15 (1907): 173–175.

25. ASP, Atti di Pubblica Sicurezza, Cat. 6. Busta 42.

26. ASP, Atti di Pubblica Sicurezza, Cat. 6. Busta 41.

27. ASP, Atti di Pubblica Sicurezza, Cat. 6. Busta 41.

28. Aldo Pace, *Banco di Napoli: L'emigrazione e le rimesse emigranti* (Naples: Istituto Banco di Napoli, 2007).

29. Lacava, "Sulle condizione economico-sociali della Basilicata," 117.

30. Gino Massullo, "Economia delle rimesse," in *Storia dell'Emigrazione Italiana*, Vol. 1, eds. Piero Bevilacqua, Andreina de Clemente, and Emilio Franzina (Rome: Donzelli, 2002), 162.

31. R. J. Bosworth, *Italy and the Wider World, 1860–1960* (New York: Routledge, 1996), 6.

32. De Clementi, "Gender Relations and Migration Strategies in the Rural Italian South," 93.

33. Massullo, "Economia delle rimesse," 170–176.

34. Adolfo Rossi, "Vantaggi e danni dell'emigrazione nel mezzogiorno d'Italia (Note di un viaggio fatto in Basilicata e in Calabria dal R. Commissario dell'Emigrazione," *Bollettino dell'Emigrazione* 13 (1908): 1644, 1564, 1567.

35. Quoted in Massullo, "Economia delle rimesse," 161.

36. "Relazione del Commissario Generale dell'Emigrazione," *Bollettino dell'Emigrazione* 7 (1904): 18.

37. "Le ombre nel quadro della nostra emigrazione," *Bollettino dell'Emigrazione* 15 (1907): 173–175.

38. ASP, Atti di Pubblica Sicurezza, Cat. 6. Busta 41.

39. *Il Lucano*, March 1899.

40. *Il Lucano*, March 1905.

41. *Il Lucano*, March 1905.

42. *Il Gazzettino di Basilicata*, May 1888.

43. *Il Lucano*, March 1899.

44. *La Libera Parola*, September 1909, 4.

45. *Giornale di Basilicata*, December 1912, 4.

46. *Giornale di Basilicata*, December 1911.

47. *L'Intransigente*, May 1892, 4.

48. *La Libera Parola*, September 1909, 4.

49. *La Libera Parola*, December 1909, 4.

50. *La Libera Parola*, March 1910, 4.

51. *Il Lucano*, March 1899.

52. *Il Lucano*, March 1900.

53. *Il Lucano*, March 1905.

54. *L'Intransigente*, May 1892.

55. *Il Lucano*, March 1905.

56. *Giornale di Basilicata*, March 1912, 4.

57. Vincenzo Solimena, *Educhiamo la donna: Conferenza letta al circolo degli artigiani* (Rionero in Vulture: Tipografia di Torquato Ercolani, 1888), 9.

58. Solimena, *Educhiamo la donna*, 10.

59. ASP, Atti di Pubblica Sicurezza, Cat. 6. Busta 43.

60. Solimena, *Educhiamo la donna*, 11.

61. ASP, Atti di Pubblica Sicurezza, Cat. 6. Busta 41.

Chapter 4

Women and the State
Forging Citizenship

In November 1878, Rosa P. appealed to the mayor of Palazzo San Gervasio, a small town in Basilicata, asking for his assistance in writing to the prefect. She sought news of her husband, Paolo T., who emigrated to Buenos Aires six years prior, "leaving a wife and two children of tender age." Rosa's request stated that she had not heard from him in two years, and the family was experiencing great hardships. She decided to turn to the mayor, "imploring him for support to discover the location of her husband." Since there seems to have been no response, eight months later Rosa sent another petition, again asking for news of her husband. The mayor added a comment when he forwarded the second petition to the prefect, writing that this request, "deals with a miserable mother of two children perplexed over the abandonment of her husband." Three months later, just shy of a year after the first request, the Foreign Ministry finally responded, saying it could not locate Rosa's husband. Five months later, in March 1880, Rosa wrote once again, hoping she would obtain news of her still missing spouse. At that point it had been eight years since he emigrated and almost four years since he sent money to support his wife and children. Rosa received another response from the Foreign Ministry in January 1881, stating it still could not find him, and informing her that "the name of Paolo T. was published on a list of persons being searched for by the consulate in Buenos Aires, without presenting himself or anyone else having news of him."

The file ends here, and the fate of Rosa and her two children is unknown. She was in a desperate situation, abandoned by her husband and in need of money to support her children. Like most women in Basilicata, Rosa had limited opportunity to earn wages, and it was difficult for her to find paid work without marital authorization. She could not remarry because there was no proof of her husband's death, so she would be forced to find a way to provide for herself and her children. The numerous requests made in attempt to locate her husband show her persistence. She did not give up after the first petition went unanswered and wrote various times for news of her husband.[1]

When young married men left Basilicata in search of work or fortune elsewhere, many married women were left behind on their own. The previous chapters have shown how these women were responsible for taking care of the household, managing the family funds, raising the children, and performing any tasks their husbands may have left in their care. Scholars have used the idea of "women who wait" as a label for those who remained behind.[2] Yet this designation perpetuates the stereotype of passivity and dependence and gives the impression that the lives of these women rested completely on the actions of their husbands.[3] Other scholars have labeled the situation as temporary widowhood, or *vedovanza temporanea*.[4] This may be a more appropriate label, yet still not completely accurate since married women did not share the same legal rights as widows. Women's situations varied, but they could not and did not simply wait for men to return, and their lives did not halt because of their husbands' absence. Instead, with men away, some women turned to local officials for aid and support, forging a new relationship with the state and using it to their advantage when in need.

In order to better understand the situation of these women, the chapter begins with an in-depth analysis of the phenomenon of migration in Italy at the turn of the twentieth century, examining who migrated and why, with particular focus on those from Basilicata. As migration increased over the course of the Liberal Period, not only did the state become more heavily involved in protecting migrants, particularly through two major pieces of legislation, but it also became more involved in protecting the women who remained behind. Examining the process, the factors that went into making the decision to emigrate, the governmental response, and the shift in how Rome perceived migration, demonstrates that emigration greatly impacted the place of departure and *all* people involved in the process.

When left on their own and in need, women contacted their local mayors and prefects, requesting passports and information to search for missing husbands and relatives abroad. Mayors not only forwarded their requests to regional officials and international consulates but in doing so also assisted and protected women who remained behind. Many officials added in their observations and comments about the women and seemed to advocate for them, especially if their circumstances appeared to be dire. A further look at the language in the requests also shows the emotional impact of emigration on women, and how some mayors displayed sympathy for their situations.

Not only did emigration change women's roles within marriage, family life, and the economy, but it also helped shape a new relationship with officials of the Italian state. In their requests, it is clear that women knew their rights, especially within marriage, and recognized that they could rely on government officials to help protect those rights. Yet in appealing to the state, women stepped out of prescribed gender roles and norms, as men would traditionally be the ones who interacted with state officials as head of the family. Women, however, were not passive, and in fact took active steps to stand up for themselves, even if it meant turning to a state that at times seemed out of touch or alien to them. They developed a new relationship with the Italian state, one in which women interacted with officials in the public sphere, traditionally the realm of men, and thus cultivated a sense of modern citizenship.

THE MIGRATION DECISION

As outlined in the introduction, migration had always been part of Italian life, well before the great wave of emigration that began in the late nineteenth century. In Basilicata, laborers migrated seasonally to nearby towns or provinces searching for agricultural work. After unification in 1861, internal migration in the south slowed, mainly due to brigandage and the resulting difficulty and dangers of traveling. The promises of Liberalism and the newly unified state also gave Lucanians hope that the government would enact policies that would improve their lives and stimulate the local economy. By the 1880s however, higher grain prices, as well as taxes and other economic pressures, led Italians to emigrate in search of better wages. Large-scale Italian emigration truly began about twenty years after unification. In most cases, this relocation was not permanent, but a temporary solution to earn more money. Although traveling a lot farther to find work, many emigrants still intended to return home after they had earned and saved money. Thus, migration was not a new phenomenon in Basilicata, and the decision to leave was one that many families had previously considered.

Italian emigration patterns changed from the beginning of the nineteenth century to the early years of the twentieth century. In the early nineteenth century, emigration was limited to skilled workers and was small in number. Later in the century, emigration boomed after the agricultural crisis of the 1880s. Government protections favored proprietors and hurt small landowners, thus affecting the wages they could pay their workers and pushing those workers to emigrate.[5] Before 1900, a majority of Italian emigrants left from northern regions, such as the Veneto, Friuli, and Piedmont. Generally, most emigrants from the north went to other European countries, such as Germany, France, and Switzerland. This migration also was largely temporary. Only after 1900 did the south overtake the north in the total number of emigrants per capita. Southern Italians tended to go to the Americas, with the United States, Brazil, and Argentina as some of the leading destinations.[6]

Basilicata was among the southern regions that would eventually send millions of emigrants to the Americas and all over the world. Emigration from the region began in large scale in the late nineteenth century and picked up even more after the turn of the century. The heaviest emigration came from the western part of Basilicata: the mountainous area surrounding Potenza and towns in the districts of Lagonegro and Melfi. The eastern part of the region, especially the area near Matera, had a lower rate of emigration, due to a more favorable climate and somewhat better agricultural conditions.

Emigrants from Basilicata were mostly young, working-age males, many of them either newlyweds or only married a few years. They were illiterate laborers who survived on daily wages. These men often had their own families which they had the obligation to support, and knew that going abroad to work would most likely allow them to do that. Despite the separation and the long journey, they believed they would be able to provide for their families better than if they remained in Italy. Emigration ostensibly required an agreement between husband and wife. Ideally, the husband would emigrate to work, with every intention of returning, and in the meantime, the wife would stay behind, care for the family's interests, and receive money that the husband sent in remittances.

Men accounted for an overwhelming percentage of Italian emigrants. According to numbers collected by the Department of Statistics (*Direzione di Statistica)* between 1876 and 1900, 81% of emigrants were male, and 84% of them were over the age of fourteen.[7] This pattern holds true in Basilicata as well. Between July 1880 and June 1881, the district of Lagonegro had 1,280 emigrants (83% male and 17% female), and the district of Potenza had 1,440 (74% male and 26% female).[8] Overall, more emigrants left Basilicata individually than with families; in 1905, 68.86% of emigrants left alone, while only 34.14% left with family members.[9] These figures may indicate that migrants intended to return home after a period of time. In terms of age, 82.4% of all southern Italian immigrants to the United States between 1899 and 1909 were between the ages of fourteen and forty-four.[10]

Between 1876 and 1914, Basilicata's emigration rate was one of the highest in Italy. Emigration was so pervasive that in the 1901 census, 11,000 women in Basilicata were living without their husbands.[11] Statistics from the same census show that of the 124,872 families in Basilicata, roughly 20% of the households reported the head of the family was absent or dead. In comparison to Pavia (in the Lombardy region), an area in the north with similar population, there were 108,700 families and the number with absent or deceased husbands was roughly 5%.[12] Thus, a higher number of women were living alone in Basilicata, likely due to heavy male emigration.

Only a small percent of emigrants were women, and a majority of those who left did so with their husbands. Between 1876 and the early 1900s, women made up at most 20% to 25% of emigrants, and in most cases, they were traveling with or joining their husbands or other family members abroad.[13] Unlike their counterparts in the north who occasionally emigrated to other European countries for work, southern women rarely emigrated on their own. The mentality of a patriarchal society deemed female emigration inappropriate, and many officials feared women traveling alone would become deviant or fall into an immoral lifestyle if not regulated. Thus, most females emigrated under the protection of a spouse or male relative. Their emigration tended to be permanent, as they would usually travel with or join their husband or family members already settled abroad.[14]

Most emigrants originated from rural areas and worked as day laborers.[15] For example, in 1905, 10,035 out of 17,009 emigrants from Basilicata were agricultural workers.[16] Since they did not own land, unskilled laborers depended on their wages to survive and took on a variety of jobs in the places to which they emigrated, from agriculture to industry. In northern Europe, Italians worked in industrial factories and mines. In Brazil, where slavery was abolished in 1888, emigrants helped cultivate coffee on former slave plantations. In North America, Italian migrants did everything from farm work, mining, factory work, to construction projects, like digging the subway tunnels in New York City.[17]

Italian migration differed from that of other groups arriving in the Americas in the same period in that it was not always permanent. Many migrants planned to stay abroad for a determined amount of time and then return home to Italy. In fact, a number of them even went back and forth multiple times. These "birds of passage," as they were called, were similar to seasonal migrants who traveled within Italy, except they now made a longer transatlantic journey, facilitated by the use of the steamship. Birds of passage went abroad for certain seasons, saved money, sent remittances home, and then returned. For example, in Argentina and Uruguay, landowners depended on Italian workers who arrived in October and left in February or March when the harvest was complete.[18] Following labor opportunities was in line with historical migratory patterns in southern Italy.

With emigration, several towns witnessed a transformation in socioeconomic structure and class distinctions. Emigrants from Basilicata and Italy overall were generally poor, but property owners, both small and large, saw their ablest workers emigrating and returning with more earnings. Both small and large landowners were hurt by emigration. Unable to find or pay workers, often they were forced either to cultivate their own land or abandon it. Because of lack of workers, they often had to leave much of their land uncultivated, which decreased profits. Selling their property was difficult because few were interested in buying it. Many property owners chose to emigrate despite their elevated social position, knowing they could earn more working abroad.

Many landowners thus abandoned their holdings and became wage laborers, showing just how much more wage laborers earned in America than most others in Basilicata. A report in the *Bollettino dell'Emigrazione* pointed out the unusual phenomenon; "it is no longer the poorest social classes leaving the country . . . (but) especially small property owners, who leave their poor possessions to go abroad as wage laborers."[19] Other small landowners emigrated to improve their social position, knowing that in America they could make higher wages, then return to Italy and buy more land, improve their homes, and afford new luxuries.[20] A politician from the town of Corleto Perticara noted that "a shepherd lives better than a schoolmaster."[21] Thus, emigration disrupted the social hierarchy within many villages.

The state of agriculture was one of the main reasons for emigration from Basilicata. Farmers used outdated, if not antiquated, techniques, resulting in poor yields. Combined with the state of the land, which was described as "sterile" and insufficient, inhabitants either had to resign to a life of uncertainty or emigrate.[22] Originally from Basilicata, Francesco Saverio Nitti wrote that despite emigration being difficult, people left because they knew what they had to endure could not be worse than life as it was.[23]

Another article in the *Bollettino dell'Emigrazione* observed that even the unskilled or those with no profession could hope to go to America and make a fortune. The reporter told the story of fourteen-year-old Filomena, who spoke to him with wide eyes full of hope about America. She said that even people with no experience or skills could go to America and make money, including her former coworker. This colleague was a seamstress who was always scolded for her lack of ability and carelessness. Yet when this coworker went to America, within two months, she earned more than double what Filomena made.[24] Her story may have been an exaggeration, but it demonstrates the high hopes people had about finding success abroad and the relative ease with which they expected to achieve it.

Basilicata was and remains one of the least densely populated regions of Italy. In many areas, agricultural production was also low, resulting in fewer opportunities for work. The laborers who stayed behind thus became more demanding and wages became more competitive in the late nineteenth century. Lack of able workers also forced small landowners to raise wages, even for women, or recruit workers from other Italian regions, as discussed in the previous chapter. Laborers in many other southern Italian regions, in contrast, experienced difficulty finding work and wages were not competitive because of the large number of available laborers. In addition, work was seasonal with laborers working for a few months at a time. In Basilicata, peasants struggled to make enough to support their families. Even when landowners paid higher wages, the land was often infertile, and earnings were not enough to retain workers. The situation was similar in the north, yet many wage laborers were able to move to nearby cities and find work there, especially in factories. In the southern mainland, Naples was the only big city in the area (Bari to the east was much smaller), and work was difficult to find there because of poverty and lack of major industry in Naples itself. This pushed many southern Italians to emigrate to America.

Emigrants reported that work was easier in America. Adolfo Rossi, who traveled throughout the region as part of an inquest into the lives of farmers (*Commissione d'inchiesta per i contadini*), interviewed a man who explained that in Basilicata, laborers woke up at dawn, and walked up to seven miles along mountainous terrain carrying their tools. By the time they arrived at work, they were exhausted. Workers did not have to travel as far each day in America, and in addition, they earned more money. The emigrant told Rossi, "the farmer cannot resist the temptation to go. This is what is called the contagion of America."[25]

Perhaps hearing the success stories of others was the most influential reason for emigration. Rossi also interviewed an emigrant from Albano di Lucania who returned to the town to bring his parents and sister to America. When asked why he had emigrated, he responded saying: "here I was poor and ragged, I went around barefoot and earned fifty cents on the days which I could work. In New York, as a simple barber I earned twelve to fourteen dollars a week. Then I had my own shop. Before leaving I sold it for $500 and now I will return to New York to open an even better one."[26] Emigrants told stories of success and prosperity in America when they returned, surely inspiring those who may have been contemplating emigration. In Laurenzana, a town with heavy emigration, the mayor reported that initially people left because of poverty, but "now it is the spirit of imitation and the hope of savings."[27] Many Lucanians thus left because they heard of the successes of their family, friends, and neighbors and wanted to experience that same luck.

Emigration agents also traveled into towns to try to convince people to emigrate. The law sanctioned licensed companies (*Comitati comunali e mandamentale per l'emigrazione*) to send representatives to Italian towns to provide information to and recruit prospective migrants. Over 3,000 Comitati existed in all of Italy by 1904, the largest number in the province of Potenza, with 123.[28] Yet, these agencies were less effective in convincing people than word of mouth. By 1908, the mayor in Pignola reported that there was no longer a need for emigration agents to come to the town; every family had relatives or friends in America.[29] Emigration was pervasive even in small and seemingly isolated villages.

Yet, some decided not to emigrate. A man interviewed in the town of Latronico discussed why he chose to remain, despite not earning enough for daily expenses and having his wife and four children sleeping in one room with two beds. He explained that he did not have the money to pay for the journey. Migrants generally borrowed money from friends or relatives to pay for the initial passage, and then repaid the sum after earning wages abroad. The interviewee also asserted that unlike some others, he could not leave his wife and small children.[30] While some migrants may have been willing to leave their families for the opportunity to give them a better life, others simply did not want to take the risk.

It is difficult to recreate or even imagine the thought process of prospective emigrants. Surely they had seen their family members, friends, and neighbors emigrate, and witnessed the monetary and material benefits of that decision. They must have evaluated their own situation and calculated the costs and benefits of emigrating themselves. Indeed, they saw women, children, and the elderly left behind, and probably wondered how their departure would affect their own family. It could not have been an easy decision for anyone. The prospect of crossing an ocean had to be disconcerting to someone who may have never even left his own village. Yet, many migrants saw the reward as being well worth the inherent risks.

GOVERNMENT RESPONSE AND LEGAL LIMITATIONS

Italian laws regulating emigration changed drastically over the course of the late nineteenth and early twentieth centuries, from barely any oversight to complete government intervention in the process. Yet, one constant through-out this period was a commitment to Liberal principles and individual liberties, including the freedom to emigrate. The increasing number of emigrants, the enormous economic benefit of remittances, and the budding interest of the state in the millions of citizens who were leaving the country, especially in the post-unification period, were major causes for the government's radical shift. Consequently, these national laws impacted the women of Basilicata on a local level as well.

In the years after Italian unification in 1861, the government was still working on incorporating the diverse regions of the peninsula into one state. A lack of knowledge and a great deal of misunderstanding about the south persisted. As a result, the state did not initially look favorably upon emigration from its southern regions, viewing it as a means of escape for criminals and vagrants, especially brigands. Others argued that most emigrants were young men who wanted to avoid compulsory military service. In general, officials felt that large-scale emigration tarnished the image of the new state.

According to historian Richard Bosworth, it undermined the government and tested its legitimacy.[31]

In the years following unification and before major emigration legislation, Italians migrated at their own risk, with little government oversight.[32] Emigration was "tolerated" by the government, which rarely intervened in the process.[33] The state was slow to change its position. Discussions about emigration began to increase by the 1870s, as Parliament debated how much the government should intervene, but little was resolved. A circular from January 1873 demonstrated the attitude of the government as it encouraged prefects and mayors to dissuade emigrants and to give "suitable advice so as to discourage dangerous illusions."[34] In 1876, the government began keeping statistics on emigration, and as the growing number became apparent in the following years, Rome could no longer ignore the issue. The first piece of major legislation regarding emigration was passed in 1888, and a subsequent, more comprehensive law passed in 1901. Each of these laws reflected the politics at the time and demonstrated a shift in government interest which overlapped with an ever-increasing rate of emigration, especially from the southern regions. The government's changing position also coincided with the arrival of large sums of remittances, which many officials considered a possible solution to the south's economic and social problems.

Passed on December 30, 1888, the Crispi Law (n. 5866) was the first major response by the state to large-scale emigration. Prime Minister Francesco Crispi was from Sicily, which at that time was just beginning to experience mass migration. Serving as Prime Minister from 1887 to 1891 and then again from 1893 to 1896, Crispi played a key role in the passing of the legislation. Much of his first term dealt with social and economic issues, such as the penal code, prison reform, emigration law, and an overhaul of public health and welfare. The law which bears his name was based on his view of the positive effects of emigration, especially for economic improvement in Italy, a viewpoint which was still quite rare from politicians in Rome at the time.[35]

The law confirmed the freedom of Italians to emigrate, yet imposed some restrictions. It reaffirmed the need for marital permission for women to migrate. Young men needing to fulfill military service obligations were not issued passports, especially if officials suspected they were emigrating to avoid it. If young men had appeared for service and were placed in reserve, they could obtain a passport. Criminals or those who were condemned to serve a prison sentence were also prohibited from emigrating.

A major concern of the Crispi Law was to prevent prospective emigrants from being duped by malicious agents looking to profit off their naivety. Thus, the law placed controls over the activities of emigration agents.[36] Scammers lent money to prospective emigrants and charged high rates of interest. In a letter to the prefect, the mayor of Savoia di Lucania elucidated

his concerns, saying that those who decided to emigrate desperately took
loans from speculators who charged exorbitant interest rates.[37] The law aimed
to protect emigrants in these circumstances. Any agent acting as an interme-
diary between emigrants and steamship companies, including those who sold
tickets to emigrants, was required to obtain a license.[38] The cost of a license
was high, which prevented just anyone from obtaining one, and even some
who had worked in the business prior to the law could not afford a license to
continue working.[39]

The 1888 law aimed primarily to prevent abuses by those wanting to take
advantage of the migrants. Yet, its main focus was on the initial phases
of emigration: buying a ticket and transporting individuals to ports of
departure. The law did not consider the protection of emigrants once they
boarded the ships and departed Italian soil. Thus, fewer recourses existed
for emigrants once abroad, where citizens lacked the protection of the
Italian government. Volunteer societies or members of the Catholic Church
established local groups or organizations to fill that gap in an attempt to
assist emigrants abroad. Overall, the law called for government intervention
in the regulation of the emigration process, but it was not meant to encour-
age migration.

At the time the Crispi Law was passed, the rate of emigration was still low,
but very much increasing. Thirteen years later, in light of the continued rise
in the numbers of emigrants, another major piece of legislation was passed
on January 31, 1901, which again redefined the state's role in the process.
This legislation was much more comprehensive, and indeed, more paternalistic, than the previous law. It focused on safeguarding migrants through all
phases of the journey from buying a ticket, leaving the village, boarding the
vessel at the port of embarkation, and arrival abroad. Coinciding with many
other pieces of progressive legislation of the Giolitti Era (1901–1914), the
law focused on direct government management of emigration by protecting
migrants and making the journey more secure.[40]

The 1901 law reiterated that emigration was free for all, except for those
with military obligations or those who had to serve a prison sentence.
Passports were to be issued within twenty-four hours of the request, and the
law eliminated the necessity of those intermediaries that tended to fool or
swindle prospective emigrants.[41] It reiterated that only agents licensed by the
state could advertise and sell tickets to emigrants.[42] The law also addressed
the issue of emigrating minors. As discussed in Chapter 2, schemes set up by
traffickers and scammers to pay families for young children to work abroad
were not uncommon in the years after unification. These professions were
outlawed and the agents promoting them were largely eliminated by 1900.
However, the 1901 emigration law did address children workers, and reiterated that it was illegal to send minors abroad for work.[43]

The 1901 law shifted responsibility for emigration from the Ministry of the Interior to the Foreign Ministry (*Ministero degli Affari Esteri*), granting it the power to limit or suspend emigration to certain locations for reasons of public order or due to a specific danger for emigrants.[44] The creation of the *Commissariato Generale dell'Emigrazione* (CGE) was an important part of the legislation. This agency helped emigrants in all facets of the journey, from buying the ticket in their home village, to searching for work through contacts and agencies abroad, and all the processes in between.[45] The law stipulated that an inspector of emigration be placed at all the ports of embarkation—Naples, Genoa, and Palermo—and the shipping carrier was responsible for any damages to emigrants.[46] The law also created the *Bollettino dell'Emigrazione,* which became the means of correspondence and dissemination of pertinent information relating to emigration within the CGE. Published between 1902 and running until 1928, the *Bollettino dell'Emigrazione* helped agency workers remain abreast of the latest emigration information, statistics, and warnings so they could pass that news on to the appropriate officials. The publication also included articles by various contributors, who conducted surveys and even case studies on aspects of Italian migration.

The law also made the *Banco di Napoli* the official institution for sending and receiving remittances, which facilitated the process for emigrants sending money home. In 1901, the *Banco di Napoli* opened a branch in New York, and within a few years, the bank established over seventy affiliated branches in the Americas, Africa, and Europe.[47] This network of banks made the process of transferring money easier and more reliable. Financial institutions could more easily and reliably track the flow of money back to Italy. By 1907, over 550 million lire were sent back to Italy from locations abroad.[48] The establishment of the *Banco di Napoli* as the official bank of remittances was yet another way that the 1901 emigration law protected emigrants even after they left Italy.

The 1901 legislation capped a radical shift in state policy toward emigration. Within a little less than thirty years, the state went from having little to no interest in emigration, to taking on a paternalistic and protective role. Historian Casimira Grandi contends that in the time between the two laws, the government's attitude clearly shifted, and emigration became more political.[49] Similarly, historian Samuel Baily argues that the 1888 law treated emigration as a private decision, with the role of the state as eliminating abuses, but by 1901, state oversight increased, bringing it into the public realm.[50] The state took years to recognize the effects of emigration, both on its people and its economy, and went from an opposing to an intervening position. While initially the government was not favorable toward emigration because it seemed to reflect its inability to help its own people and was considered a source of shame, Rome had little choice but to accept the reality of this growing nationwide phenomenon and pass legislation to intervene and assist migrants.

LOCAL INTERACTIONS WITH THE STATE

As in the rest of Italy, emigration laws were enforced locally in each region. The mayor of each town and prefect of each province were intermediaries between the state and citizens on a local level. As noted, a father or a husband as head of household represented the family in the eyes of the state and would interact with these officials when needed. Married women traditionally kept to the private sphere and did not have many legal rights. Yet, a closer examination reveals that women were able to interact with the state and use it to their benefit, especially in times of great need. They could not get around their legal limitations, but they could demand that the state uphold and protect their few rights. Thus, a positive relationship developed, one where wives, as de facto heads of the family, petitioned the state, which would in turn offer services to support women in need.

Rural women in Basilicata turned to the structures of the new national government to assist them with hardships and difficulties that arose due to emigration. These secular authorities provided assistance that women did not otherwise obtain through social or religious means. If a wife depended on her husband's wages to support her and the family, communication between the couple would be crucial during their time apart. Emigrants could write letters or send messages through other migrants traveling to and from the village. Yet, women left on their own sometimes had the unfortunate circumstance of not hearing from their spouse or receiving any sign that he was alive. If husbands did not send remittances from abroad, then it was their dependents—women and children—who suffered the most. Finding themselves on their own and in these difficult circumstances, some women approached local officials to search for their spouses abroad, whether to implore them to return home or to force them to send money. Even though they may have acted out of desperation, women saw appealing to the state as an option and decided to utilize it to their benefit. They contacted their mayors to assist them with requesting passports, asking for financial help, pleading their cases, and demanding their husbands comply with their duties.

One option for women in these situations was to petition the Ministry of Foreign Affairs to search for news of their relatives abroad. Written with the help of the local mayor, their requests were then sent to the prefect, who passed them along to the Ministry of Foreign Affairs. The Ministry then contacted consulates abroad, which in turn would search for the missing person, generally through word of mouth, bulletins, newspapers, and registers of people trying to be located. In most cases, the petitioning woman received a response once consulates abroad considered the request. Case files in the state archives conserve this paper trail, with documented notes from the various offices through which petitions passed. These documents offer a rich glimpse into the way requests to various state agencies were made, as well as how the state handled such requests and communicated among themselves. Unfortunately, unless women sent subsequent petitions, their reactions upon receiving a response from the state are unknown.

All of the women's petitions were unique and used certain persuasive language in appealing to officials. Because of high illiteracy rates, many women wrote these requests with the help of the mayor, so it is impossible to know if the actual words were directly from the women or if they were embellished by the mayor (a male) who knew what to say to make the requests heard. Nevertheless, since each letter differed, and there was no specific template, it is probable that mayors did listen to each individual woman while composing their petitions. Some women simply wrote for information, without making their case or expressing their suffering. Other women pleaded their case using strong, emotional language, citing their poverty, misery, and inability to feed their children. No evidence exists that either method was more successful than the other. The differences in wording might be attributed to the different personalities of women requesting assistance. While there are a large number of requests, it is also impossible to know the percentage of women who *did not* appeal to the state for assistance.

Legally, the mayor would be aware of the emigrant's duties as a husband and father, and he would also attest to the presented condition of the woman who came to make the request. It is difficult to gauge whether the women were exaggerating in their petitions, but if the mayor forwarded their requests and added his own commentary imploring the prefect to act, it may demonstrate that the women did not overstate the gravity of their situations.

Responses from the consulates also indicate the type of comprehensive searches that various agencies conducted abroad. If an individual from Italy was searching for a family member's whereabouts, the consulates abroad attempted to make this public information. They posted lists of names in newspapers and even used social networks and word of mouth to search for missing people. The process took time, which meant that the women at home who requested information often waited months for a response. These had to be difficult periods of anguish and uncertainty, especially for women in desperate financial situations.

REQUESTING SEARCHES

Women commonly turned to the state to help them search for a husband abroad who had not been heard from for some time or had lapsed in sending remittances. Various examples of this were seen in Chapter 1. In the opening story of this chapter, Rosa, an abandoned mother with young children, turned to the mayor when she could no longer depend on her husband. In most of the petitions, wives requested news of their husbands and financial assistance for survival. Their needs seemed to be more material and economic than emotional. Children, on the other hand, were treated differently in the petitions.

Women made petitions searching for children abroad and pleaded to the mayor for help if their children were missing or had been out of touch. Mothers in Basilicata sent search requests all over the world, from Argentina, to Paraguay, to the United States, and other countries in Europe. All these women were desperate to hear news of their children. In most cases, mothers searched for their children because they generally were concerned about their well-being. In one request, a woman described as a "derelict mother" asked for information about her son, whom she had not heard from in over a year. She simply asked for news of his whereabouts and hoped a response would bring her "peace."[51] Although, children may have also been sending money to parents, the motivation for searching for them was largely emotional, as mothers desperately desired to know if their children were well.

Besides searching for their husbands and children abroad, women also requested information about other family members. One woman from Moliterno wrote on behalf of her parents, asking for news of her brother in Cincinnati, Ohio, whom they had not heard from in several years. The letter suggested that the family also had some business in the town and needed his permission to proceed. They asked him to contact the consulate immediately and send a power of attorney.[52] No response accompanied this request, so it is unknown whether or not the brother was located or replied to their petition. However, the letter shows the circumstances in which many families had been placed: a family member was missing and could not be contacted abroad and those at home needed his authorization for some type of transaction. The daughter made the request on behalf of her parents, who entrusted her to help locate their son and her brother.

As stated above, the women who remained behind are often referred to as "widows in white"; however, some women actually did become widows if their husbands died while abroad. These women were put in a particularly difficult situation, as they had to arrange for the return of the body and ensure that their town's civil registers recorded the death. Requesting the death certificate of husbands who died abroad was crucial, especially if a woman wanted to remarry. The only way she would be permitted to wed was with the death certificate confirming her first husband was deceased. In one instance, the Foreign Ministry wrote to a woman in Potenza to inform her that her husband died in a hospital in Bolivia. In fact, he died as a result of injuries after the husband of his mistress physically assaulted him. The widow, Angela Maria P. wrote to the Foreign Ministry three years later to request an official death certificate because she was required to present the document in order to remarry.[53]

Widows not only requested death certificates but also obtained the power to take care of other legal business. For example, in 1881, Beatrice R. of Lauria sent an appeal to the Foreign Ministry after her husband died abroad. She requested that the possessions he left there be sent back to her.[54] Women also made requests to arrange items from other family members be returned as well. Angela Maria N. wrote asking for the return of her deceased brother's goods from Africa.[55] Normally other male family members would make this sort of request, but from the records it appeared their father was also deceased, and Angela Maria was likely the only remaining sibling.

Another concern for abandoned women was learning their civil status. Several wives petitioned because they wanted to find out whether their husbands were alive or dead. This would indeed change a woman's legal position and would give her a great deal more freedom, including the possibility of remarrying. Even if she had been abandoned with no sign that an emigrant husband would send remittances or ever return to Italy, she needed a death certificate to gain the rights of a widow or eventually remarry. Thus, women searched for husbands and other family not only when they were alive but also if they were deceased, in order to deal with bureaucratic work and settle affairs at home.

Overall, the national and local governments took women's requests seriously and made every attempt to follow up on them. Many petitioners received a response. Some were more comprehensive, others were short, answering inquiries, and explaining the situation if necessary. For example, the wife of Francesco C. of Picerno received a brief response when she requested a search for her husband: "C. resides in Mercedes (Buenos Aires) and promises to write without delay to the named woman."[56] Others were pages long, and officials took time to add detail to their responses. Women's requests were handled with as much attention as male requests, demonstrating the state was available to help women, and they in turn could trust the state to follow up on their petitions.

LANGUAGE IN THE REQUESTS

Women continued to petition the state when in need, using emotionally charged language that appealed to the perceived weaknesses of their sex, compelling the state to advocate for their rights against their husbands' neglect. The prevailing attitudes of the time were based partly on Cesare Lombroso's positivist analysis of women as less intelligent, weak, and prone to hysteria. Lombroso argued that their physical characteristics demonstrated this inferiority. In order to improve their situation and force answers to their petitions, women played on their helplessness and their inability to work outside the home, as well as their husband's duty to provide for his family. The language used in their petitions and sent to government officials from various agencies demonstrates that women consciously used their subordinate position to appeal to officials for sympathy.

There were several strategies women used in petitioning authorities. The most common approach was mentioning that they lived in poverty or misery. Often, the letter related a story of the woman's situation and described her as being poor and miserable. In one example, a woman requesting a passport without authorization, Maria Felicia D., claimed that she was "going through the most extreme miseries, would like to go and find him, and to present his own faithful daughter to remind him of his conjugal duty."[57] This woman expressed she was living in deplorable conditions and wanted to go find her husband. Her request also referred to their daughter and marital duty, two important reasons her husband ought to send money back home.

Many other petitioners presented as a "poor woman" and demonstrated poverty as a way to show their desperation. Maria Antonia V. wrote a letter on her own, without the help of the mayor, so the words were directly hers. In her petition, she humbly expressed her situation to the prefect. She explained that her husband migrated seven years prior and had not sent any money, just letters. After pleading her case, she begged the prefect to issue her a passport in order to "wash away her misery."[58] Here she used her inferior position and inability to work to gain sympathy and support from the official.

Authorities did not want women to beg on the streets or turn to prostitution, so they helped seemingly desperate women. Perhaps officials believed that if husbands knew their wives and children were poor and living in misery, even if exaggerated, they would be more likely to send remittances. While Maria Antonia was not issued a passport, her situation caught the attention of the mayor, who forwarded along her request. Mayors were sympathetic, but in the end, they could not bend or change the law; they did as much as they could, but the system of patriarchy remained.

The petitions allow outsiders a glimpse into not only a practical but also an emotional aspect of emigration. Although one cannot know if the petitions were exaggerated or even fabricated, they played on the weakness and vulnerability attributed to women. Each petition was distinct and told a unique story. They were imaginative and inventive, using rhetorical strategies to state their problems. As mentioned earlier, women did not simply fill out a form letter when requesting assistance, but each letter told of an individual family and its own unique circumstances. Within each petition, the use of specific words and phrases portrays the desperate state of these women.

The language used in many of the petitions was meant not only to pull at emotions but also to require husbands to comply with their legal duties and obligations toward their wives. The wording that Serafina C. from Lauria used in her request for information about her husband in Montevideo employed this dual purpose. She informed the mayor about her husband, stating that "about eleven years ago he emigrated to America and in the first years he sent some small relief to the family, but in the past five years he has persistently forgotten the obligations he has in this town." She asked that the consulate in Montevideo search for her husband and inform him that his wife and five children "yearn repatriation" and that he "return to his family as a good father and husband as he was before emigrating to America."[59] There was no response in the file, but the letter gives insight into some of the feelings women may have experienced in regards to their husbands emigrating to America. While a good economic decision for the family, provided that the husband kept his promise and sent money home, others might have considered emigration a bad decision. Some perceived America as a place husbands went to escape from their duties and obligations and to forget about their wives and families. This letter implies that emigration to America made this husband stray from his role as a provider. The wife felt that if he returned home, he would escape the negative influence of America and once again comply with his duty.

Although rare, letters written by women themselves were especially powerful and show suffering and abandonment were not limited to the poorest or least educated. In 1883, Rosina C. of Potenza wrote pleading her case to the prefect. Her letter is notable, as she used elegant script and bolded certain words for emphasis. She wrote that her husband, Bonaventura G. "abandoned his country and his large family consisting of *five* children and emigrated to the *Americas*, promising to lift his family from the hardest misery." When he first went to New York, he sent provisions home, which she claimed were barely enough to provide bread to their five children. But, she wrote, for the last six months, not only had he not sent anything but also the family received no news of him. She was turning to the esteemed prefect "taking to heart the unhappy position of her five unfortunate children who ask for *bread*, let this news reach their father and force him to succor *his own blood* and to repatriate."[60] The Foreign Ministry's response stated that her husband could not be located at the address she provided, but they would publish his name in the newspaper *L'Eco d'Italia*, hoping someone would know of his whereabouts. Written by an abandoned woman, this letter demonstrates that despite education or social position, married women had the same restrictions, and most depended on their husbands to provide for their families, especially the children. The letter also made reference to "blood," when the woman asked her husband to return to take care of his family. This was another appeal to the duties and responsibilities of men and the ties that bound them to their children, for whom they were required to provide.

Children also saw the effects abandonment had on their mothers and attempted to assist them. Sons and daughters could also petition the mayor and the prefect for news and information, using language intended to emotionally move state officials. In 1882, Guglielmo M. from Armento wrote a petition on behalf of his mother, stating, "I live in the most squalid misery at my mother's expense, who because of her advanced age is hardly able to secure a piece of bread."[61] He requested a search for his father and brother, who had been living in America for about two years. Apparently, they wanted Guglielmo to migrate, but he expressed concern about leaving his mother. His petition used some of the same language as those written by women, particularly that they were living in poverty and not able to afford a meager piece of bread. His letter shows that both men and women knew the particular effect language had in making their appeals heard.

Furthermore, women were not the only ones using strategies and appealing to certain values in their petitions. The responses from abroad show that men also knew how to appease officials and gain sympathy. For example, a woman wrote to the prefect, asking for word from her spouse and to request he return home. Her husband, Domenico T., was located in Spain and responded that he would not repatriate, but instead he would send a remittance.[62] As long as men replied stating they would send money in the future, it appeared as if husbands were complying with their marital duties, temporarily appeasing wives and authorities. Those not wanting to comply claimed they were in the right and accused wives of being unfaithful or of mishandling funds previously sent. Others made promises to send remittances, even though in the end they did not act on those pledges.

Mayors also used persuasive language as they forwarded requests to the prefects. On the petition form, there was an area in the margin for officials to include their own comments or notes. The mayors often sided with the women and used the requests to help them obtain their legal rights. Even if these officials knew in some circumstances that they legally could do nothing for the petitioners, they added their observations anyway, urging the prefect to find a way to help the women in need.

Mayors often remarked on the appearance or state of the women who presented themselves before them. For example, in 1880, the mayor of Trecchina wrote on behalf of Carmela A., whose husband Nicola D. was located in Brazil, observing that the woman appeared "in a sad condition" and that her husband "has not even written for some years." In another request, the mayor of Potenza referred to a woman as "a poor petitioner" (*la povera esponente*) whose husband emigrated eleven years prior, and for two years had not sent "a morsel" to the family. She decided to appeal to the prefect "in despair."[63] The petitioner was able to provide her husband's exact address in Montevideo, but she received a response stating that they could not find him, even though his name was published in local Italian language newspapers. The mayors did not pass judgment about the women or their circumstances, at least not with their words.

Though they were limited in what they could actually do, the mayors' observations suggest that they felt bad for suffering mothers. It was common for them to refer to the women making the requests as *la infelice supplicante*, or the unhappy supplicant.[64] One mayor commented in the margin when an "unfortunate mother" petitioned a search for her son in Marseilles, with no luck.[65] Another woman, Arcangela D., a widow from Pignola, had not heard from her son since he emigrated one year prior. The mayor asked the prefect in her request to "please give peace to this derelict mother."[66]

The choice of words in some instances conveyed powerful pleas and emotions. For example, many of the requests were entitled *preghiera* or prayer, indicating the desire and desperation that came along with it. In a letter from 1880, the mayor sent a letter to the prefect on behalf of Maddalena P. with the subject "prayer." The letter stated that her husband, "left with the best intentions in the world . . . and for a long time he had never been burdened to send his wife and two young children anything, and they are destitute and lack means, languishing in the hardest misery."[67] She asked that the prefect have compassion for her. In this letter, the mayor emphasized the desperate nature of the woman in question and the horrible conditions in which her husband left her.

Even responses from the prefect show an interest in protecting and helping the women. In one instance, a wife requested a passport to join her husband in France. She did not have marital authorization and authorities could not issue her the passport. In his note to the mayor, an official from the prefecture responded, "I have done all I can in favor of the petitioner," but he could not issue a passport without marital consent, so he called for a search for her husband.[68]

Whether or not the language choices used in the petitions and requests helped in any way is unclear, especially since officials were required to follow the law which prioritized the patriarchal role of the father and limited the position of women. However, the mayors' words show that they felt sympathy and compassion for those suffering as a result of emigration. Through these seemingly simple acts, the state took on a greater role in advocating for and protecting women. Turning to the state and requesting assistance was probably not easy and may have even been embarrassing for some individuals.

However, the requests made by women to state officials humanize them, and show that they had apprehensions and fears about their loved ones emigrating and being left on their own. They worried about their spouses and children and in many cases were desperate when they did not hear news from them. Although reasons for searching for spouses and children may have differed, these requests show the complexity of emotions that women experienced as a result of emigration and the reaction of state officials to their dilemmas. Most importantly, the petitions give agency to rural, southern Italian women, a rarity in the history of Basilicata.

The decision to emigrate was not easy and was filled with uncertainties and risks. Leaving the familiarity of home required courage, resourcefulness, and strength. Yet, certain factors may have made the decision easier for some: friends or relatives who were already settled and established abroad, work opportunities, support from the family at home, and the safety net of the church and local community. These factors helped persuade prospective migrants and push them to make a decision about when to leave and where to go. Though some had difficulties, most individuals were issued a passport if requested, regardless of profession or socioeconomic status. As rates of emigration increased, the government view of migration shifted and became much more accepting and protective of emigrants. In the midst of this evolving stance on emigration, and reflected in the major legislation of 1888 and 1901, the government steadfastly not only upheld the freedom to emigrate but also the continued patriarchal protection of women.

Emigration also helped integrate women as citizens of the new Italian state. Women who remained behind were not living in an isolated and closed world, accepting of their fate. Largely uneducated rural women had knowledge about their rights and actively sought out the help of the government to assist them with issues dealing with emigration. Southern Italian women, often assumed to be apolitical, were drawn to a new relationship with the state as a result of large-scale emigration.[69] This behavior was revolutionary for women because of their legal limitations and subordinate role. Men were the heads of the family and the liaisons between the state and the family. They maintained legal authority over their wives and children, and the power to vote for their families. Yet, with men absent, women had to step in and deal directly with the state. Some women who remained behind depended on government agencies to issue passports, search for relatives, provide them with information, and possibly even coerce men into fulfilling their duties. These actions show women were desperate, but determined, and knew they could turn to the mayor when in need of assistance. They were not passive, accepting, or inactive, but concerned wives and parents, persistent, desperate, and knowledgeable about the law and their rights.

Some of them were literate, but more were not, a difficulty which did not impede their attempts at petitioning government officials. While impossible to know what percentage of women turned to the government, it was not an insignificant number. One may speculate as to the motives of these women: poverty, desperation, greed, and loneliness. This trust in the state and state agencies was a direct result of emigration and the absence of men. Yet there were probably also a significant number of women who chose not to appeal to the state and to deal with their situation in silence or privately within the family. These women may not have known their options, or they may not have wanted others to know the hardships or challenges they faced. The next chapter will demonstrate how difficult this type of secrecy was in the close-knit communities of Basilicata. Overall, these petitions demonstrate that emigration not only changed the relationships and responsibilities among members of the household but also transformed the relationship women had with the state.

NOTES

1. ASP, Atti di Pubblica Sicurezza, Cat. 6. Busta 40.

2. See: Linda Reeder, *Widows in White: Migration and the Transformation of Rural Italian Women, Sicily, 1880–1920* (Toronto: University of Toronto Press, 2003).

3. See: Andreina De Clementi, "Gender Relations and Migration Strategies in the Rural Italian South: Land, Inheritance, and the Marriage Market," in *Women, Gender and Transnational Lives: Italian Workers of the World*, eds. Donna Gabaccia and Franca Iacovetta (Toronto: University of Toronto Press, 2002).

4. Casimira Grandi, *Donne fuori posto: L'emigrazione femminile rurale d'Italia postunitaria* (Ann Arbor, MI: University of Michigan Press, 2008), 44.

5. Giuseppi Masi, "Tra spirito d'aventura e ricerca 'dell'agognato peculio:' linee di tendenza dell'emigrazione calabrese tra ottocento e novecanto," in *Emigrazione e storia d'Italia*, ed. Matteo Sanfilippo (Cosenza: Pellegrini, 2003), 124.

6. Luigi Favero and Graziano Tassello, "Cent'anni di emigrazione italiana (1876–1976)," in *Un secolo di emigrazione italiana, 1876–1976*, eds. Gianfausto Rossolli and Francesco Balletta (Rome: Centro Studi Emigrazione, 1978), 16.

7. Antonio Golini and Flavia Amato, "Uno squardo a un secolo e mezzo di emigrazione Italiana," in *Storia dell'Emigrazione Italiana*, eds. Piero Bevilacqua, Andreina de Clemente, and Emilio Franzina (Rome: Donzelli, 2002), 48.

8. ASP, Pubblica Sicurezza, Cat 6, Busta 40.

9. Direzione Generale di Statistica, *Statistica della emigrazione Italiana per L'estero negli anni 1904 e 1905* (Rome: Tipografia Nazionale di G. Bertero, 1906), xiv.

10. The Immigration Commission, "Emigration Conditions in Europe," (Washington, DC: Government Printing Office, 1911), 25.

11. de Clementi, "Gender Relations and Migration Strategies in the Rural Italian South," 96.

12. Pietro Lacava, "Sulle condizione economico-sociali della Basilicata," *Nuova Antologia* (March–April 1907): 113.

13. Franco Ramella, "Reti sociali, famiglie e strategie migratorie," in *Storia dell'emigrazione Italiana*, eds. Piero Bevilacqua, Andreina de Clemente, and Emilio Franzina (Rome: Donzelli, 2002), 146.

14. de Clementi, "Gender Relations and Migration Strategies in the Rural Italian South," 78.

15. Felice Lafranceschina, "I lucani in Argentina, Brasile e Cile," *Basilicata Regione Notizie* 94 (2000): 73.

16. Cesare Cagli, "L'emigrazione e l'agricoltura in Basilicata," *Nuova Antologia* CXLVIII (July–August 1910): 137.

17. Paola Corti and Maddalena Tirabassi, eds. *Racconti dal mondo: narrazioni, memorie, e saggi delle migrazioni* (Turin: Fondazioni Agnelli, 2007), xi.

18. "Italy Stops Emigration," *The New York Times*, September 24, 1911, C4.

19. "L'emigrazione italiana per l'estero nell'anno 1906," *Bollettino dell'Emigrazione* 11 (1907): 21.

20. Antonio Checco, "L'emigrazione siciliana: i luoghi e le comunità di partenza (1881–1913): una proposta di ricerca," in *Emigrazione e storia d'Italia*, ed. Matteo Sanfilippo (Cosenza: Pellegrini, 2003), 169.

21. The Immigration Commission, "Emigration Conditions in Europe," 223.

22. Maria Falvella, "Flussi migratori della Basilicata: Situazioni e dimensioni nel periodo 1861–1940," *Basilicata Regione Notizie* 98 (2001): 87.

23. Francesco Saverio Nitti, *Scritti Sulla Questione Meridionale, Vol 1: Saggi sulla Storia del Mezzogiorno Emigrazione e Lavoro* (Bari: Laterza, 1958), 327.

24. "L'emigrazione delle donne e dei fanciulli dalla provincia di Caserta," *Bollettino dell'Emigrazione* 13 (1913): 16.

25. Adolfo Rossi, "Vantaggi e danni dell'emigrazione nel mezzogiorno d'Italia (Note di un viaggio fatto in Basilicata e in Calabria dal R. Commissario dell'Emigrazione," *Bollettino dell'Emigrazione* 13 (1908): 1557.

26. Rossi, "Vantaggi e danni dell'emigrazione nel mezzogiorno d'Italia," 1555.

27. The Immigration Commission, "Emigration Conditions in Europe," 223.

28. "Allegati alla relazione sui servizi dell'emigrazione," *Bollettino dell'Emigrazione* 7 (1904): 235.

29. Rossi, "Vantaggi e danni dell'emigrazione nel mezzogiorno d'Italia," 1556.

30. Rossi, "Vantaggi e danni dell'emigrazione nel mezzogiorno d'Italia," 1575.

31. R. J. Bosworth, *Italy and the Wider World: 1860–1960* (New York: Routledge, 1996), 116; Mark Choate, *Emigrant Nation: The Making of Italy Abroad* (Cambridge, MA: Harvard University Press, 2008), 2.

32. Dino Cinel, *The National Integration of Italian Return Migration* (New York: Cambridge University Press, 1991), 72.

33. Maria Rosaria Ostuni, "Leggi e politiche di governo nell'Italia liberale e fascista," in *Storia dell'emigrazione Italiana*, eds. Piero Bevilacqua, Andreina de Clemente, and Emilio Franzina (Rome: Donzelli, 2001), 310.

34. Quoted in Casimira Grandi, *Donne fuori posto*, 27.

35. See Christopher Duggan, *Francesco Crispi 1818–1901: From Nation to Nationalism* (New York: Oxford University Press, 2002); Ostuni, "Leggi e politiche di governo nell'Italia liberale e fascista," 310.

36. Choate, *Emigrant Nation*, 59.

37. ASP, Pubblica Sicurezza, Cat. 6, Busta 40.

38. Legge 31 gennaio 1901 n. 23 sull'emigrazione, Art. 2.

39. "Italian Emigration: How It Will Be Affected by the Crispi Bill," *The New York Times*, July 5, 1888.

40. Choate, *Emigrant Nation*, 60.

41. Legge 31 gennaio 1901 n. 23 sull'emigrazione, Capo 1, Art 5.

42. Legge 31 gennaio 1901 n. 23 sull'emigrazione, Capo 2, Art 13.

43. Legge 31 gennaio 1901 n. 23 sull'emigrazione, Capo 1, Art 2.

44. Legge 31 gennaio 1901 n. 23 sull'emigrazione, Capo 1, Art 1.

45. Legge 31 gennaio 1901 n. 23 sull'emigrazione, Capo 2, Art 7.

46. Legge 31 gennaio 1901 n. 23 sull'emigrazione, Capo 2, Art 24.

47. Choate, *Emigrant Nation*, 61.

48. Cited in Bosworth, *Italy and the Wider World*, 118.

49. Grandi, *Donne fuori posto*, 30.

50. Samuel Baily, *Immigrants in the Land of Promise: Italians in Buenos Aires and New York, 1870–1914* (Ithaca, NY: Cornell University Press, 2004), 52.

51. ASP, Atti di Pubblica Sicurezza, Cat. 6. Busta 42.

52. ASP, Atti di Pubblica Sicurezza, Cat. 6. Busta 43.

53. ASP, Atti di Pubblica Sicurezza, Cat 6, Busta 43.

54. ASP, Atti di Pubblica Sicurezza, Cat 6, Busta 42.

55. ASP, Atti di Pubblica Sicurezza, Cat 6, Busta 41.

56. ASP, Atti di Pubblica Sicurezza, Cat 6, Busta 40.

57. ASP, Atti di Pubblica Sicurezza, Cat 6, Busta 40.

58. ASP, Atti di Pubblica Sicurezza, Cat 6, Busta 40.

59. ASP, Atti di Pubblica Sicurezza, Cat 6, Busta 42.

60. ASP, Atti di Pubblica Sicurezza, Cat 6, Busta 43.

61. ASP, Atti di Pubblica Sicurezza, Cat 6, Busta 40.

62. ASP, Atti di Pubblica Sicurezza, Cat 6, Busta 41.

63. ASP, Atti di Pubblica Sicurezza, Cat 6, Busta 41.

64. ASP, Atti di Pubblica Sicurezza, Cat 6, Busta 42.

65. ASP, Atti di Pubblica Sicurezza, Cat 6, Busta 41.

66. ASP, Atti di Pubblica Sicurezza, Cat 6, Busta 42.

67. ASP, Atti di Pubblica Sicurezza, Cat 6, Busta 41.

68. ASP, Atti di Pubblica Sicurezza, Cat 6, Busta 40.

69. Jennifer Guglielmo, *Living the Revolution: Italian Women's Resistance and Radicalism in New York City, 1880–1945* (Chapel Hill, NC: University of North Carolina Press, 2010), 3, 12.

Chapter 5

Family, Community, and Church

Coping with Emigration

Domenica G. married Donato F. in 1882 in the small town of Picerno, just outside of Potenza. The couple had several children, but at some point during their fourteen years of marriage, Donato began an affair with another woman. Domenica could not have been pleased, even if infidelity was not uncommon among married men. Donato and his lover, Mariantonia R, also known as Zerba, however, were bold, and flaunted their relationship for the entire community to see. Zerba, who was also married, was seventeen years younger than the thirty-eight-year-old Domenica. The length of the affair is unclear, but neighbors and acquaintances surely knew about it. One summer day in June 1896, witnesses saw Donato and his mistress returning from a walk together. Later that evening, Domenica stabbed Zerba in the stomach with a sharp object. She did not intend to kill Zerba, but cause harm, which she did, as court records indicate that Zerba was unable to perform ordinary activity for seventeen days.

Domenica was accused of causing personal injury toward Mariantonia and the *Corte d'Assise* heard her case. Witness accounts from the trial revealed that Donato's actions were well known to many in the village. It was no secret he had a lover and paraded her around the town, even bringing her into his household. In giving testimony about the circumstances of the case, one neighbor stated: "In this town there is no one who ignores the fact that Donato has taken Zerba as a lover." He continued, testifying that he often observed Zerba and even her young son in Donato's house. They came and went together often, and the witness claimed that just a few days prior he saw them leaving the house together and heading for the forest. Another female neighbor also testified that the two were lovers, claiming she frequently saw Zerba at Donato's house. She even stated that she heard Domenica tell Zerba that she did not want her there. A third neighbor confirmed the previous witness accounts, stating that Zerba was "continuously" in Donato's house and she often ate meals there as well.[1] The situation no doubt was humiliating for Domenica, who likely was frustrated and fed up, and subsequently attacked Mariantonia.

This case demonstrates that the community witnessed the intimate and private lives of their neighbors. They clearly knew who was coming and going and could see and hear the acts and secrets of others. These fellow villagers might have passed judgment on Donato's actions, but more so on those of Zerba. They may have felt badly for Domenica and sympathized with her frustration, as she could do nothing to stop her husband from bringing his mistress into their house where she and Donato had young children. In this tight-knit atmosphere, neighbors observed and witnessed tragedies like Domenica's story.

While the above story does not relate to emigration, it does concern how inhabitants of the small villages of Basilicata lived. In a rural town of a few thousand, Lucanians would have known their neighbors and possibly even the private details of their lives. They would have been aware of who emigrated, which wives were left on their own, the effects of emigration on those women, and might even attest to their level of suffering. Those neighbors likewise helped one another when in need, perhaps out of a sense of friendship, community, or mutual suffering. Some married women may have experienced a greater sense of freedom with their husbands absent, but at the same time, community surveillance may have limited their activities. Villages, like their residents, adjusted to large-scale emigration, and in doing so, the meaning of community was transformed.

Many people in small towns were connected by marriage, and intermarriage among certain families was common, making some groups part of extended families. Thus, the network of neighbors and community was crucial, especially when many of them may have been close or distant relations. These connections took on greater meaning during the age of mass emigration, when the support of the community became even more important. Neighbors looked out for one another and could not only assist each other during difficult times but also provide company to fill the void of family members abroad. In the village, neighbors and friends supported each other, the mayors assisted women when they requested state support, and the church and local parish provided comfort and assistance to families. In short, the community helped women survive while men were absent.

Communities themselves also transformed in this period, as hundreds, if not thousands, emigrated, leading to concerns about the resulting demographic makeup. While people left behind coped with emigration, mayors and prefects expressed fears about the future of their villages and the region. The

sense of alarm permeated communication among local officials and even concerned residents. Some thought the solution would be to limit emigration, but
other officials believed doing so would go against liberal values of freedom
of movement. While emigration rates were high from a number of towns, in
many cases, these fears tended to be exaggerated.

This chapter surveys the small communities that existed in Basilicata,
examining relationships and the dynamics that shaped them. The government
and the inhabitants dealt with migration differently, as all parties attempted to
come to grips with its impact and to overcome the local challenges it posed.
Prior chapters have shown how women sought help from the state, but some
women also turned to the Church. Though a major part of life in Italy, the
Catholic Church had a severed relationship with the Italian state in this period,
and mention of it is notably absent from government and migration records.
Mayors and prefects did not refer to the Church in their communication, and
religious organizations likely acted independently when assisting women and
families. Unfortunately, source material on the local role of the Church during
this period is scarce. While women sought help from both Church and state,
they did not do so in tandem. Examining both the community and the role of
the Church in the lives of Lucanians offers another perspective on how migration impacted the world in which the women who remained behind lived.

DEMOGRAPHIC EFFECTS OF EMIGRATION

interi paesi si svuotano
entire villages are emptying[2]

By the early twentieth century, millions of Italians left their towns and villages to emigrate, greatly impacting entire communities. A magazine on
colonization reported that the number of Italians abroad by 1924 was close to
ten million, a number that had doubled since 1901, and was far greater than
the estimated 270,000 Italians that emigrated by 1871.[3] These numbers show
just how much migration increased in a little over fifty years. Many of those
emigrants, around half, returned to Italy. They had gone abroad to earn higher
wages and to save money and came home after earning a sufficient amount.
Others returned home to retire in Italy. Between 1880 and 1950 over 50%
of emigrants returned from the United States alone.[4] Yet these numbers vary
widely, depending on the year and the location abroad. For instance, in 1903,
35% of emigrants returned from the United States, while 66% returned from
Argentina.[5] Because of the proximity to Italy, emigration to other European
countries such as France, Germany, or Switzerland was more likely temporary and had a higher return rate.

It is impossible to calculate the exact number of Italian emigrants, or how many returned. Passport requests, local town registries, and ship manifests aid in estimating the amount of emigration from each region, but the figures are not exact. Some emigrants used foreign ports, such as Le Havre, Marseilles, or even Hamburg, to which they traveled by land before embarking. Even Francesco Saverio Nitti commented on how unreliable statistics were, since many Italians left from French ports and Italy often relied on American statistics for their own migration numbers.[6] Furthermore, tracking the number of returnees is difficult, especially those returning from the Americas, because passenger manifests of migrants returning to Italy were not preserved. Either way, emigration overall was not a small phenomenon, and it affected residents all across the Italian Peninsula.

Yet, the circumstances in Basilicata were somewhat different from the rest of Italy. Men left in droves, leaving towns to be occupied largely by women, children, and the elderly. Historian Dino Cinel cites statistics that show Potenza and Matera, the two provinces of Basilicata, had low return rates.[7] Although some men come back and many still considered their village home even if living abroad, all accounts show that reality was quite different. The toll emigration took on the towns in Basilicata was far worse than the rest of Italy, greatly impacting demographics. In general, migrants returned to regions with better economies and more opportunity. Thus, the provinces of Potenza and Matera had the lowest return rates in the Mezzogiorno mainly because they were among the poorest regions in the south. Between 1881 and 1901, Basilicata was the only region in all of Italy with a population decline, a decrease of over 50,000 inhabitants in twenty years.[8] A closer look at these numbers shows that Potenza and Lagonegro, and the mountainous areas surrounding the two cities, were largely responsible for the drop in population. The towns near Matera had continued population growth, particularly because emigration was slower from the eastern areas of the region.[9]

Statistics taken from Picerno, a town in the province of Potenza and referenced in the opening story, demonstrate how emigration may have affected the population. In the 1880s, the average number of births in the town was 214.1 per year. By the 1890s, that number decreased to 172.1 per year, and in the 1900s, it dipped even further to 146.3 per year.[10] As for marriages, there were an average of 45.2 per year in the 1880s, but only 34.6 per year by the 1900s.[11] In terms of overall population, there were 4,401 registered inhabitants of the town in the 1881 census. This number decreased to 3,828 by 1901, and 3,579 in 1911.[12] These declines can be attributed to emigration, but other factors cannot be ignored, such as a falling birth rate in Italy and in much of Western Europe by the early twentieth century. Although the numbers cited are those for one town, they are representative of many in the vicinity of Potenza that experienced large-scale emigration in the late nineteenth and early twentieth centuries. Decline in the male population was significant because it meant that young single women were less likely to find a husband, get married, and have children.

Many other towns around Potenza had similar population shifts due to emigration. A 1908 report from the *Bollettino dell'Emigrazione* noted that in the town of Albano di Lucania, the population rapidly declined due to emigration. Not only men left, but also entire families. The town registered 2,400 residents in 1908, 600 of whom were reported to be in the Americas. The same 1908 report found that emigration was continuing to increase throughout the region, especially in the ten years prior, resulting in a population decrease in many areas. For example, in 1901, seventy-one municipalities in Italy had a decrease in population of 800 or more people, and of those, twenty-four were in Basilicata. In the town of Pignola, the mayor reported that the population almost halved as a result of emigration. There were 4,000 residents in 1881, a number that dropped to 2,557 in 1901, and further decreased to 2,100 by 1908. In Laurenzana, the population was 7,300 in 1881 and dropped to 4,300 in 1901. By 1908, the population fell to 3,000, a decrease of about 60% in nearly thirty years. In Viggiano, the population also decreased from 7,000 in 1881 to 5,000 in 1908. The mayor of another town, Latronico, reported that the village had 2,300 inhabitants in the country and 1,500 in America, and by 1908 entire families were emigrating.[13] Similar statistics exist for most towns in western Basilicata. Low return rates combined with ever increasing emigration led to severe population loss in the region. The dramatic decrease in the population is evidence that unlike the situation in other Italian regions, emigration was, more often than not, permanent in Basilicata.

FEARS OF TOO MUCH EMIGRATION

I greet you in the name of the 3,000 people of Moliterno who have emigrated and of the 5,000 others who are preparing to leave

(Vincenzo Valinoti Lattorraca, mayor of Moliterno,
to Prime Minister Giuseppe Zanardelli in 1902).

Emigration from the Italian Peninsula peaked between 1876 and 1914 causing widespread alarm about the inhabitants and the land left behind. During this period, about three million people emigrated from the Veneto, 1.45 million from Campania, and 870,000 from Calabria.[14] In those same years, about 375,000 people emigrated from Basilicata.[15] While the numbers on their own may not be as high as those from other regions, between the period of 1876 and 1905, Basilicata had the second largest emigration rate per population after the Veneto.[16]

The large number of people leaving caused alarm in many regions, especially in Basilicata given the high percentage of men emigrating. The newspaper *La Stampa* reported that in 1887 one-third of the male population emigrated from some towns of Basilicata.[17] The article expressed concern among residents because the youngest and ablest men left, and it seemed no one would remain to work in the fields. They also feared population loss, and towns filled with only women, children, and the elderly. A 1902 article about emigration from the *Bollettino dell'Emigrazione* stated, "Women and children remain in Italy; only the able-bodied men emigrate . . . the proof is the low number of Italian births."[18] One small landholder noted that "emigration does not leave anyone in the countryside besides the old and the invalid, because the best leave and sometimes they take their entire families."[19] By the 1880s, at least two decades before large-scale emigration reached its peak, officials in Basilicata already worried about the large number of emigrants.

The changing ratio of men to women in the region also caused concern. In a study on Basilicata from 1907, Pietro Lacava noted that in 1881, there were 251,621 men and 272,883 women living in the region (approximately 48% men to 52% women). By 1901, those numbers reduced to 231,763 men and 258,942 women (approximately 47% to 53%).[20] Although women already outnumbered men earlier on, within a twenty-year period, there was an overall population decrease, and the gap between the number of women over men increased by 7,000. Lacava points out that in other regions, men made up the majority of the population. Emigration continued to pick up in the early decades of the 1900s and concern began to grow over the increasing number of women and the likely demographic impact on the village of large-scale male departure.

At the local level, mayors expressed concern about emigration from their towns. In a letter to the prefect of Potenza in February 1882, the mayor of Savoia di Lucania wrote that emigration from the town had increased so much that there was a severe danger to the population and the local economy because of loss of farm labor. The prefect responded, saying his complaints were not unique to his town, and that "an inordinate desire is manifesting itself in many communes of this province for emigration abroad." He stated that officials could do little because the government must "respect the right of individual freedom."[21] A 1910 article on Basilicata from *La Stampa* reported that the region, along with Calabria, was completely depopulated (*sono spopolate miseramente*).[22] The mayor of Laurenzana recounted that many inhabitants closed up and left houses in the town and abandoned land because of lack of workers. The dismal tone of several mayors reflected the concern about the future of the villages.[23]

Outsiders observers also commented on the region's large demographic shifts. Nitti commented on the population loss in various towns, saying "I represent one of the towns most devastated by emigration, the area of Muro

Lucano; in it emigration . . . has become morbid. The population is reduced in some municipalities by half or at least half: San Fele, Balvano, Ruoti, Ruvo, perhaps all the towns in my area are decimated by emigration."[24] Carlo Levi observed the effects of emigration during his stay in the region in the 1930s, writing that "the villages of Lucania, with half their people on one side of the ocean and half on the other, were split in two."[25] While emigration to America had slowed by the 1930s, Levi witnessed the impact it had on the village with half its population abroad, many inhabitants with relatives overseas, and others who had returned themselves.

Information gathered from the Royal Italian Agricultural Commission's investigation into Basilicata and Calabria also demonstrated the fears of local officials about the effects of emigration on their towns. Despite employers offering higher wages, the towns of Albano di Lucania and Viggiano lacked workers, and during harvest season farms recruited peasants from the province of Lecce (Puglia). Officials in Albano di Lucania, Pignola, Laurenzana, Viggiano, Moliterno, and many other towns, all reported that wages had doubled since emigration increased, and workers had become more demanding, often asking for food. All towns reported heavy losses of population due to emigration.[26]

Local officials wondered what they could do to slow the exodus of its residents. A priest from Laurenzana commented that the best way to deter migrants would be by not issuing passports so readily, making emigration more difficult and encouraging prospective migrants to reconsider.[27] An article from a local newspaper, *Primavera Lucana*, noted that migration had doubled over the four-year period between 1902 and 1906. The article proposed various solutions to curb high rates of emigration, like denying passports to the illiterate. Another long-term suggestion posited that improving the economic situation in the region would eliminate the need to emigrate.[28]

Communication between mayors and the prefects show how local officials even felt pressure from the community to monitor emigration. In an 1883 letter to the prefect of Potenza, the mayor of Picerno complained that emigration agents told stories of how spectacular the Americas were, and thus many residents came to request passports to emigrate. However, he asked the prefect to give him "the necessary orders to repress the abuses of agents in order to prevent the best cultivators from leaving." He also asked the prefect for advice on how he could slow down or stop emigration, fearing that the growing attraction of success in America will result in extreme emigration and the fields would go uncultivated.[29]

Many of Basilicata's inhabitants shared the same fears as officials. Emigration affected a number of villages, some more than others. In almost all towns, fears focused on the shortage of young, able men, and the insufficient number of people to work in the fields. An article from the *Bollettino dell'Emigrazione* described the situation, noting, "Basilicata, like other regions is affected by the damages of emigration: good workers leave and those who remain are the old, women, and children, unproductive individuals in short. There is a lack of workers and the land lies fallow."[30] Likewise, according to an article in *Primavera Lucana*, anyone capable of working left, and the piece quite bluntly stated that those who remained were the "undernourished, epileptics, idiots, invalids, incapable." Clearly demonstrating eugenic fears, some worried that emigration would cause the "less desirable" types of people to remain and reproduce, further impacting the Italian population. The article also expressed fear over the future of the military; if all of the most capable men emigrated, it asked "who-in an eventual conflict-would defend Italy?"[31]

Indicative of the concern and desperation of Lucanians, a 1906 article in *Primavera Lucana* reported that emigration continued to increase at an alarming rate, without remedy, and predicted that in a few years Basilicata would be "a true land of death."[32] An article in the *Bollettino dell'Emigrazione* the following year also pointed out that "emigration has become morbid: entire villages are losing the strongest men and they move to America, accompanied by priests . . . women, the elderly, and children remain."[33] Houses in the communities were closed up and abandoned, farmlands went uncultivated, and fears persisted that the only residents remaining in the village would be women, children, the elderly, and those who failed to succeed in America. Thus, by 1914, it seemed that many towns would cease to exist if emigration continued. While many locals may have supported or understood the reasons for emigration, others feared for the future of their town, region, and country.

Many of the above-stated fears were exaggerated and unrealistic. For Italy overall, migration did not have that great of an impact on the population. Few opportunities existed for Lucanians at home, which was the main factor in their decision to emigrate. Many of those emigrants would return, however, alleviating several of the aforementioned concerns. Yet these fears must have permeated the communities, who while coping with the situation, also worried a great deal about the local impact of emigration.

Francesco Saverio Nitti's words demonstrate that the government was aware that emigration was temporary and not a cause for great alarm. He pointed out that more than half of emigrants returned, many through the ports of Naples, Genoa, Palermo, Catania, or any of the other ports (including foreign) accepting ships from abroad. Nitti also stressed that Italy had one of the highest birth rates in Europe at the time. The population rose from 25,016,801 in 1861 to 29,699,785 in 1885, despite the growing number of emigrants leaving each year. Nitti argued that these factors, along with falling mortality rates, proved that there was no need for alarm: population growth occurred despite emigration. He also tried to quell fears by reporting that emigration rates were also increasing in other European countries, not just Italy. He cited that the United Kingdom, Germany, Switzerland, and Sweden all had rising emigration rates in the 1880s.[34]

EMIGRATION AND THE COMMUNITY

Many of the villages of Basilicata were relatively small and close-knit, containing less than 5,000 residents. Most Lucanians lived in the hilltop town centers, while the rest lived in more rural locations in the surrounding territory. Although technically considered rural, inhabitants lived quite closely to one another in town, and frequently interacted with friends, neighbors, and members of the community. It was also quite common for residents to be familiar with their neighbor's habits and movements, as they would be hard to ignore living in such close proximity. Shops lining the main thoroughfares and crowded markets that frequently visited town were places where townspeople, especially women, could gather and socialize. Networks of gossip facilitated the spread of news about local matters among the villagers. Occurrences such as emigration, illness, pregnancy, poverty, and other life events would spread. This type of community setting could be a blessing and a curse—neighbors could help each other when in need, but it also could mean prying eyes and little privacy.

As seen in the chapter's opening story, court cases and witness testimony elucidate the inner workings of how communities operated and the extent to which people were aware of their neighbors' everyday affairs. A witness giving testimony in an infanticide trial stated she noticed that the accused was pregnant and trying to hide her growing stomach. She also knew the husband of the accused was in America.[35] Neighbors and townspeople would also report walking by houses and hearing discussions or arguments between spouses or among family members. Some appeared to know the intimate details of their neighbors' lives. This monitoring seemed especially targeted at women with husbands abroad, almost as if the townspeople felt compelled to "keep an eye on them" and ensure they remained out of trouble. Surveillance, whether innocent or purposeful, was a key aspect of community relations. When women's husbands were absent, not only family but also their neighbors would keep a watchful eye on them, making sure they did not bring dishonor to their families. Other neighbors noticed when women gained weight due to pregnancy or lost weight due to illness. In small towns, it was difficult to hide from friends and foes, and townspeople were quick to notice and form opinions about what occurred in other's lives. Some women were not even safe from the watchful eye of relatives or extended family. In many cases, emigrants' mothers wrote to their sons abroad, informing them of what occurred in the village. Evidence presented in this and the following chapter demonstrates that eyes and ears were always observing and listening to events occurring outside their windows or in their villages, and for most residents, privacy was nonexistent.

As evidence of the importance of family when husbands emigrated, one mother wrote to the Foreign Ministry on behalf of herself and her daughter-in-law to find the whereabouts of her son. The letter explained that eight years prior, Nicola L. "abandoned" his wife, leaving her "in the most desolate misery."[36] He was a coppersmith living in Africa, but he did not respond to letters and the family did not know his location. Both the emigrant's mother and wife lived in poverty, surviving on bread. The consulate responded that he was in Algeria, and although a good worker, he had poor conduct and wasted the money he earned. The letter was quite frank and informed the family not to expect any aid from him. Here a woman and her daughter-in-law worked together and depended upon each other after their son/husband emigrated. Despite receiving bad news, this petition shows the importance of family and the support system that women had after men emigrated.

As seen in previous chapters, the state also took on an important role and, in a sense, substituted for husbands, advocating for women if their spouses were abroad. Correspondence between government agencies reflects this concern. In one case, the mayor of the town of Rotonda and the prefect disagreed over the issuing of a passport to Catarina D., a woman seeking to emigrate. Because she was single and had all the correct documentation, including the *nulla osta*, the prefect issued the passport to Catarina. However, the mayor later received evidence to invalidate it. It turned out that she had a lover living in America and he was the one who called her to join him there. Her lover's mother intercepted and wrote to the mayor, telling him that Catarina, who was pregnant with someone else's child, was having illicit relations with her son. The prefect wrote that the mayor was correct to dispute the issuing of her passport, because "there is no doubt that the lover living abroad who has sent the money for the trip, seeing her arrive pregnant, will turn to brutal acts."[37] The documents also reveal that Catarina was underage, another reason for revoking her passport.

This complicated case reveals the relationships and power dynamics that existed within the community. The emigrant's mother was aware that her son had a mistress, and that this woman had engaged in relationships with other men while he was overseas. She was also aware that Catarina was pregnant. Catarina, on the other hand, knew that her lover abroad would soon discover her pregnancy, yet still wanted to emigrate. Perhaps she felt he would be supportive since they would be living abroad, away from the social stigma that came along with pregnancy out of wedlock. The mayor, after discovering the truth about the situation, refused to issue the passport, fearing for Catarina's safety. His intervention prohibited her from emigrating, and possibly prevented her from being physically harmed by her boyfriend abroad when she arrived pregnant. Perhaps the mayor overstepped his authority, but this particular official seems to have felt a certain responsibility toward his fellow villagers. Mayors were also members of the community, often coming from prominent or influential local families and being acquainted with most residents. In the state's view, single and underage women required special attention, as they were not deemed capable of making decisions on their own. Women had few legal rights, and the petition from her boyfriend's mother prevented Catarina from emigrating, demonstrating again how women in the community helped police behavior in the absence of men.

While it is apparent that neighbors came together to help each other when necessary, some worried about the negative effects of emigration and the lack of men in certain towns. Fears abounded of increased crime, especially as more children were raised in the absence of a father figure in their lives.[38] An article from the *Bollettino dell'Emigrazione* expressed fears about the possible moral effects of emigration on family and children, stating,

> prolonged absence breaks family ties; the husband loses the love for his wife, who is often scorned, because the man, who, living abroad amongst educated people, has learned to appreciate education and desires a more human way of life, becomes condescending towards humble companions, who remained boorish in the distant village, absorbed in the work of the field and the care of the children.[39]

A local newspaper article from 1908 spoke of similar fears, stating that "the family is dissolving. A thousand factors contribute to its decline, among them those that come from socialist action, from the emancipation of women, the organization of the classes, workers far from home, and many others."[40] Emigration was no doubt among these reasons. The article placed the burden on the state and called for it to step in and take responsibility for education of the young. Another article in *La Stampa* also went so far as to say that the weakening of family ties also led to a rise in illegitimacy.[41] These claims may seem exaggerated, and while emigration did separate families for long periods of time or even permanently, family troubles did not begin with emigration. As noted earlier, men working in agriculture were often away for extended periods of time depending on harvest seasons.

Little evidence exists that crime greatly increased as a result of the absence of men in areas of high emigration. According to statistics from the *Direzione Generale di Statistica* for the years 1898 to 1903 in Basilicata, most instances of crime decreased. For example, the number of murders in the region declined from ninety-three reported in 1898 to seventy-four in 1903. Robberies, extortions, and blackmails decreased from sixty-seven in 1898 to twenty-four in 1903. The number of thefts did slightly rise, increasing from 296 to 313 in the same period, perhaps because there were more consumer goods or possessions in people's homes. However, statistics only included reported crimes. It is impossible to gauge the number of offenses that actually occurred both before and during the period of mass migration. Overall, crime did not increase a great deal, considering the population decreased during this period.[42] Of course, the connection between decreasing crime rates and emigration cannot be directly determined, even though the two occurred during the same period. Crimes committed by women will be examined in the next chapter.

Government assistance for those in need was inadequate in this period. After unification, the newly formed state attempted to take charitable institutions out of religious hands and make them secular. Various towns requested governmental assistance, particularly seeking aid for local soup kitchens, as well as for kindergartens.[43] A note from the town of Bella in 1913 contained a list of the names of the poor, which included sixty-three people, forty-three of whom were women. The document does not give any information about their situation, and it is unclear if their poverty was a result of emigration. However, two-thirds of the people on the list were women. Some may have been widows, others might have been abandoned by their emigrating husbands. These impoverished residents were sent a sum of 300 Lire in state subsidies. Though not a lot of money, it did provide some assistance and would have allowed families to feed themselves and survive.[44] Despite the region being one of the poorest in Italy at the time, some inhabitants were worse off than others. There is some evidence in the archives of communities working to assist the poor. Although it is impossible to know if individual poverty stemmed from emigration, either way the communities took steps to care for the less fortunate.

Each locality differed. Some communes had heavier migration than others, and some had larger overall populations. Members of certain communities came together to help each other as best they could. Unofficial mutual aid societies were likely created to assist villagers in need. Even if they had their own economic difficulties, inhabitants took steps to make sure others, such as the poor and impoverished women who remained behind, received assistance. Much of this charity was likely carried out with the help of the local church, since neither state nor religious charity was enough on its own.

ROLE OF THE CHURCH

The Catholic Church was at the heart of southern Italian communities. Although the Church's dogma and official practices differed from local beliefs and customs that evolved over the centuries, many Lucanians were likely faithful churchgoers. Yet, the Church was much more than a place of worship. The local parish often provided assistance and social welfare that formed the backbone of the community. It helped the sick at a time when most towns did not have a sufficient number of doctors, not to mention a hospital. The Church cared for orphans and foundlings, as well as widows, and provided shelter to the poor and needy. Church teachings dictated proper behavior, influenced people's worldviews, and shaped their beliefs and morals.

The Church was also the center of cultural life, especially in the small towns and villages of the region. Before the state became involved, the Church was largely responsible for education in the community. It was not rare for lessons to be held in the sacristies of local churches. In the period before Napoleonic law required civil registration in 1809, the parish additionally served as a registry office, recording the births, marriages, and deaths of parishioners, and keeping track of families in the town (*stato delle anime*), some as far back as the fifteenth century.

Beyond the boundaries of Basilicata, the Church and the Italian state had a fractured relationship during the Liberal Period. During the process of unification, the newly formed Italian state incorporated lands of the Papal States, confining the Church to Rome and its surrounding region of Lazio by the time the Kingdom of Italy was proclaimed in 1861. Rome was finally incorporated into the Kingdom of Italy and made its capital in 1870, when French troops protecting Pope Pius IX withdrew to fight in the Franco-Prussian War. In the decades following unification, the Vatican did not recognize the Italian state, nor did the Kingdom of Italy recognize the authority of the Church in its territory.

On a practical level, this meant that marriages which took place in church, but not with a civil ceremony, were not recognized by the state, and any children of that union were deemed illegitimate unless their parents wed in a civil ceremony.[45] To distinguish these children from those born of a lawfully married couple, on the original birth record a child would either be labeled with unknown parents, with just the mother's name, or state that it was the result of a union of an unmarried couple. If the parents later married in a civil ceremony, a notation in the margin would indicate the child had been legitimized, referring to the marriage date. For example, in 1905, forty-one-year-old Vito L. and thirty-seven-year-old Maria Rosaria R. married in Marsiconuovo. We do not know how long the couple had been together, but earlier in the year they had a son, Giovanni. On their marriage record, the state officially recognized their son.[46] While it is impossible to know why couples did not get married civilly in this period, as seen in the above example, opposition to civil ceremonies continued into the early 1900 and demonstrates that the tension between the church and the newly formed Italian state extended into the private lives of inhabitants of Basilicata.

As mentioned in Chapter 3, the state also sold off a great deal of Church property in the years after unification, greatly impacting the local landowning patterns. This greatly decreased church income, resulting in many religious orders becoming impoverished.[47] In his study on the Catholic Church in modern Italy, historian John Pollard argued, "The reduction in landowning by the religious orders and the charitable congregations and confraternities of the parishes also inevitably reduced their capacity to serve the needs of the poor."[48] When large-scale emigration became more common in the following decades, this may have impacted the local Church's ability to assist the women who remained behind. Many parishes in the towns of Basilicata were small and poor themselves, and did not have the resources to assist others in the community.

The Church on the local level differed vastly from its center in Rome. While many Italians followed the major beliefs of the Church, practices and traditions differed depending on the area. In all of Italy, and particularly the south, the patron saint of the town held an important position and was especially revered. San Gennaro in Naples is the most well-known example in the south. St. Nicholas of Bari is the patron saint of a number of towns in Basilicata. These local patrons all had (and continue to have) festivals in their honor, and whole towns mobilized to show their devotion. On June 13, residents of Stigliano, a town in the province of Matera, throw the biggest feast of the year to celebrate St. Anthony of Padua. The festivities are capped by parading the statue of the saint through the streets and celebrating a mass in his honor. Celebrations continue into the night, with music and fireworks. Year round, the saint was an object of devotion for the residents. In many cases, migrants named churches in their communities abroad after the patron saints of their hometowns. The most well-known example is San Gennaro in New York, where parishioners still honor him with a major feast every September in Little Italy.

It is difficult to reconstruct the role of the Church on the local level in Basilicata. In a special report on the region in 1887, *La Stampa* reported that the Catholic Church had a significant moral and material presence in the region, despite its rift with the Italian government.[49] Unfortunately, there are no statistics on church attendance during this period. The paper also reported that local priests often tended to originate from poorer families. They did not sequester themselves from society, and the priests even went to the local bar and drank coffee with the townspeople.[50] The parish priest was frequently someone from the town, meaning he knew the inhabitants and was familiar with their family situations. The priest himself may have had family and friends who emigrated, so he could relate to the plight of his fellow villagers.

Some priests even migrated and served in churches in Italian communities abroad.

The Church generally supported the decision to migrate, and as an international organization, was also concerned about its members, regardless of location. While papal encyclicals and various publications express the views of the Church concerning emigration on a macrolevel, they give little information about local issues. Publications like the *Civiltà Cattolica* frequently published information about emigration, especially notices, statistics, and various factual reports, but this information was unlikely to be consulted by mayors and prefects, who received it from other sources, like the *Bollettino dell'Emigrazione*. Occasionally, religious newspapers also published opinion-based articles, many of which were critical of the Italian state's handling of emigration. An article from 1888 condemned Francesco Crispi's government, and stated that if the state was "honest, wise, Christian, concerned with universal well-being," then there would be little need for people to emigrate.[51] The same article also pointed out that Italy did not have an empire like other nations, so their emigrants went to foreign lands, making it more difficult for immigrants to adjust to life in a new country. The Church feared that living in unfamiliar lands would lead to degeneration of the family, loss of the native language, and weakening of religious practices.[52]

In 1888, Pope Leo XIII issued a papal encyclical related to emigration, entitled *Quam Aerumnosa*, the first major statement a pope made addressing the growing phenomenon. In the encyclical, Leo XIII addressed the troubles and hardships of emigrants in America. His main concern was the lack of priests who spoke Italian in foreign lands. Without local priests, believers could not receive the sacraments or take part in the religious community, which Leo XIII feared would result in young people distancing themselves from the Church. The encyclical announced the opening of an institute in Piacenza, under the auspices of Monsignor Giovanni Battista Scalabrini, which would train priests to send abroad to serve in Italian emigrant communities.

The encyclical shows the concern of the Church for emigrants, especially in regard to maintaining their faith after emigrating. It focused mainly on migrants going to the United States, where Protestantism was the dominant religion. Despite the pope's encyclical, concern persisted, and a 1094 article from the *Civiltà Cattolica* indicated continued alarm over the lack of Italian priests and spiritual guidance for Italian Catholics in America, exposed to a number of other cultures and religions.[53]

From these sources, the Church seemed sympathetic to the emigrants and not interested in limiting or preventing their movement. It was primarily interested in the well-being of their followers in foreign countries and wanted to ensure Catholics could continue to practice their beliefs. Thus, the family and maintaining faith were key issues for the Church, more so than the quality of life or living conditions of emigrants. The Church set up organizations to aid migrants both in Italy and abroad. Monsignor Scalabrini was perhaps the most notable, helping to establish groups for migrants in Brazil and the United States. These organizations would provide assistance to migrants looking for work or housing, or even assist in distributing food and provisions. The work of these groups aided not only Italians abroad but also even individuals who remained in Italy, as the efforts to help migrants in America meant helping dependents at home who would share the fruits of their success abroad.

The Church also played an important role in supporting men and women both in Italy and in communicating with consulates abroad. It was common for religious institutions to conduct and respond to requests made for missing husbands abroad. For example, Rosa M. from Abriola wrote for news of her husband, who had emigrated fifteen years prior. She wanted him to return home, and to send "means of sustenance, being that she lives with an unmarried sixteen-year-old daughter in the most squalid misery."[54] She received word four months later that her husband was located in Brazil, living in good economic conditions. The parish of the locality had informed the consulate of his location. The priest there added that Nicola C. lived "in concubinage" with a woman, but he would speak with him on his wife's behalf.[55] In this case, a local priest in the Americas intervened, responding to a state request, and promised to talk to the husband on behalf of his wife in Italy. Priests abroad advocated for women and families and pushed husbands to take care of their responsibilities. They also knew their parishioners and could assist authorities in helping to locate individuals. Whether in Italy or abroad, churches assisted those impacted by migration on a local level.

While the Catholic Church was present in the community and no doubt assisting women, the extent of this intervention has been difficult to measure. There are few references to the Church in state and government documents and archives. It is likely that parish priests and local Church organizations, often poor themselves, took on a heavy burden to support women who remained behind, especially those without family to support them. They were surely communicating among themselves and with bishops about the situation locally. More research is needed in this area, especially in Church archives, to demonstrate the role the local church played in the lives of the women who remained behind.

Community was always an important part of life in Italy, particularly during times of heavy emigration. The phenomenon introduced a number of challenges to the communities of Basilicata. Demographic shifts and loss of population due to emigration greatly impacted life in the region. As they witnessed thousands leave and villages seemingly depopulate, local leaders feared the effects departure would have not just on the town and the economy but also on the individuals who remained. The Exaggerated alarm about population loss and demographic change in Basilicata echoed larger fears about the population of Italy, reflecting the fact that concerns in the region were not isolated, but connected to the nation as a whole. For the women left behind, friends and neighbors could be there when husbands or other relatives were absent. A new sense of community may have formed among those who remained in the village, but this also led to increased surveillance. Interactions among villagers may have been purely social, or they could have involved economic assistance. As in many of the cases, situations differed. The divided relationship between the Italian state and the Catholic Church also reached the women in Basilicata. While the Church offered moral support for women, it often did not have the resources to offer material assistance for impoverished families. Nonetheless, the women who remained behind had a network of support if they so choose, especially because many other members of the community also experienced emigration firsthand. This shared experience surely helped many women get through difficult times and perhaps allowed them to redefine the meaning of community and forge shared attitudes and values regarding emigration.

NOTES

1. ACM, Corte d'Assise. Busta 417, a. 2371.

2. Nicola Lisanti, "L'emigrazione lucana dall'unità al fascismo," *Lucani nel Mondo* (1998): 14.

3. Anna Maria Di Tolla, "La presenza dei lucani in Nord Africa," *Basilicata Regione Notizie* (1998): 39.

4. Francesco Paolo Cerase, "L'onda di ritorno: i rimpatri," in *Storia dell'emigrazione Italiana*, eds. Piero Bevilacqua, Andreina de Clemente, and Emilio Franzina (Rome: Donzelli, 2002), 115.

5. "Relazione de Commissario Generale dell'Emigrazione," *Bollettino dell'Emigrazione* 7 (1904): 17.

6. Francesco Saverio Nitti, *Sctitti sulla questione meridionale, Vol I: Saggi sulla storia del mezzogiorno, emigrazione e lavoro* (Bari: Laterza, 1958), 308.

7. Dino Cinel, *The National Integration of Italian Return Migration, 1870–1929* (New York: Cambridge University Press, 1991), 109.

8. Adolfo Rossi, "Vantaggi e danni dell'emigrazione nel mezzogiorno d'Italia (Note di un viaggio fatto in Basilicata e in Calabria dal R. Commissario dell'Emigrazione," *Bollettino dell'Emigrazione* 13 (1908): 1640; Maria Falvella, "Flussi migratori della Basilicata: Situazioni e dimensioni nel period 1861–1940," *Basilicata Regione Notizie* 98 (2001): 88.

9. Falvella, "Flussi migratori della Basilicata," 89.

10. Statistics compiled using the Stato Civile di Picerno, Atti di Nascita, 1880–1910.

11. Statistics compiled using the Stato Civile di Picerno, Atti di Matrimonio, 1880–1910.

12. Statistics taken from the Picerno Wikipedia.it page which cites ISTAT as the source. https://it.wikipedia.org/wiki/Picerno.

13. Rossi, "Vantaggi e danni dell'emigrazione nel mezzogiorno d'Italia," 1550–1640.

14. Mark Choate, *Emigrant Nation: The Making of Italy Abroad* (Cambridge, MA: Harvard University Press, 2008), 25.

15. Raffaele Giura Longo, "Dall'unità al fascismo," in *Storia della Basilicata*, eds. Gabriele de Rosa and Antonio Cestaro (Rome: Laterza, 2006), 98.

16. Falvella, "Flussi migratori della Basilicata," 88.

17. "Un lembo ignorato d'Italia: La Basilicata IX," *La Stampa*, October 11, 1887.

18. "L'emigrazione italiana delle provincie tedesche del Reno e della Westfalia," *Bollettino dell'Emigrazione* 10 (1902): 7.

19. Rossi, "Vantaggi e danni dell'emigrazione nel mezzogiorno d'Italia," 1552.

20. Pietro Lacava, "Sulle condizioni economico-sociali della Basilicata," *Nuova Antologia* (Marzo–Aprile 1907): 112.

21. ASP, Atti di Pubblica Sicurezza, Cat. 6, Busta 40.

22. Giuseppe Bavione, "Lettere dall'Argentina: Le colpe della Madre Patria," *La Stampa*, November 1, 1910.

23. The Immigration Commission, "Emigration Conditions in Europe" (Washington, DC: Government Printing Office, 1911), 223–224.

24. Cited in "Discusione dei disegni di leggi: stati di previsione dell'entrata e della spesa del Fondo dell'emigrazione per l'esercizio finanziario 1905–906 e assestamento degli stati medesimi per l'esercizio 1904–905." *Bollettino dell'Emigrazione* 15 (1905): 37.

25. Carlo Levi, *Christ Stopped at Eboli* (Turin: Eunaudi, 1945), 93.

26. The Immigration Commission, "Emigration Conditions in Europe," 223–224.

27. Rossi, "Vantaggi e danni dell'emigrazione nel mezzogiorno d'Italia," 1563.

28. "L'emigrazione transoceanica ed i proposti del governo," *Primavera Lucana*, February 12, 1907.

29. ASP, Atti di Pubblica Sicurezza, Cat. 6, Busta 44.

30. "Adunanza del 15 giugno 1906," *Bollettino dell'Emigrazione* 1 (1907): 67.

31. "L'emigrazione transoceanica ed i proposti del governo," *Primavera Lucana*, February 12, 1907.

32. "L'emigrazione in Basilicata," *Primavera Lucana*, December 25, 1906.

33. "Le ombre nel quadro della nostra emigrazione," *Bollettino dell'Emigrazione* 15 (1907): 173–175.

34. Nitti, *Scritti Sulla Questione Meridionale*, 308–09, 314.

35. ASM, Corte d'Assise, Busta 216, a. 1353.

36. ASP, Atti di Pubblica Sicurezza, Cat. 6, Busta 42.

37. ASP, Atti di Pubblica Sicurezza, Cat. 6, Busta 40.

38. Lacava, "Sulle condizioni economico-sociali della Basilicata," 113.

39. "Le ombre nel quadro della nostra Emigrazione," *Bollettino dell'Emigrazione* 15 (1907): 173–175.

40. "La delinquenza nei fanciulli," *La Provincia: Quindicinale Cattolico di Potenza*, May 24, 1908.

41. "Mali e dolori dell'emigrazione," *La Stampa*, January 5, 1907.

42. Francesco Campolongo, *La delinquenza in Basilicata* (Rome: Unione Cooperative Editrice, 1904), 17.

43. ASP, Prefettura, Gabinetto Io Versamento, B. 267, Operie Pie.

44. ASP, Prefettura, Gabinetto Io Versamento, B. 267, Operie Pie.

45. David I. Kertzer, "Religion and Society, 1789–1892," in *Italy in the Nineteenth Century, 1796–1900*, ed. John A. Davis (New York: Oxford University Press, 2000), 194.

46. Stato Civile, Marsiconuovo, 1905 Births and Marriages.

47. John Pollard, *Catholicism in Modern Italy: Religion, Society and Politics since 1861* (New York: Routledge, 2008), 30–31.

48. Pollard, *Catholicism in Modern Italy*, 31.

49. "Un lembo ignorato d'Italia: La Basilicata," *La Stampa*, October 1, 1887.

50. "Un lembo ignorato d'Italia: La Basilicata," *La Stampa*, October 1, 1887.

51. "Della emigrazione Italiana," *La Civiltà Cattolica* XI, no. 916 (1888): 401.

52. "Della emigrazione Italiana," *La Civiltà Cattolica* XI, no. 916 (1888): 403.

53. "IV: Cose Varie," *La Civiltà Cattolica* 3, no. 1298 (1904): 252–253.

54. ASP, Atti di Pubblica Sicurezza, Cat 6, Busta 43.

55. ASP, Atti di Pubblica Sicurezza, Cat 6, Busta 43.

Chapter 6

Deviant Women

Criminal and Dishonorable Activity

Anna L. and Filomena L., both from the town of Grassano, had an ongoing antagonism. Both women were married—forty-two-year-old Filomena since 1876 with one living daughter, and thirty-five-year-old Anna since 1879. In June 1890, Filomena accused Anna of having an affair with her husband, Leonardo. The length of the affair is unknown and both denied the accusation. The animosity between the two women apparently existed for some time and culminated in the summer of 1890 when they came across one another one evening. It is uncertain who provoked whom, but a confrontation ensued. In the confusion, Anna took out a dagger and stabbed Filomena multiple times, piercing the femoral artery and killing her almost instantly.[1] It was unclear why Anna had a dagger on her. The allegations about the affair between Anna and Filomena's husband may or may not have been true, but the suspicion was strong enough to provoke an emotional reaction and confrontation.

Anna was arrested and accused of homicide and carrying a dangerous weapon, and her case was brought before the Court of Assizes. Court documents labeled it a case of love and jealousy, similar to the opening story of Chapter 5, where Domenica G. also attacked her husband's mistress. In these cases and others, women violently acted upon their emotions. As this chapter will demonstrate, many contemporaries believed that women were too often subject to passion and too weak to control their desires in the heat of the moment. These beliefs offered another reason why society deemed women vulnerable and needing to be guarded and protected, especially during this period of large-scale male emigration.

In exploring the actions of the women who remained behind, it is impossible to ignore the likely negative or deviant aspects of their behavior. As seen in previous chapters, many women took advantage of their husbands' absence to carve out a new space for themselves and to claim a role above and beyond their legal limitations. At the same time, some women, either out of necessity or desire, turned to various dishonorable or criminal acts. Crime did not dramatically increase in Basilicata during this period, but widespread fears persisted among citizens and officials alike, especially because large numbers of women were left on their own. Indeed, women committed crimes regardless of the presence of their spouses, but it might have been easier or more tempting for them if they were on their own. Turning to criminal or dishonorable acts was not likely the norm for most women because family and neighbors closely guarded them, especially when husbands were absent. Women knew their deviant actions might damage their reputation and impact the position of the family and their children in the village.

The women examined in this chapter committed various types of misdeeds, both criminal and moral. While it is difficult to track petty crimes or those neither reported nor prosecuted, a small group of crimes relating to honor serve as good indicators of the types of female crime. In particular, instances of prostitution, abortion, or infanticide demonstrate how some women left behind committed transgressions and then afterward attempted extreme actions in an effort to save their honor, reputations, and financial security. While by no means affecting a large number of individuals, this chapter discusses these crimes, particularly highlighting cases of infanticide to show that despite changes brought about by emigration, women did not always conform to legal or societal norms, and some traditional elements persisted in society, specifically a strong honor culture.

CRIME AND ANXIETY ABOUT MEN LEAVING

The inhabitants of Basilicata were familiar with violence and crime. As described in the Introduction, the region was the epicenter of the widespread brigandage occurring in the Italian south in the 1860s. In the decade following national unification, outsiders considered it one of the most violent regions in Italy. Brigands defied national authority, destroyed property, and essentially wreaked havoc in the countryside. Even women were known to have joined their husbands or take part in the brigandage themselves.[2] The phenomenon subsided by the 1880s, but it left its mark on the region's population. Despite the widespread violence throughout the region in these years, Basilicata did not have a mafia like other regions of the south, and so it lacked the crime resulting from its presence.

In the years of mass migration, crime generally increased in Italy. Between 1887 and 1889, the country experienced an increase from 526,300 to 571,427 crimes reported.[3] Statistics from the first decade of the twentieth century demonstrate that the trends of the late nineteenth century continued. The number of reported crimes in all of Italy between 1905 and 1909 rose from 811,487 to 928,707. The prevalence of most offenses increased, from homicide to crimes against the family, as well as those against public order. Overall, more men committed crimes than women, a fact reflected in court and prison statistics. The number of women found guilty of crimes in all of Italy decreased between 1906 and 1909, from 28,404 to 24,478. During that same period, the number of men condemned increased from 116,759 to 120,790.[4] Italy was not unique, and crime rose in other European countries as well during the same period. However, Italy did have the highest percentage of homicide, with a rate of 7.59 per 100,000 in 1894. The next lowest country was Spain with 5.02. For context, France had a rate of 1.77, and Britain .48 per 100,000.[5]

Certain crime rates rose in Basilicata in this period as well. According to an 1892 article in *La Cronaca Lucana*, there was a decrease in homicides but an increase in other offenses, such as robberies and thefts in the countryside.[6] In fact, Basilicata (along with Sardinia, Lazio, and Abruzzo) had a particularly high rate of thefts (*furti*), and also increased reports of injuries and beatings (*ferrite* and *percosse*).[7] It is difficult to analyze such general numbers, or to know what type of impact emigration had on crime rates, especially in Basilicata. News reports do not analyze the specific causes of the rise in crime; however, the article from *La Cronaca Lucana* indicates the spike might have been due to lack of public security or poverty among the inhabitants.

Similar to emigration, crime increased in Basilicata when people were desperate or impoverished. A local newspaper, *Il Lucano*, included a quote attributed to Napoleon, stating in part "if crimes increase, it is proof that misery is growing and that society is poorly managed, their decrease is proof of the opposite." The article continued, stating, "in our days, crimes are growing dramatically and suicides are increasing, not out of love delusions or scams . . . but by those seeking relief from misery in the silence of the grave."[8] The region was impoverished prior to large-scale emigration, and many Lucanians may have sought emigration, not criminal activity, as a remedy to their condition.

Nonetheless, during these years of mass emigration, crimes committed by women did not increase drastically. This is not to say that women did not commit petty offenses, especially if hungry and desperate. Unfortunately, there is no way to quantify the extent to which this occurred. Yet, many observers were not concerned about women committing criminal offenses, but about the connection between emigration and possible moral misconduct.

In a patriarchal society, an abundance of women with husbands abroad led to anxiety and suspicion about their actions and behavior. Thousands of migrants left Basilicata during this period, and about 80% of those leaving were men. The largely uneven pattern of migration resulted in numerous social and demographic effects. Some villages lost a significant percentage of their male population, usually the youngest and ablest members of the labor force. If migrants remained abroad, fewer men in town meant fewer women could marry, often leading to a decline in childbirths. Basilicata was the only region with a population loss between 1881 and 1901 not only because thousands were emigrating but also because there were fewer at home to reproduce.

With men leaving and women remaining behind, public fears increased about women committing crimes or having illicit relations. Local officials expressed anxiety over the large number of wives left on their own and the potential for misconduct. Historian Donna Gabaccia points out that officials viewed "widows in white" as more of a threat to public morality than actual widows because oftentimes thousands of young, newly married women were left at home without the protection of their husbands. Many feared these women would turn to immoral behavior, resulting in a breakdown of morals and family structure. Yet, Gabaccia provides statistics to argue that in Sicily, illegitimate births and infanticides did not increase in this period as a result of emigration.[9] Husbands might have been uneasy about leaving young wives on their own and entrusted them to the care of family, friends, or neighbors who would watch over them.[10] As seen in Chapter 5, the importance of community cannot be overstated, as it remained a key arbiter of those in the village, especially women. Networks of surveillance and gossip served to keep women in line, for fear of the consequences of their actions being known to all. Nonetheless, leaving behind a family for months or years at a time constituted a great risk for some husbands.

Scientific reasoning of the late nineteenth century concluded that women were not completely responsible for their actions because they were psychologically inferior and thus legally less culpable when committing crimes. Under the law, and even in practice, women were considered impulsive, hysterical, and not able to control their emotions. In the late nineteenth century, positivist scholarship, spearheaded by criminologist Cesare Lombroso (1835–1909), attempted to demonstrate women's mental inferiority through an analysis of their physical features. Measurements of their skulls provided evidence of their limitations. Paradoxically, the image of the nurturing mother as an innate female quality also became popular in this period.[11] Thus criminal behavior and dishonorable crimes like abortion or infanticide baffled some who believed these were crimes against nature.

Legislation is indicative of larger societal ideas about the capacity of women, their potentially unstable emotional state, and the acts they might be capable of committing, especially if left on their own. The Penal Code in

Italy during this period, which will be examined later in the chapter, treated people who committed crimes in the name of honor as victims themselves. For example, the possibility of a reduced sentence due to the *causa d'onore* for infanticide was written with the understanding that childbirth emotionally affected women. Therefore, committing such a crime could be considered a "momentary aberration," because the offender was not otherwise a danger to society. In his study on infanticide written in 1896, lawyer Pasquale Arena stated "it is not out of perversity of the soul that a woman commits such a misdeed, but because it is a painful necessity of which she herself is the victim. It is the effect of an instantaneous psychological episode."[12] Thus, a woman should not be considered a criminal, but a victim, because in that instant she had to choose between the life of her child or her own dishonor. The crime occurred in a moment of weakness when, largely influenced by societal pressure and moral prejudices, a woman allowed her impulses to win over. By the time of an accused woman's trial, not only would the public know she committed infanticide but also her pregnancy and tainted honor would be discovered. In a small village of Basilicata with only a few thousand people, a woman would not be able to escape her dishonor or tainted reputation. Thus, some legislators may have considered the crimes of these women understandable, in part out of sympathy for the women facing such a dilemma.

By the turn of the twentieth century and amid the age of mass migration, the image persisted of the "immoral woman alone, unable to resist the attentions of men or to exercise the necessary authority over her children, abandoned to a destiny of criminality."[13] While not accurate, this depiction indicates prevailing mentalities about women at the time. To some extent, women may have had more independence as a result of emigration, as shown in previous chapters. However, with fewer men in the town—husbands, brothers, fathers, or other family members—women, whether married or not, potentially had more freedom to engage in illicit relations. Such encounters had to remain secret and hidden from the scrutinizing eyes of relatives and neighbors as they threatened the honor and reputations of the women involved and perhaps their social and economic position in the community. Some of the most severe crimes women committed when their husbands were absent were those which affected their honor and standing in the community.

HONOR AND THE LAW

Honor was a major component of Italian life, especially in the south. With men absent, women would be responsible for preserving both their honor and that of their families. Poor behavior could impact one's good name and reputation in the community. An honor culture centered around the values and actions that guided a person to behave in a certain way in order to earn respect and status in the community. In this type of society, honor and shame dictated acceptable and reprehensible conduct. Good or honorable behavior brought respect and dignity to oneself and one's family, while poor conduct brought dishonor, shame, and the possibility of being shunned by the community. Honor codes were complex, and in most cases, gender-specific, reflecting a highly patriarchal society. While a man's honor was generally tied to his masculinity, virility, and strength, a woman's honor was tied to her chastity and sexual fidelity. Maintaining honor for single women meant refraining from sex before marriage, wearing modest clothing, and maintaining self-control in social relations with men. For married women, honor was also tied to behavior and fidelity. Dishonorable acts could range from inappropriate contact with a male stranger, to prostitution, or even illegitimate pregnancy. There was much less societal pressure on the sexual activities of men, who were free to engage in sex before and even after marriage or seek prostitutes. In many honor cultures, including in Italy, men protected and defended the honor of their female relatives. Any transgression against female honor reflected on the men of her family and demonstrated to the community that men were not able to protect or control their female family members. Dishonorable or shameful behavior might also lead to ostracism in the community, which could further result in financial loss. Despite changes in society by the turn of the century, the mentality of the honor culture persisted.[14]

If a family's honor was stained in any way, members went to great lengths to try to restore it, including the use of violence, which was justified in those cases and to some extent sanctioned by the Italian law code. Honor codes and the law in the modern period were largely based on the theories of Cesare Beccaria (1738–1794), who began to analyze crime and called for mitigated culpability and punishment based on the causes and social conditions surrounding it.[15] The Penal Code of 1889, also known as the Zanardelli Code and in effect from 1890 to 1930, upheld the importance of honor and was lenient regarding crimes committed in its name. Punishment was less severe for cases of adultery, abortion, homicide, and infanticide if committed to defend one's honor. This aspect of the law was not unique to Italy. European law codes included exceptions for crimes of honor since the early nineteenth century, and penal codes in Austria (1803 and 1852), France (1824 and 1832), and Germany (1872) incorporated reduced penalties if the *causa d'onore* was invoked. The honor excuse remained in subsequent Italian law codes until 1981.

If an individual (male or female) committed a crime to save his or her honor or that of a relative, the sentence could be reduced significantly. For example, the penalty for voluntary homicide was imprisonment for eighteen to twenty-one years, but reduced to three to twelve years if the crime was committed to protect one's honor. To use the excuse of *causa d'onore*, a number of conditions had to be present. For cases of infanticide, the child had to be illegitimate, the crime had to have been committed to hide one's dishonor, and the woman should have had her honor intact.[16] That is, she should not have been a dishonored woman, such as a prostitute. Historian Maria Sophia Quine argues that this provision in the criminal code was a result of a general acceptance of honor crimes in society. She argues that "the high degree of tolerance which Italian society exhibited toward infanticide arose partly from the conviction that this was primarily a crime against children who should not have been born in the first place."[17] It is also important to note that the honor excuse within the Penal Code was in effect for all of Italy, despite honor culture being closely associated with the south.

The use of the honor excuse was an important feature of Italian law, but it was largely a way for women (and men) to justify criminal behavior and the actions they committed in order to save their names, their social position, their economic position, and in some cases, their marriages. All of these aspects were interrelated—if one was damaged, so were the others. If men were absent, women took it upon themselves to restore their own honor and defend their reputation, even if they had been the ones who put them in jeopardy.

Persisting cultural values based on a code of honor led women and families to commit extreme acts. Many women attempted to abort fetuses, abandon infants, or commit infanticide in a moment of desperation, fearful of the consequences when the community, their husbands, or their families might learn of their supposed transgressions. If a woman became pregnant out of wedlock or by a man other than her husband, the baby would become a sign of her dishonor for all to see. Women would have to deal with the stress of hiding a pregnancy, avoiding neighbors' suspicions and speculations, and feeling shame over possible adultery. Attempting to obtain an abortion, hiding an unwanted pregnancy, abandoning an infant, and if necessary, committing infanticide were all ways to conceal a transgression, repair dishonor, and save one's reputation. Thus, some women in this period found themselves in a difficult situation, having to decide between honor or shame and the life or death of their babies. The willingness to commit such acts shows the strength of these forces on the lives of women. David Kertzer has argued that the community justified crimes committed to save one's honor because of the vital role it held in southern Italian culture.[18] Women who remained behind may have felt exceptionally alone and vulnerable and took matters into their own hands to preserve their honor.

PROSTITUTION

The most common dishonorable practice women participated in when left on their own was prostitution. Women likely turned to prostitution for economic reasons, or even survival. There was no typical prostitute—she might have been young or old, married or single, and childless or already a mother. Women could resort to the practice once or repeatedly. It is difficult to track how many women turned to prostitution, especially if casual or occasional. It is also easier to track prostitution in major cities than in the small, rural villages of Basilicata, where most residents knew each other, and were aware of which women were considered "respectable" or not. As seen in Chapter 5, many residents found it difficult to hide their circumstances or private actions with the watchful eyes of neighbors always on them. In major cities or larger towns, potential clients were more numerous and greater anonymity existed, so it is unlikely that many women turned to prostitution in a village of two or three thousand people. However, it is possible that some women used their bodies to acquire food or other goods for themselves and their children, especially those in dire need. Thus, most prostitutes were likely hidden from the historical record, and the nature of prostitution in Basilicata can only be gauged by those who were detained and/or arrested by authorities, surely not a representative sample.

Documents do show evidence of prostitution in the region, and authorities tracked many "repeat offenders." Records of Public Security documented the regulation of prostitutes. Files were maintained on women of all ages, some as young as fourteen, and others in their forties. Many were women who the police picked up, arrested for public safety violations, and sent to the *sifilicomio*, or an institution where doctors examined women—mostly suspected prostitutes—for syphilis and other sexually transmitted diseases, and offered treatment to those infected.[19] Although Basilicata was small, with a population of less than a half a million before the turn of the century, there were *sifilicomi* in Potenza, Matera, and Melfi, three of the largest municipalities in the region. Women likely fled from the confines of the *sifilicomi* if they were able to, and authorities even picked up some women for a second or third time. Evidence from Public Security documents cases of girls as young as fifteen arrested and badly infected with syphilis, exhibiting ulcers and high fevers. These cases were few, and the motives behind their actions is difficult to gauge.

Women with husbands abroad might have turned to prostitution out of financial need, regardless of whether or not their husbands were sending remittances. A sixty-year-old aunt of Gerarda L., a woman accused of infanticide, gave insight into her niece's situation, testifying, "my niece has a husband in America for various years . . . (she) told me that it has been ten months that he has not written, nor sent money, and she was forced to live as God intended."[20] This and other statements in the court records imply that Gerarda lived a life of poverty and perhaps turned to prostitution to survive after her husband abandoned her. While not excusing the behavior, the aunt justified her niece's actions. Another accused woman gave insight into her situation with the statement, "I am married to Antonio P. and my husband has been in America for four years. I have remained alone without the help of anyone, I had to sell my body to buy life."[21] Statements like these show the desperation of abandoned women, often turning to prostitution to survive.

It is difficult to determine if emigration was the cause for these women turning to prostitution. The practice could be a profession for some, while others might turn to it during a time of temporary necessity. Women whose husbands abandoned them were likely more prone to resort to it for financial reasons, especially if they had no family to assist them. These women would still want to protect their name, even if they did not necessarily rely on having a good reputation, in order to potentially receive remittances from abroad. Perhaps in these circumstances a reassessment of common perceptions of prostitution is necessary. Women might have simply turned to the care and financial protection of another man, while still married, because he offered to support her and her children after marital abandonment. While prostitution was legal, it was not considered an honorable practice. If a woman, especially a married woman with a husband abroad, was labeled a prostitute, it would lead to shame, dishonor, and economic ruin for her and her family.

INFIDELITY

Prostitution for women left behind may have stemmed from an economic necessity. Other women gave in to a more emotional necessity. With husbands away for prolonged periods of time, wives may have sought love or affection from other men. Although difficult to measure, evidence shows that infidelity rates among women did not rise significantly as a result of emigration.[22] Yet with many men leaving, some wives would inevitably turn to other partners, especially if their husbands were absent for a number of years. These actions were risky for several reasons. If a husband abroad was sending remittances that a wife depended on, this inflow of money would most likely end if he discovered his wife's infidelity. In many instances, friends and relatives watched wives and would quickly inform husbands if they sensed or witnessed misbehavior. Women had to be secretive, knowing they could be discovered at any time. These encounters are hidden from the historical record, and it is difficult to gauge the percentage of unfaithful wives. Like prostitution, infidelity could be a one-time occurrence or transpire on a more regular basis. Nonetheless, it was crucial to be seen as an honorable member of society, and having an affair and a possibly a child out of wedlock could tarnish one's name and cause irreversible damage to the whole family, more so for the woman involved than the man.

Men were also unfaithful, but their actions were much less scrutinized. Emigrants living in New York, London, Buenos Aires, and other locations benefited from the anonymity of a major city and were not subject to the same rigid honor codes of their small village. Away from home, there were fewer consequences, and their behavior would not threaten their standing in their new community. Anecdotal evidence of emigrants in the Americas having a second wife or other children is common, but it is unlikely that these were legal unions. Even at home in Italy, men were allowed much more leeway in terms of infidelity. A clear double standard existed, and behavioral expectations differed greatly for married men and women.

UNWANTED PREGNANCY, ABORTION, INFANT ABANDONMENT

Infidelity was especially risky for women if it led to pregnancy, making their transgression visible to the whole community. By the late nineteenth century, little, if any, birth control was available in rural Basilicata and abortion was illegal. After discovering they were pregnant, women would have to face a stressful decision, one that might include how to terminate their pregnancy before others discovered it.

Italian society did not deem it dishonorable for men to father a child out of wedlock. In fact, a father was not required to provide for an illegitimate child and had no legal responsibility regarding the baby unless he later recognized it. The Civil Code of 1865 prohibited paternity searches, and fathers were rarely mentioned in court documents involving abortion and infanticide cases, unless others in the community knew who they were and named them. Even if the father was known, the civil birth record only listed the mother's name. Thus, the social and economic burden of an illegitimate pregnancy fell solely on the woman and her family.

Women had few options for unwanted pregnancies. A woman could keep the baby, which not only meant shame and dishonor for her and her family, but also an end to financial support from her husband if he was abroad. For a single woman, a pregnancy out of wedlock could mean a loss of respectable marriage prospects, resulting in possible financial hardship or economic loss for her and her family. Many women did not want to risk living life as a dishonored spinster.

Abortion was an option, albeit illegal—it was not legalized in Italy until 1978—and, as demonstrated by court records, women would be in legal jeopardy if caught trying to procure one. The practice was also extremely risky and posed a danger to the mother's life if complications occurred. In everyday parlance, abortion was not labeled as such, but as bringing on menstruation, especially in the first few months of pregnancy. It seems that women in this circumstance knew other women who could give them a mixture to drink that would lead to miscarriage. Women would have to acquire in secret these remedies, which were very dangerous to ingest and could result in other health complications. They could also attempt other ways to miscarry, such as purposefully causing injury to themselves. These methods may or may not have been successful.[23]

If pregnancies reached full term, but the mother did not want or could not keep the baby, infant abandonment was an option after giving birth. Kertzer points out that infant abandonment was quite common in all of Europe, as well as in Italy, where hundreds of thousands of babies were abandoned over the centuries.[24] Abandonment of an illegitimate child meant that a woman would have to keep her pregnancy secret—not always an easy task in small southern Italian towns. There was much more anonymity in a larger city than in the villages of Basilicata, where it may have been harder to conceal and secretly give up a child.

Infant abandonment was common in Italy, and even encouraged by the Catholic Church since medieval times to spare the lives of babies that might have been aborted or killed. Most infants were abandoned on the wheel (*ruota*).[25] The wheel was a contraption, like a turntable, attached to a church or convent on which a woman could anonymously place a baby, spin the wheel, and deposit the baby inside, where it would be reared. In early modern times, infant abandonment centered around moral concerns; the wheel was originally intended to receive illegitimate infants anonymously as a form of Catholic charity, thus freeing unmarried women of the burden of a baby that brought her shame or dishonor. With high child mortality rates, especially in orphanages, abandoning a child was almost a form of infanticide. By the late nineteenth century, a growing number of parents abandoned legitimate babies for economic concerns, a marked shift in the reasons for abandonment, causing a crisis in foundling homes over how to care for the many babies.[26] The *ruota* was used all throughout Italy but had higher usage in the south.

Foundlings were children given up by their parents, and it is difficult to know if they were illegitimate or offspring of married couples who likely gave them up for economic reasons. Italian localities kept statistics of births in each town and foundlings were identified in civil registers, but listed separately, with an entry made for each, describing how the baby was clothed when it arrived and also giving it a name. After 1883, all babies were listed together in the registers, but abandoned babies and those by single mothers with unknown fathers were labeled as illegitimate children, or *figli naturali.*

Changing attitudes about infant abandonment led to the abolition of the wheel in most Italian provinces by the 1880s, but the practice persisted well into the early 1900s.[27] By the end of the century, the state took charge, and the anonymity of abandonment gave way to a state increasingly open to assisting single mothers. As Maria Sophia Quine argues, a shift from church to secular state control of infant abandonment occurred, and "under liberalism, the unwed mother was transformed from an anonymous sinner into an object for rehabilitation, experimentation, and control."[28] Secular authorities aimed to change the perception of single motherhood so that it would be deemed socially acceptable to raise illegitimate children. While the law shifted enormously, society adapted slowly. Quine has pointed out that when the wheel was abolished, there was an increase in infant deaths and stillbirths reported, which could point to women committing infanticide when anonymous abandonment was no longer an option.[29]

Generally the south had higher rates of infant abandonment than the north, but the rate in Basilicata was low, at just under 3% in the years following unification.[30] One of the most notorious foundling homes in the south was the Annunziata in Naples, which took in babies from the surrounding areas, including Basilicata, especially if nearby small rural towns did not have an establishment to care for abandoned children.[31] Churches in the small towns of Basilicata did have the wheel, and statistics for 1902 to 1906 reveal that some towns, despite new laws, still used the wheel. A total of seventy-eight babies were abandoned during those years. Basilicata had a relatively small number of infants abandoned compared to other regions still using the wheel. For example, during those same four years, Sicily still had 126 municipalities using the wheel with over 10,329 babies collected. The only regions with no reported use of the wheel were all in the north and center: Piedmont, Liguria, Veneto, Tuscany, Umbria, and Lazio.[32]

The number of women who may have gotten pregnant and found a method of aborting the fetus or abandoning the baby is difficult to determine. Women often committed these acts anonymously, and no record of them has been left behind. Infanticide was another, more grave choice, but its frequency also cannot be measured. This crime was committed by women who likely tried to abort their child or may not have been able to anonymously abandon their baby.

INFANTICIDE

Article 369 of the Italian Penal Code of 1889 defined infanticide as a crime committed against an infant fewer than five days old and not yet entered into the civil registers. Infanticide, the killing of a newborn infant, was an act likely committed under extreme circumstances. Women who were single, married, or widowed all had reasons to commit infanticide in late-nineteenth and early-twentieth-century Italy, particularly if the baby was illegitimate or if it would be an extreme financial burden. If authorities discovered their crime, the accused regularly claimed they committed infanticide to protect their honor, as permitted under the Penal Code, which resulted in mitigated culpability and could lead to a reduced sentence. Earlier law codes, such as the Piedmontese Penal Code of 1859, only allowed the mother to use the honor excuse. The Italian Penal Code of 1889 extended the use of honor for the crime of infanticide to include other family members, such as those defending the honor of their wife, mother, descendant, adopted daughter, or sister. Italian law considered infanticide a homicide, unless committed to save one's honor. While some women did commit infanticide to preserve their honor, and indeed, it was their only legal excuse, social and economic reasons also influenced their decision, especially during this period of mass emigration.

Infanticide was not a crime committed often, at least as indicated by court documents. Many cases of infanticide in this period were committed by women with husbands abroad. Of all the cases tried in the Court of Assizes (*Corte d'Assise*) in Basilicata between 1876 and 1914, there were at most one or two cases yearly in each province (Potenza and Matera). The files of each case contain a description of the crime, statements from the accused, medical reports—including autopsies—and witness testimonies, from both men and women, friends and neighbors in the community. The numbers represented in these cases are in no way an indication of the actual amount of infanticides that occurred. Court documents reflect the cases of women who were caught, and there is no way of knowing how many women in fact committed infanticide and concealed all evidence. Despite limitations, court documents reveal how rural, southern Italian women left behind by their emigrating husbands perceived their honor and justified their actions.

There was no one stereotypical woman who committed infanticide in Basilicata during this period. The accused women were of all childbearing ages, and many already had other children. In fact, of the twenty-one cases examined, twelve of the accused women were married. Eight of those women had a husband in America and two had husbands not present in the village. The women were also all from the poorer classes, coming from families of farmers or working as servants. If they had wanted to risk the societal consequences of having an illegitimate child, they were not women who had the financial means to take on single motherhood while being shunned by society. Those with husbands abroad did not want to risk the loss of remittances that would likely occur after an unwanted pregnancy. Despite the circumstances or motives, all the men and women accused in the infanticide cases claimed they acted to defend their honor.

Understandably, all the accused women attempted to conceal their pregnancies, some more successfully than others. One woman said she was able to hide her condition because of her tall stature and gave birth secretly at home during the night while her other three children slept nearby.[33] Another woman, Maria Annunziata G. hid her pregnancy because her husband was in America and he was not the father of the child.[34] She feared the consequences of him learning of her condition. Women with a spouse abroad also had to ensure that no one in the village found out about and related news of their infidelity to their husbands who might stop sending remittances. In many cases, neighbors testified that they observed the accused women getting bigger and were therefore pregnant, but the accused always denied it. Neighbors, especially other women, were hard to fool.

In most cases, authorities discovered a crime not because neighbors or friends reported a woman, but because of carelessness in disposing of the body and/or evidence.[35] Women and their accomplices attempted to hide the corpses, but in their desperation, did not conceal them well. In rural Basilicata, women disposed of bodies in a number of places in and around the village, such as in a pile of rocks, in a crevice in a stone wall, in a cellar, in the cemetery, and even in a fountain. Most wrapped the bodies in cloths, which eventually aided investigators in connecting the women to their crimes. When a body was discovered, investigators had to figure out how the baby died and who might be the mother, and often took witness statements from others in the community who could attest to women with recent pregnancies. It might be easy to narrow down the suspected mother, especially if a woman's attempts to conceal her pregnancy were unsuccessful.

When accused of infanticide, women, out of desperation, gave various arguments to authorities to at first protect their innocence, and if caught lying, to then lessen their culpability. As mentioned, women commonly lied about being pregnant. In one instance, when it was apparent to neighbors that Catarina B. was pregnant, she negated it, feigning a "uterine malady" when questioned. She later testified, "I did not know I was pregnant and I was surprised when with the sudden abdominal pains, I gave birth." According to the report in her case file, "some believed her."[36] In another instance, thirty-two-year-old Rosaria D. was a domestic worker in a home in Baragiano when she got pregnant. At first, while denying her condition, she claimed to have suffered from hydropsy, or a buildup of blood in her abdomen, attempting to hide her condition so as not to lose her job.[37] She eventually lost her position when her supervisor discovered that she misled him and was indeed pregnant. In a case of blatant lying, a local doctor testified that another accused woman, Teresa D., whom he had examined at four months, told him he was mistaken and that she definitely was not pregnant. Not surprisingly, the doctor stated he did not want to examine her again after that visit.[38]

Despite feigning ignorance, most women knew they were pregnant and tried to plan a way to dispose of the evidence of their dishonor. In cases where they hid their pregnancy, women often gave birth alone at home, trying not to alert anyone in the house or their neighbors. Many inhabitants in small towns most likely resided in homes with a few rooms. If there was a separate bedroom, it was often shared among family members. Some case files reported that women gave birth silently in their beds during the night, while others were asleep in the same room.[39] One official recounted the story of Maria Annunziata G. giving birth silently in bed so as to hide from her family, saying "the woman gave birth and had the rare courage not to scream and to keep the little one from crying."[40] This woman's case captures the fear and desperation felt by many women who hid their pregnancies, and emphasizes the threat of gossip and social stigma if the community discovered their secret. It also reveals the risks some women were willing to take: giving birth alone could be dangerous, especially if there were complications. It is difficult to imagine how these women were able to give birth alone in these circumstances.

Women often denied pregnancy, but once discovered, blamed others, claiming they were attacked, or even raped. Mentioned earlier, Teresa D., whose husband had been in America for three years, denied being pregnant, explaining her pregnancy-like weight gain by claiming she also had hydropsy. When doctors refuted that claim and she could no longer deny her condition, she desperately accused her sixteen-year-old brother of fathering the child. The brother vehemently denied the accusation, and she later dropped the allegation against him. She then testified the father was a stranger who raped her. After she stated the baby was stillborn, authorities further discredited her testimony when they discovered the injured corpse of the baby in a box in her home.[41] In another instance of an outrageous allegation, Porzia O. accused the father of her child, who was involved with her sister, of raping her. During the case, her claim was discredited when authorities discovered that the relationship was consensual, and they had been having an intimate relationship unknown to others until she became pregnant.[42] Rosa G. from the town of Laurenzana denied committing infanticide and attempted to blame a woman described as a *mediatrice* who she claimed knew about her pregnancy and helped her with the birth. After Rosa G. tried to place the blame on her for committing infanticide, the "mediator" testified "if that woman did not want to kill her own child, she would not have first hid the pregnancy and then attempted to abort it."[43] Such cases demonstrate that even as evidence mounted against them and their lies were discredited, the accused women used multiple excuses to deny allegations facing them, and often went as far as blaming others for the crimes.

The accused also tended to mislead investigators about the child being alive at birth, frequently reporting it was stillborn, a believable scenario since infant mortality rates were still very high. Autopsies and medical examinations often negated these claims, yet many women insisted on their stories, despite medical evidence demonstrating the contrary. In one case, Rosaria D. denied her pregnancy and then lied about the child being born dead, even though evidence indicated the accused mother strangled the baby. She eventually admitted it was in fact her baby but claimed, "he was dead even before she had cut the umbilical cord."[44] When the accused women were confronted with overwhelming evidence and they could no longer deny giving birth, they continued to try to mislead investigators, all in order to exculpate themselves from their crimes in a desperate attempt to defend their honor.

The testimony of accused women shows that they made outrageous claims and committed extraordinary acts to save their reputations. They gave desperate and often misleading testimonies in an effort to exonerate themselves or blame others for their actions. Perhaps they were uninformed and not aware that an autopsy could prove they misled investigators. They may have been outright lying in a frantic attempt to plead for their innocence, fearful of going to prison. Perhaps, as some believed at the time, these women were in a psychological state that prevented them from seeing reality. Fear of tarnished honor could have indeed had psychological side effects, and officials might have believed the women's fragile mental state could not handle such societal pressures. Nonetheless, these various excuses and explanations demonstrate the extreme emotional pressure women were under and allow for the possibility of ongoing postpartum psychosis or depression which affected their actions, even after committing the crime.

The reactions of members of the community to the accused infanticides reveal how others thought about the crime. Accomplices—mothers of the accused, close friends, or other family members—often lied to authorities, denying pregnancies or claiming ignorance. When learning a friend or an acquaintance in the community was accused of infanticide, many witnesses reasoned that the accused could not possibly be guilty of their crimes because they were good women who came from honorable or respectable families. Most residents expressed their opinions about the accused women in their testimonies. Others showed outrage and doubt that the accused women committed such horrible acts, even if justified by honor. One witness expressed her disbelief that the accused actually committed infanticide, stating, "it did not appear true because no mother could harm her own child."[45] In another case, a neighbor doubted a woman was guilty of hiding her pregnancy and subsequently committing infanticide because "she came from a good family."[46] A neighbor in another instance who knew the accused for about five years testified, "I always believed she was an honest woman."[47] These statements show honor culture at play: women from respectable families in good standing in the community were not expected to commit such acts. At the same time, honor and respectability extended to all social classes, and in some cases, honor might be the most valuable possession poorer people had to protect.

Members of the community knew what occurred with their neighbors and especially kept an eye on women who were on their own with husbands in America. One witness stated of an accused woman that "after the departure of her husband for America she had many dishonest relations."[48] A neighbor of Teresa D., whose husband had been in America for three years, stated she knew the accused lived alone with two children, but never saw or heard of anyone visiting or staying the night. This same female witness said she was hurt when she learned the truth and did not want to know anything more about the accused.[49] Keeping secrets in small villages and close-knit communities was difficult, and often everyone knew who had emigrated and which wives were on their own. Even inside the home, family members had little privacy from one another. Various members of the family commonly slept in the same room, and children were often present while adults conversed. The ten-year-old daughter of a woman accused of infanticide testified that she heard her mother speaking about an abortion. She also witnessed her mother asking a doctor for pills to terminate a pregnancy, which the doctor refused to provide.[50] Perry Willson has argued that often the community itself, especially other women, helped enforce gender roles by calling out transgressions which could bring shame or social stigma to a family.[51] In an environment of large-scale emigration and a higher proportion of women left in towns, this may very well have been the case in a number of local communities. Women giving testimony were observant and aware of what went on in the village. Unfortunately, the truthfulness of their testimony was uncertain, as they may have used the platform to act on a grudge, to protect friends or neighbors, or to try to manipulate the verdict of a case for some reason.

When cases went to trial, both the accused and their accomplices used honor as a defense. As mentioned above, the *causa d'onore* was a legal excuse that defendants could use in cases of infanticide. While initially many of the accused women denied the crime, lied about being pregnant, or misled investigators, they all claimed they were acting to protect their honor. For instance, Rosa G. admitted to giving birth but said the child was born dead, and no one assisted her during childbirth because she was home alone. Afterward she brought the baby to the cemetery and abandoned it there. In her testimony, Rosa stated, "I took the child away in secret just to save my honor, being that I was seen as young and honest in the village."[52] Preserving her honor and reputation drove her to conceal her actions. In this case, as in many others, women admitted to having an illegitimate baby, but still denied committing infanticide. The women may have considered infanticide a horrible crime, one they did not want to admit to having committed. Nevertheless, they used the honor excuse to justify disposing of a child that they hid from the public and claimed was born dead.

Similar to tactics used by women who petitioned to the mayor in earlier chapters, some of the accused used the strategy of appealing to the stereotypical characteristics of a weak woman controlled by her emotions. After giving birth, Porzia O. claimed she committed the crime as emotions overtook her. She wrapped the baby in a cloth without even looking to see its sex because "in that moment I was overcome by a hysterical episode, during which I lost all reason."[53] Although her husband had been in America for over four years, she claimed her husband sent her money, so she did not commit the crime because she lived in poverty. Instead, she was weak and could not resist the man who took her honor.[54] Here she appealed to the reputation of women as impulsive and unable to control their emotions, hoping for sympathy from an all-male jury. It is also possible that women in these cases knew how men perceived them and used the discourse designed to oppress them in order to escape culpability. It did not matter if these arguments were illogical, in fact, that often helped prove their point.

The case of Domenica L. further shows how women may have manipulated investigators feigning a fragile mental state despite overwhelming evidence to the contrary. After a denial in her initial testimony, she later admitted to the crime, stating her actions were the result of a momentary lapse, which led the jury to consider mental instability or insanity.[55] While this defense may have been plausible, she also lied about other aspects of the case. She claimed the baby was born dead, but the autopsy clearly demonstrated trauma which caused its death. She was also accused of giving a false name and information to a public official. The various lies and manipulations added together challenged the initial claim of momentary insanity.

Preserving honor was important not only to the pregnant woman but also her family. In a number of cases, family members, mostly women, assisted with the crime or in hiding evidence in order to help preserve the honor of the family. Angela T., a twenty-four-year-old single woman, had an affair with a married man, resulting in pregnancy. It is unclear whether or not others knew of her pregnancy, but after she gave birth, her mother helped her get rid of the baby. Claiming she acted to save her daughter's honor, Angela's mother, Rosa S., buried the corpse near a hill. A man walking his dog later discovered the body.[56] A similar situation occurred with Maria S., a thirty-three-year-old widow, who claimed her baby was born dead and she tried to bury it in secret to save her honor. She gave misinformation about whether or not her mother helped, at first claiming she assisted with the delivery, then saying her mother did not help at all, so as not to implicate her. Chances are, the mother was involved in order to protect the honor of her daughter, because both were sentenced to four years and two months detention.[57] Another widow was brought to trial on charges of infanticide alongside her mother-in-law, who was named as an accomplice. This case involved a mother helping her deceased son's widow maintain her honor, indicating that protecting the family's reputation continued after death.[58]

While one's standing in the community was a key motivator, the distinctive aspect of these cases from Basilicata is that several accused women had husbands abroad and depended on money sent from America. They must have feared their husbands would no longer send remittances if they found out about their misdeeds. The summary of one case explicitly stated that the defendant's husband had been in America for a year, and she committed infanticide to avoid him finding out about her infidelity. In another case, the mother of an absent husband testified in defense of her son, stating, "My son about two or three years ago left Potenza to look for fortune in America, but even far away he did not forget his wife, to whom he sent up to this day about 150 lire and with that aid she was able to live well . . . I did not know she had taken to a bad life, and when from neighbors I was told, a few months ago, that she was pregnant, I confronted her, and she negated it, acting offended."[59] This mother reiterated that her son continued to perform his marital duty by sending his wife money, but that his wife dishonored him with her infidelity. The wife's actions threatened not only her honor but also her remittances and source of economic survival.

Court documents also demonstrate the dynamics of the relationships between husbands and wives, especially if they were living separately. One woman accused of infanticide claimed that she hid the pregnancy from her husband fearing for her life. A neighbor reported that the accused woman told her she did not have the courage to tell her husband for fear of his reaction. That same husband said he received a letter while in New York from his mother, informing him that his wife was pregnant. He told the authorities that he did not believe the rumors about his wife and surprised her by coming home. He testified that if she had told him the truth, he would not have been violent with his wife, but would have separated from her.[60] This case clearly shows the husband as a figure of authority, and violence and/or abuse was acceptable in marriage, although this particular man claimed he would have refrained from using it. The mother acted on behalf of her son and protected him from the lies and deceit of his wife.

These women's stories highlight the economic nature of marriage, the close relationship between honor and reputation, and the financial consequences of dishonor. Most couples in this period likely did not marry for love, and wives did not generally express longing for husbands who had emigrated, especially if the men abandoned them. Rather they were concerned with their economic well-being and that of their children. This, of course, does not mean they did not care about their husbands or develop a loving relationship. Perry Willson points out that while some women did marry for love, most women were afraid of ending up as spinsters, so they were more likely to marry an available suitor rather than wait to fall in love. Furthermore, because families closely guarded young unmarried girls, there was little opportunity to meet and fall in love with a potential match.[61] Many times families selected spouses for their children based on social or economic considerations. In sum, married women left on their own worried that their actions would lead to shame or financial loss, and single women feared the financial insecurity of not marrying or being socially shunned before selecting a spouse. Dishonor could ruin a woman's life.

The honor excuse was not always effective because one needed to possess honor worth saving in order to claim it. Catarina L. hid her pregnancy and when it became apparent that she was getting bigger, she told others she was sick. The accused had a husband in America for two years and two other children, and perhaps had committed other dishonorable offenses. After being accused of committing infanticide, she nonetheless claimed *causa d'onore.* Yet documents from the court stated, "She cannot be ashamed because those who habitually work in a brothel can no longer feel shame for shameful acts."[62] Despite her plea, the court did not believe her excuse and found her guilty because she was apparently a prostitute, and already a socially stained woman.

In general, women initially gave misleading information to investigators, at first denying pregnancy and then having committed a crime. All of the accused used the honor excuse when the case went to trial, but defending their honor was not their first defense in the heat of the moment when initially accused. Moreover, the crime did not have to be impulsive for one to claim defense of honor. Women knew they were pregnant and had months to think about how to deal with their situation or what they could do if they gave birth to a live baby. In some cases, family members or friends helped women commit the crime. Yet according to law, the honor defense could be applied whether the crime was committed in a moment of psychosis after giving birth, or if it was planned with the help of others, demonstrating the nature of the honor excuse at the time.

If one committed infanticide to protect their honor, the Penal Code of 1889 called for a reduced sentence to three to twelve years of detention from eighteen to twenty-one years of reclusion. This important distinction between *reclusione* and *detenzione* was that the former was more legally severe, and detention had slight advantages, such as the ability to send letters or receive more visitors. While both were forms of incarceration and in practice were similar, reclusion was considered more dishonorable. Information about the verdicts is not present for all cases, but most of the women accused of infanticide were convicted, along with their accomplices, who received similar or equal sentences. In 1908, Maria V. was sentenced to four years detention, and the woman who helped her commit infanticide was sentenced to three years and nine months.[63] Maria S. and her mother Rosa B., who was found guilty of assisting her daughter, both received four years and two months detention.[64] In another case, Domenica L. was sentenced to eight years and four months of detention, but the sentence was reduced to seven years and ten months for "amnesty."[65] The longest sentence among the examined cases was ten years. There is no information in the case files concerning whether or not the women served out their sentences and what their lives were like after. The information available about sentences indicates that courts tended to take a middle road in assigning penalties, perhaps indicating that although the women were guilty of committing the crime, the all-male juries did show some sympathy for their situations.

As numbers of emigrating males increased, many in Basilicata worried about rising rates of crime, especially among women who remained behind. Fears abounded of women on their own and what they might possibly be pushed or tempted to do. Much of the evidence demonstrates that crime did not rise significantly with women left on their own. However, some women found themselves in difficult situations as a result of emigration, and much of what they did was out of need or desperation, more so than desire or pleasure. Prostitution, infidelity, unwanted pregnancy, abortion, infant abandonment, and infanticide were just some of the criminal or dishonorable acts women committed during the period of mass emigration. Unfortunately, court cases are the main source of this information, so the accused are more visible than others who were never caught. While not the only ones impacted, women with husbands abroad could more easily find themselves in these situations as a result of being left on their own. The files containing these cases are one of the most direct sources relating to the women of Basilicata in this period.

Cases of infanticide, as well as instances of attempted abortions and infant abandonment, reflect the convergence of a complicated set of circumstances for these women: economic hardship, emigration, social position, and reputation in the community. When faced with the potential loss of their honor, women were desperate to hide their transgressions and resorted to horrific acts in order to protect themselves and their family's image. Honor and one's standing in the community were extremely important for families; women's actions did not just affect them, but their husbands, children, and even extended family. This strong honor code persisted despite migration, which in fact created situations that could threaten it even more. While it would normally be the responsibility of the male head of household to uphold a family's honor, these women were forced into this role when left on their own. It is clear that in a society bound by honor culture, public image was more important than the deeds they committed in order to uphold that image. The acts examined in this chapter, particularly infanticide, demonstrate the complexity of honor in the Italian south and how it connected to many other aspects of the lives of women in Basilicata, including emigration.

NOTES

1. ASM, Corte d'Assise, Busta 172, 1060.
2. John A. Davis, *Conflict and Control: Law and Order in Nineteenth Century Italy* (London: Macmillan, 1988), 172–175.
3. Direzione Generale della Statistica, *Annuario statistico italiano: 1895* (Rome: Tipografia Nazionale di G. Bertero, 1896).
4. Direzione Generale della Statistica, *Annuario statistico italiano: 1912* (Rome: Tipografia Nazionale di G. Bertero, 1913).
5. *La Lucania Intransigente*, June 19–20, 1898, N12, 1.
6. *La Cronaca Lucana*, January 24, 1892.
7. *Annuario Statistico Italiano 1895*, 244.
8. *Il Lucano: Giornale Politico Amministrativo*, March 21, 1893, N.2.
9. Donna R. Gabaccia, *Italy's Many Diasporas* (Seattle, WA: University of Washington Press, 2000), 87–88.
10. Andreina de Clementi, "Gender Relations and Migration Strategies in the Rural Italian South: Land, Inheritance, and the Marriage Market," in *Women, Gender and Transnational Lives: Italian Workers of the World*, eds. Donna Gabaccia and Franca Iacovetta (Toronto: University of Toronto Press, 2002), 92; Maura Palazzi, *Donne sole: Storia dell'altra faccia dell'Italia tra antico regime a società contemporanea* (Turin: B. Mondadori, 1997), 373.
11. Perry Willson, *Women in Twentieth Century Italy* (New York: Palgrave Macmillan, 2010), 13.
12. Pasquale Arena, *L'Infanticidio per ragion d'onore: Studio giuridico-sociologico* (Naples: R. Tipografia de Angelis & Bellisario, 1896), 44–45.
13. Bruna Bianchi, "Percorsi dell'emigrazione minorile," in *Storia dell'Emigrazione Italiana*, eds. Piero Bevilacqua, Andreina de Clemente, Emilio Franzina (Rome: Donzelli, 2002), 259.
14. See: Steven C Hughes, *Politics of the Sword: Dueling, Honor, and Masculinity in Modern Italy* (Columbus, OH: Ohio State University Press, 2007).
15. Arena, *L'Infanticidio per ragion d'onore*, 12.
16. Arena, *L'infanticidio per ragion d'onore*, 25–26.
17. Maria Sophia Quine, *Italy's Social Revolution: Charity and Welfare from Liberalism to Fascism* (London: Palgrave Macmillan, 2002), 184.
18. David Kertzer, *Sacrificed for Honor: Italian Infant Abandonment and the Politics of Reproductive Birth Control* (Boston, MA: Beacon Press, 1993), 26.

19. For more information about *sifilicomi*, see Mary Gibson, *Prostitution and the State in Italy, 1860–1915* (New Brunswick, NJ: Rutgers University Press, 1986).

20. ASP, Corte d'Assise, Busta 345, 2001.

21. ASP, Corte d'Assise, Busta 345, 2003.

22. See: Linda Reeder, *Widows in White: Migration and the Transformation of Rural Italian Women, Sicily, 1880–1920* (Toronto: University of Toronto Press, 2003), chapter 2.

23. Jane Schneider and Peter Schneider, *Festival of the Poor: Fertility Decline and the Ideology of Class in Sicily, 1860–1980* (Tucson, AZ: University of Arizona Press, 1996), 146.

24. David Kertzer, *Sacrificed for Honor*, 12. Other studies on infant abandonment in Italy include: Maria Canella, Luisa Dodi and Flores Reggiani, *Si consegna questo figlio: l'assistenza all'infanzia e alla maternità dall Ca' Grande alla provincial di Milano: 1456–1920* (Milan: Università degli studi di Milano, 2008); Cristina Cenedella and Laura Giuliacci, *La vita fragile: infanzia, disagi e assistenza nella Milano del lungo Ottocento: convegno di studi, Milano, Fondazione Stelline* (Milan: Vita e pensiero, 2013).

25. Rachel Fuchs, *Abandoned Children: Foundlings and Child Welfare in Nineteenth Century France* (Albany, NY: State University of New York Press, 1984), 2, 42.

26. Schneider and Schneider, *Festival of the Poor*, 147.

27. See Massimo Livi-Bacci, *A History of Italian Fertility during the Last Two Centuries* (Princeton, NJ: Princeton University Press, 1977), 70; Kertzer, *Sacrificed for Honor*; Maria Grazia Gorni and Laura Pellegrini, *Un problema di storia sociale: L'infanzia abbandonata in Italia nel secolo XIX* (Florence: La Nuova Italia Editrice, 1974), 13.

28. Quine, *Italy's Social Revolution*, 219.

29. Quine, *Italy's Social Revolution*, 190–193.

30. Kertzer, *Sacrificed for Honor*, 76–77.

31. Kertzer, *Sacrificed for Honor*, 89.

32. Direzione Generale della Statistica, *Annuario Statistico Italiano, 1905–1907* (Rome: Tipografia Nazionale di G. Bertero, 1908), 234.

33. ASM, Corte d'Assise, Busta 216, 1353.

34. ASM, Corte d'Assise, Busta 216, 1355.

35. In two cases, a mother-in-law reported the crime, one to authorities, the other to her son in America. ASM, Corte d'Assise, Busta 216, 1353, 1355.

36. ASP, Corte d'Assise, Busta 431, 2446.

37. ASP, Corte d'Assise, Busta 297, 1750.

38. ASM, Corte d'Assise, Busta 192, 1189.

39. ASM, Corte d'Assise, Busta 172, 1067.

40. ASM, Corte d'Assise, Busta 216, 1355.

41. ASM, Corte d'Assise, Busta 192, 1189.

42. ASM, Corte d'Assise, Busta 216, 1353.

43. ASP, Corte d'Assise, Busta 345, 2003.

44. ASP, Corte d'Assise, Busta 297, 1750.

45. ASM, Corte d'Assise, Busta 216, 1355.
46. ASM, Corte d'Assise, Busta 192, 1189.
47. ASP, Corte d'Assise, Busta 431, 2446.
48. ASP, Corte d'Assise, Busta 364, 2110.
49. ASM, Corte d'Assise, Busta 192, 1189.
50. ASM. Corte d'Assise. Busta 216, a. 1355.
51. Willson, *Women in Twentieth Century Italy*, 9.
52. ASP, Corte d'Assise, Busta 417, 2368.
53. ASM, Corte d'Assise, Busta 216, 1353.
54. ASM, Corte d'Assise, Busta 216, 1353.
55. ASM, Corte d'Assise, Busta 194, 1196.
56. ASM, Corte d'Assise, Busta 191, 1184.
57. ASM, Corte d'Assise, Busta 191, 1182.
58. ASP, Corte d'Assise, Busta 386, 2217.
59. ASM, Corte d'Assise, Busta 216, 1353.
60. ASP, Corte d'Assise, Busta 386, 2217.
61. Willson, *Women in Twentieth Century Italy*, 9–10.
62. ASP, Corte d'Assise, Busta 364, 2110.
63. ASM, Corte d'Assise, Busta 204, 1266.
64. ASM, Corte d'Assise, Busta 191, 1182.
65. ASM, Corte d'Assise, Busta 194, 1196.

Chapter 7

Returning Men and Emigrating Women

Giovanni and Rosa Maria, the couple introduced in the beginning of Chapter 1, spent a good deal of their marriage separated because he had emigrated to America. Rosa remained home with her children, while Giovanni was a "bird of passage," migrating a number of times to New York and sending remittances to his wife and children when he was not present in the village. As Giovanni advanced in age, he decided to return home permanently. His family never moved to New York to join him, and Giovanni did not remain in America, despite his brother and other relatives settling there. While Giovanni was away, Rosa surely experienced many of the situations seen in this book. She managed the household, took care of the children, made sure to provide for their well-being, and managed family finances. Each time Giovanni returned to his small village, he was influenced by life in a big city halfway around the world. Yet despite success in America, he chose to return to Italy, rather than start a new life across the ocean.

Migration, and the subsequent absence of many of the region's men, impacted the women who remained behind in a number of ways. These situations were often temporary, however, as husbands were expected to return. Most men did indeed come back, some to remain at home or others to emigrate again, either alone or with their families. The return might not have always been easy, as it would once again challenge the family dynamics. After spending time in major cities and foreign countries, men might have looked differently upon their wives, children, homes, and villages. Women were also mobile, whether by choice or not. They may have been called by their husbands to migrate, or may have migrated on their own, with or without the permission of their husbands or families. Most obtained a passport and traveled legally, but in rare instances, some tried to emigrate clandestinely without proper paperwork. Female emigration was more likely to be permanent, so those who eventually settled abroad left family and friends, and had to adjust to a new home, language, and culture abroad. In short, women were deeply affected by migration, whether their husbands migrated and they remained behind, or they migrated themselves, either alone or with their husbands. This chapter will not only examine the impact of men returning on the women in Basilicata but also consider the many women who migrated and how that experience may have shaped their lives.

MEN RETURNING

As previously noted, both Lucanians and outsiders were concerned with the impact of emptying villages and the abundance of women when a large percentage of men emigrated. The tide of emigration seemed to be sweeping through villages of the region, taking with it the youngest and ablest of the population. These fears were unfounded for many reasons, however, most notably the high return rate of emigrants. Traveling abroad was an opportunity to earn higher wages and potentially improve the family's social status and position in the community. Migration was generally a family decision, and when the head of household emigrated, it was usually temporary. The circumstances varied in each family situation; sometimes men made the decision, other times women encouraged their husbands to migrate. Emigration might be a substitute for divorce and offer couples an opportunity to live apart without the social stigma of being separated. Nonetheless, wives knew that even if they were left on their own, their husbands would continue to provide for the family and eventually return with more money after working for some time abroad. For this reason, so many Lucanians took the risk and left, despite the difficulty of the decision and potential risks of the journey.

The rates of return migration overall were high for Italians when compared to other migrating groups in the same period. According to the U.S. Immigration Commission, 56% of southern Italians and 62% of northern Italians returned from the United States between 1908 and 1910. These return rates were high compared to other immigrating groups to the United States at the time; the Irish had a return rate of 6% and Eastern European Jews had a return rate of 8%.[1] Italians generally emigrated for economic reasons, as opposed to other migrating groups who left because of famine, religious persecution, or political turmoil at home, situations to which they were less likely to return. Statistics for the years 1906 to 1915 show that around six million Italians emigrated, and in the period of 1904 to 1914, 1.8 million returned.[2] While these numbers only include the United States, the trends were likely similar for Italians in other countries. Most married men who migrated without their family were expected to return, or at least to eventually send for their family.

The return journey for migrants was a familiar process, similar to the departure. Ports of entry in the United States and other countries were also ports of departure. The same ocean liners that brought immigrants to the Americas also brought passengers back to Europe, whether they were returning migrants or unsuccessful migrants whom authorities rejected at the port of entry. The Italian birds of passage were accustomed to the journey on the steamship. They would be familiar with the process of filling out manifests, the conditions in steerage, and the one- to two-week journey home. The main Italian ports of departure—Naples, Palermo, Genoa, and Messina—were also ports of return, and there passengers disembarked and made their way back home, most likely by taking a train. Upon arriving in their hometown, returning emigrants were required to make themselves known at the *stato civile* office. From Basilicata, there would be a nonstop flow of migrants back and forth, to and from the region, likely through the port of Naples, although the flow out was more numerous.

A number of men who returned did so temporarily, with full intentions of migrating again. Those not planning on remaining would come back for a number of reasons. Some were birds of passage, traveling back and forth between Italy and a location (or multiple locations) abroad, every few months or years. Others perhaps might have come back to their home village to find a wife, or because their parents or family had found a potential match and arranged a marriage. Other men returned to collect wives, children, or other family members to bring them abroad. If migrants knew they were going to make a permanent life for themselves elsewhere, they also returned to their home village to settle affairs, to sell property, or to conduct other business transactions before leaving for good.

Other migrants decided to return home to Italy permanently. Some might have been birds of passage, making a number of voyages, but never remaining abroad for good, like Giovanni in the opening of the chapter. These returning migrants may have had a wife and family waiting for them back home in Italy. Giovanni, like a number of other migrants, returned home to retire and live out the rest of his life surrounded by familiar people and places. Plans change, however, and some migrants might have decided to emigrate again or even move abroad permanently at a later time.

Many men saw themselves as temporary migrants and considered their permanent residence to be in Italy. Their wives, children, families, and community were in the village and that was home, no matter how long they spent abroad. Homesickness was a strong force that cannot be underestimated. Many emigrants were not able to send letters home, as they or their family members were likely illiterate, cutting off a means of connection to family.

Migrants from rural Basilicata had to adjust to life in crowded, urban settings. Others returned home because they found the streets in America were not paved with gold. Despite the success stories of others, life for an immigrant laborer was difficult, and some were not successful, especially because of the great amount of prejudice Italians faced abroad. For these men, the best option was to return home.

Returning migrants generally lived better, had a nicer or bigger house, owned more possessions, and wore newer clothing. They were exposed to ideas, attitudes, cultures, and worldviews that drastically differed from their own. Upon their return, whether consciously or not, these new concepts were transferred from husbands to wives, families, and communities. Exposure to different types of foods, social customs, consumer habits, religions, and even houses must have challenged how emigrants viewed their own world. A number of articles from the *Bollettino dell'Emigrazione* discussed some of the changes to people who returned. Reports stated that return migrants had improved hygiene, were more interested in education, especially for children, and had a higher participation rate in civic activities. They were used to a cleaner household, one without animals living inside, dressed differently, and perhaps saw the role of women in a different light. Exposure to new customs and practices also changed how returning emigrants interacted with the community. There is no doubt change at home resulted from migration.

The community viewed returning emigrants differently, as many returnees had an improved socioeconomic position. For example, return migration in Lagonegro resulted in the creation of a small bourgeoisie called *americani*— residents who returned mainly from the United States or Argentina and subsequently survived off their earnings without having to work. These individuals often had time to participate in local politics or form societies. A 1908 report claimed that Lagonegro had about one hundred families of these *americani*, a significant number in a town of only a few thousand inhabitants.[3] In contrast, Francesco Cerase, a historian focusing on return migration, noted that those who returned to retire did not play an active role in politics and were not "an innovative force within the socio-economic structure of their homeland."[4] Because migrants who returned permanently could be older and retired, they had no interest in participating in politics. Further demonstrating the connection many had to America, in his well-known book *Christ Stopped at Eboli*, which took place in Basilicata in the 1930s, Carlo Levi noted that all the homes he visited had two pictures hanging on the wall, one of the Madonna of Viggiano, and the other of President Franklin Delano Roosevelt.

Returning migrants also had a better sense of being Italian, since individuals from abroad viewed residents from all over the peninsula as Italian, not in a regional or local sense. According to historian Richard Bosworth, the peasantry was not completely integrated into the new Italian state by the end of the nineteenth century and strong regionalism still existed. Emigration brought Italians from different regions and provinces together in a foreign land. Sicilians, Neapolitans, Calabrians, and even Lucanians were among the emigrant groups living together abroad. While they recognized differences among themselves, outsiders saw them all as "Italians." Thus, migrants gained a sense of "Italian-ness" and began to shift local identities to a more nationalistic perception.[5] This new affiliation with a larger identity might also have applied to women in Basilicata, who had already been in contact with the Italian state apparatus beyond their village or region. Both women at home and men abroad, citizens of Basilicata were acquiring an Italian identity.

PROCESS OF EMIGRATION

All emigrants were required to go through the process of obtaining the correct paperwork in order to be issued a passport. Without one, an emigrant was not able to buy a ticket or receive a boarding pass from a shipping company. The need for a passport also discouraged people from flocking to Italian port cities, only to be turned away because they did not have proper permission to emigrate. Furthermore, this regulation prevented migrants from being rejected at the port of immigration or at their final destination.[6] Passports were needed to leave Italian ports, but were not always required by the port of entry. For example, before the Quota Act of 1924, which severely limited immigration, the United States did not require a passport for entry.

Applications for passports were handled on the local level. Prospective emigrants first requested from the local mayor the *nulla osta* (no objection in Latin), a certificate confirming there were no objections to emigration and granting permission for a passport to be issued. According to a letter from the prefect to local mayors, the *nulla osta* "attests to the good conduct and that the migrant has the means to travel to and from the desired place."[7] The mayor was responsible for granting a *nulla osta*. The applicant also needed to provide a birth certificate, demonstrate he was not a criminal, and certify that he was not required to complete military service.[8] He then made a written or verbal request to the prefect for a passport. A passport cost 2.40 lire until the 1901 law, after which the document was free and valid for three years. In order for the prefect to issue the passport, he needed both the completed passport request from the migrant and the *nulla osta* issued by the mayor.

The prefect was a key figure involved in the emigration process at the local level. He not only issued passports but also received warnings against emigration to certain places and forwarded that news along to local authorities. For example, in 1879, the prefect of Potenza issued an alert against emigration to Greece warning that people could not find jobs and were living in poor conditions there.[9] These types of advisories were also published in local newspapers. The prefect communicated regularly with Rome, keeping up to date with the latest information and news regarding emigration. After 1901, government officials could stay better informed through the memos and publications from the *Commissariato Generale dell'Emigrazione*, and its primary publication the *Bollettino dell'Emigrazione*.

Women preparing to emigrate also needed to obtain a passport. Single women and widows did not need authorization and were generally free to migrate, especially if accompanied by a male relative. Usually, the male head of the family obtained a passport which was valid for all members. However, if traveling alone or with children to join her husband, a married woman required her spouse's permission. These laws pertaining to women follow a paternalistic pattern and were meant to prevent them from emigrating on their own and becoming a public charge or turning to prostitution. Thus, women's passports indicated their marital status. According to a 1905 article in the *Bollettino dell'Emigrazione*:

> It is necessary that on the first page of the passport, after the name of the holder, there follows an indication of her marital status: if she is single or married, and whether or not her husband is deceased. This indication is essential because in some foreign countries women are rejected when they disembark if they cannot prove their marital status. The United States for example, rejects pregnant women who cannot prove they are lawfully married.[10]

In some cases, one spouse could oppose the issuing of a passport to the other, and if the objection was legally sound the *nulla osta* would be suspended[11] Thus, spousal objections were another potential obstacle to emigration.

Not all men received passports either. As previously mentioned, young men with military obligations could not emigrate. In addition, men with personal debts were not issued a passport. One man from Potenza requested a passport in 1881, but was denied because he had debts and still owed payment for forest damages from 1877.[12] Furthermore, individuals who were owed money could inform the mayor and prevent their debtors from obtaining a passport. A man from the town of Sasso di Castalda contacted the mayor telling him not to grant a *nulla osta* for two individuals because they owed him money. In this particular case, the mayor did not grant the *nulla osta* and the individual did not receive a passport.[13] Another group of five men and women wrote to the prefect warning him not to issue a passport to the widow Annarosa P. because of her deceitful activity. Apparently, they accused her of defrauding them of their money so she could use it to emigrate abroad with her children. While it is unknown if the prefect heeded this request or even investigated the allegations, it is important to note that those accused of crimes were not issued a passport.

Overall, because of restrictions and legal limitations, the number of passports issued was far fewer than those actually requested. For example, between 1911 and 1912, 290 people in the province of Potenza requested a passport for Argentina. Of those 290 requests, only 156 were finally issued, just over half. These numbers are low compared to other regions. For example, in Bari (Puglia) 562 passports were requested for the same period for Argentina and 433 were granted. In Catania (Sicily), 483 were requested and 336 granted, and in Reggio Calabria (Calabria), 247 were requested and 154 were granted.[14] These numbers also demonstrate that overall fewer people were emigrating from Basilicata, as its population was lower than neighboring regions.

Each municipality kept registers containing information about the number of passports issued and to whom. The books are a key source in counting the number of emigrants from each locality, however, they are not completely accurate. The registers do not take into account those who decided not to emigrate after being issued a passport. Some might have requested a passport, and for unknown reasons chose to remain in Italy or emigrate at another time. If their passport expired, they would have to request a new one. It is thus difficult to quantify how many potential migrants for which this might be the case. The registers also do not consider *emigrazione clandestina*. In 1903, the Italian government defined clandestine emigration as "he who 'with lies and deception' embarks at a foreign port eluding Italian regulations which control emigration."[15] Although there may have been a number of reasons why someone would attempt to emigrate illegally, some of these emigrants could have been criminals escaping justice or young men seeking to escape military service. Some women also attempted to emigrate in this way. In 1904, the *Bollettino dell'Emigrazione* warned that the exact number of clandestine emigrants cannot be counted, but the number was likely significant.[16] Finally, passport registers may also contain multiple entries for one person. As mentioned above, someone could have applied for and have been issued a passport, but decided not to leave and reapplied at a later date. Birds of passage also required a new passport every three years. In addition, when browsing through passport registers, it is impossible to know whether or not emigrants planned to stay abroad for a short, temporary time period, or remain abroad permanently and settle there. Prospective emigrants were asked at the time the passport was issued what their intentions were, but the answer was not always accurate or could have changed. The only way to tell whether or not residents left temporarily or permanently was to count who returned.[17] Migrants may have also intended to return, but for one reason or another changed their minds while abroad and never came back to Italy.

Once the passport was issued, emigrants made their way to the port of departure. For inhabitants of Basilicata, that port was most likely Naples. By 1910, Naples was the largest port of emigration in Italy, with twelve steamship companies servicing it.[18] The building up of infrastructure in Basilicata aided emigrants in traveling to their port of departure. From Potenza and towns in the western part of the region, migrants traveled to Naples by railroad. Prior to 1860, poor railroad connectivity hampered development, leaving many areas isolated.[19] In the years following unification, the government invested in improving the rail lines in the south, in an attempt to connect rural towns with urban centers and the rest of Italy. By the late 1860s, a rail line connected Metaponto, Potenza, and Eboli, and brought passengers to Salerno and Naples.[20] The line expanded by the 1880s and rail service connected important points on the southern mainland, including Taranto and Reggio Calabria. The journey for many emigrants traveling from Basilicata to Naples for departure became much quicker as railroad service continued to expand. Once in Naples, migrants disembarked from their train and waited for their ship's departure in boarding houses which were supervised and subsidized by the government.

Before boarding the ships, officials completed manifests and conducted medical examinations. Anyone boarding steerage on a ship going to the United States underwent a medical exam. Italian doctors, working for the U.S. Public Health and Marine-Hospital Service, conducted these exams at the port of departure. The Americans took these extra steps to ensure only healthy immigrants were coming into the country, and the Italian government permitted doctors to examine emigrants because they were interested in protecting their citizens. Ship companies were even more willing to comply, because if the United States denied entry to an immigrant, the steam liner was required to pay for the return voyage.[21] Similar procedures were carried out at the ports of Palermo and Messina, which became a departure point for emigrants after 1905. Individuals wishing to emigrate had to go to one of the four ports servicing ocean liners for migrants—Naples, Palermo, Messina, and Genoa. Once the manifests were filled out and the passengers received medical clearance, they boarded their ship for America.

WOMEN REQUESTING PASSPORTS

While a majority of those migrating were men, women did take part in the process, especially if they were traveling on their own. Women could request passports for themselves and their children by contacting the mayor's office. As discussed in Chapter 1, married women needed the authorization of their husbands, and there was little exception to this provision. While women could apply for a passport, that did not mean they would be successful. The prefect issued the passport only if the applicant presented the correct documentation and the mayor issued the *nulla osta*. If women followed these steps, they generally had few impediments when requesting a passport and received them quickly.

The passport requests and the letters that accompanied them help demonstrate the process of acquiring passports and the mindset and emotions of women hoping to migrate. Rosa V. of Tramutola wanted to emigrate, and with the consent of her husband, the *nulla osta* was issued and sent by the mayor to the prefect's office. Two days later, the prefect issued her passport.[22] Because she had the correct authorizations in order, there was a relatively short turnover time from making the request to receiving the passport. Another woman, Maria Rosa T., also of Tramutola, requested an expedited passport to join her husband in Marseilles, who was ill. Because her husband had given his consent, she also quickly received the passport.[23] In these cases, passports requested by married women with the authorization of their husbands were granted with little or no issue.

The husband's authorization extended not only to his wife but also to his children. For example, the spouse of Filomena Maria L. of Baragiano called her to join him in Buenos Aires, and she thus requested a passport for herself and her four children. Since her husband called for her emigrate, the mayor granted the *nulla osta*.[24] In a similar case, the husband of Carolina D. gave her permission to emigrate, and the mayor issued the *nulla osta* and she subsequently received her passport. She then later asked for passports for her two children, aged six and four, a request that was granted even though it was not made at the same time.[25]

Single women with custody of their children did not need male authorization and could apply for a passport for themselves and for their children. Maria F., a single mother of a child with an unknown father, requested and was issued a passport for herself. She then asked the mayor to add her two-year-old child, Adelaide, who was a *figlia naturale* (child born outside of marriage) to the passport. The mayor granted her petition.[26] These cases illustrate that single women had more rights than married women, including greater rights over illegitimate children. Fathers who held *patria potestà*, or custody, had to authorize passports for their children. Yet, single mothers did not need such authorization. Ironically, these laws were designed to protect men by absolving them of any potential responsibility regarding illegitimate children, but in practice gave women more rights in certain circumstances.

With few exceptions, the husband's consent had to be clear to authorities issuing passports to women. In one instance, the husband of Gaetana L. of Pignola called her to join him in Montevideo (Uruguay). She wrote to the prefect because even though her husband sent a ticket, he did not send the required documentation giving his consent. In this case, however, the prefect issued the passport, arguing that since her husband bought a ticket "there is no doubt that this woman was called by her husband so that she can join him in Montevideo."[27] This type of implied consent was the closest instance of "bending the rules" or granting exceptions to women.

Women requested passports for various reasons. As seen above, a wife could easily obtain a passport if her husband was abroad and called her to join him. Husbands trusted their wives to be compliant and responsible; women could obtain passports, prepare themselves and their children to emigrate, and leave the village on their own to join an emigrant husband. Some women, however, took matters into their own hands, especially when they had not heard from their husbands or lost contact with them after emigrating. These women, most likely knowing that they could not obtain a passport on their own, requested them anyway. They were in desperate situations and wanted to travel abroad themselves to find their missing husbands or to emigrate on their own to locations where they had family. These women turned to the state for assistance.

Married women requesting passports without the authorization of their husbands were denied, no matter what reasons or excuses they expressed to government officials. Though unsuccessful, many requests gave a reason as to why women wanted to emigrate and a glimpse into what their lives may have been like. For instance, Rosaria C. of Brienza wrote to the prefect asking for him to issue her a passport. Her husband emigrated over fourteen years prior and in recent months she had not heard from him. She wanted to emigrate to Buenos Aires to search for her husband, and she wrote that she had enough money to pay for the round-trip voyage. She added that she had relatives in Argentina who would receive her, hoping to assuage fears of a woman traveling on her own. In the response, the prefect wrote that "the forwarded demand to obtain a passport to travel abroad cannot be considered," because "married women cannot emigrate and join their husbands without expressed authorization by their husband, which is done through a legalized act at the local consulate."[28] This woman's appeal seems to provide solutions for issues that might concern officials with her emigrating alone. She had enough money and a place to stay with relatives upon arrival in Argentina, so she was not likely to turn to prostitution or become a public charge. Yet, her request was denied. This woman was not desperate for money or aid, but anxious to locate her husband. These regulations demonstrate the paternalistic and protective nature of the state. Despite his long absence, the husband had legal authority over his family, and the law was meant to protect women in these circumstances.

The need for marital authorization caused difficulties if a husband could not be located. A woman from Viggiano requested a passport, writing that her husband emigrated eight years prior. She had three young children and he did not send her any money. She said that she did not even know if he was alive. She requested a passport to Boston, where she had family, hoping that fact might convince the prefect to grant it, despite her not having permission. However, the prefect sent his response to the mayor, saying that she needed the consent of her husband to obtain a passport. He continued, writing that "the mere fact of the lack of news for about five years is not sufficient to justify the likewise permission in a legal sense."[29] In this case, her option was to request that the office conduct a search for her husband abroad, so he could grant her the necessary permission. In response, she wrote that she did not know the location of her husband, as he was last in Rio de Janeiro in 1876. In this letter, she begged the prefect for mercy, reiterating that her relatives in Boston would host her. The answer remained the same. She could not be issued a passport without the consent of her husband, unless she presented a death certificate proving he was deceased. Women appealed to officials on an emotional level hoping that they would overlook legal impediments. In these cases, their pleas were unsuccessful.

Many married women still appealed to the prefect, even if they knew it was futile. Perhaps it was their only hope. For example, Rosa P. from Savoia di Lucania had an expired passport and requested a new one so she could travel abroad to her husband. The dilemma here was not that she needed a completely new passport, but an updated one. The response she received was that she did in fact need her husband's consent again and that if he was abroad, she would have to wait for him to call for her and authorize her trip before a new passport could be issued.[30] Angela S. of Balvano was also refused a passport. Her husband Angelo N. emigrated clandestinely and when she made her request for a passport it had been almost seven years since she or any other family member had heard anything from her husband. She petitioned the mayor despite not having her husband's permission, wanting to emigrate to the Americas to join him. Arguing that she was aware of the law, she had hoped the prefect would grant an exception. She received the prefect's response three days later, which stated "without the permission of the husband . . . a passport cannot be issued."[31]

No matter the circumstances, officials held firm. Women may have tried to work around the law or manipulate officials with their letters describing their unfortunate circumstances, but most were unsuccessful. Yet, despite denying them a passport, officials were able to offer assistance to women in other ways, such as by facilitating requests to search for and contact husbands abroad. The prefect and mayor often included these suggestions in their responses. So even though women received a denial, they were offered some hope for assistance.

WOMEN EMIGRATING

Women made up about 20% of Italian emigrants between 1876 and 1914, and they were more likely than men to remain abroad (i.e., not be birds of passage) rather than migrate temporarily for work. In addition, as the period of large-scale emigration continued, more and more families left. In line with Italian trends, the number of female emigrants from Basilicata rose drastically in the late nineteenth century. In 1876, there were 193 recorded female emigrants from the region; in 1901, the number rose to 5,565.[32]

Once married women obtained permission and received their passports, they were free to emigrate. Married women generally migrated with or upon request of their husbands. Since men tended to travel back and forth, many came back to the village to accompany their wives, children, or other family members on the journey abroad. Sons or husbands likely already had a steady job and a place to live before allowing female members and children to migrate to a location abroad.

Some men, without returning, requested that their wives emigrate and join them abroad, whether willingly or unwillingly (*il richiamo*). In these cases, husbands sent the appropriate permissions and funds from abroad, and the women obtained passports, bought tickets, and prepared for the journey on their own. Some women may have wanted to migrate, others might have wanted to remain at home with familiar people and places. Prospective emigrants weighed the risks and benefits and must have believed that overall, migrating would be worth it, despite the probable hardships, such as unemployment, unfamiliar culture, lack of opportunities, and a long and uncomfortable journey. Most women, on the other hand, were not as free to choose whether or not to emigrate, and often did so because their spouses or family members emigrated. They were required by law to follow wherever their husbands chose to make their home. For most families, the decision to migrate was likely a joint decision based on their future and well-being. If there was a disagreement, wives could object, but had little legal recourse. They may have been a part of the conversation, but the final decision was in the hands of their husbands.

Italian women almost always emigrated following the head of the family. Once abroad, they faced a new set of hardships, living in a foreign country, adapting to foreign customs, and learning a new language. These women were limited in what they could do, and unlike in Basilicata, often had to work outside the home for wages to help support the family. They mainly found work in domestic service or in sweatshops.[33] Focusing on the United States, an article by Italian journalist Amy Bernardy, born in Florence to an Italian mother and American father, told of struggling emigrant families who depended on their spouse's wages. If husbands got injured and could no longer work, families could be left in misery and poverty. Without the social support from their family and home village, many of these widows were forced to work, or in some cases, return to Italy. Bernardy provided the story of an Italian family in San Francisco as an example. The husband, who worked as an ice cream man, was hit by a car and killed. At the time, his wife was three months pregnant. He left her a small amount of money, but she soon found herself in debt and unable to pay for expenses. Working as a washwoman to earn money did not suffice. Siblings and family tried to help her, but her life in America was difficult. She finally decided to return to Italy. Bernardy's reporting shows that women who emigrated faced challenges and difficulties and also had to take on new responsibilities.[34]

Women's interactions with the mayors demonstrate the unwillingness on the part of some to migrate. One woman, Giulia F., expressed that she did not want to join her husband abroad in Philadelphia, despite him calling her to join him. She explained that when her husband emigrated, he sold many of their possessions, but had not sent any remittance back home to support the family. She expressed that she had no intention of joining her husband in America, and actually sent back the two tickets he bought for her passage.[35] If her husband insisted, she would not have a choice.

The requests to find missing husbands also demonstrate some of the fears and emotions that accompanied emigration. A petition by a woman from Lauria asked for news of her husband in Algeria and requested that he send aid. Her husband was located five months later, but he refused to send money to his wife. He told officials he stopped writing to his wife because "she did not respond or pay off the debts with the money for which he had entrusted her."[36] He continued, saying that he wished for his wife to join him in Algeria, since he had no intentions of repatriating and that he would send the necessary paperwork and documents for her to make the voyage. The contents of this petition give a rare glimpse into how a woman reacted to the news she received in the response. Only two weeks later, the mayor wrote back, stating, "I communicated the contents of your note to the wife . . . she is willing to join her husband, but she does not know how to travel on her own, especially on a trip of this length."[37] She then asked her husband to return home to accompany her on the journey abroad, adding that his elderly mother wanted to see him and give him a hug. The husband received the letter and wrote that unfortunately he could not travel home at the time because of work, but he would do so if possible when time permitted.

Alone and without recourse, left to fend for themselves if their husbands did not send them money, women had to have been scared and uneasy. The above woman appeared willing to join her husband, yet did not want to take the long journey by herself. The idea of traveling abroad on a lengthy voyage had to be daunting to someone who probably never went very far from her own village. Women often had little choice when called by their husbands to join them, and they often made the long journey on their own or with small children. In this case, the wife asked her husband to come back to accompany her. She also used the fact that her husband's elderly mother wanted to see him in order to try to convince him to return home. This story reinforces the permanency of migration, and serves as a reminder that parents at home suffered when their children emigrated, not knowing if they would ever return.[38]

Another aspect of emigration impacting women was the difficulty of leaving children at home. As seen in Chapter 2, mothers had to make difficult choices concerning migration and their children. Mothers of adult children might have left them behind, especially if their husbands decided to settle abroad. Families might also migrate to different locations. Although not common because of networks of mutual assistance among migrants from the same village, sometimes parents and children migrated to different cities or countries, placing an additional emotional strain on migrating women.

Some grandmothers were also charged with caring for their grandchildren if their own children migrated. In one instance, Chiara B. wrote to obtain information about her daughter Rosa M., who had emigrated to New York and left her young daughter in her care. Chiara could no longer maintain her granddaughter, who had just turned fifteen years old, and she requested her daughter return from abroad. The marital status of her daughter, as well as the location of the girl's father, is unknown. The consulate located Rosa in New York, and through it she sent a message promising she would write home soon. A month later, Rosa indeed wrote to her mother, saying that she could not return at that time, nor did she have the means to call her daughter to join her in America or send money home for her care. However, she did send a sum of 100 lire along with a message that she desired her daughter be placed in a "pious retreat."[39]

While some women may have been happy to leave their small village and emigrate to a new location, it is difficult to know how women truly felt about emigration. An article in *Basilicata Regione Notizie* on female emigrants conveyed the desperation they may have experienced; "we think of a woman as one who emigrates not for work, but to join her husband. The confusion of the present, the nostalgia of the past, and uncertainty of the future . . . the emigrant housewife is a silent victim of emigration itself."[40] Whether forced or not, emigration must have had a number of mental and physical health effects on women. In fact, medical studies conducted on emigrants found that women constituted the most frequent cases of hospitalization and therapy for mental issues, such as anxiety and depression, as a result of emigration.[41] More research is needed on this fascinating consequence of migration on women.

ABANDONMENT

Some women were abandoned, and, as highlighted already in previous chapters, left by their husbands to fend for themselves and raise their children alone. An observation by Carlo Levi in *Christ Stopped at Eboli* sums up the experience of some abandoned women: "Emigration has changed everything. Men are missing and the town is full of women. Many wives have husbands in America. He writes for the first year, writes again the second, and after nothing is known of him, maybe he has made a new family over there."[42] Abandoned women were put in an especially compromising position. While still legally married, they needed spousal authorization, not just for a passport, but for other activities and transactions. One recourse was to appeal to the courts, but wives' hands often remained tied nonetheless. They could not sign contracts or possess custody of their children. Wives could not remarry without definitive proof that their husbands were deceased. Married women could not buy or sell property or take out a loan. As discussed earlier in this chapter, they could not even request a passport to go abroad to search for their husbands. Thus, abandonment left women with few legal options.

The Civil Code of 1865 had clear laws defining abandonment. After three years of absence (or six if the person left a power of attorney), the family could go to court to receive a statement of absence confirming the individual had not been heard from. Married women could appeal to the courts to receive a small pension if the family was in dire need. Women could also gain custody of their children if the husband abandoned the family.[43] However, without definitive proof of the absent person's death, his wife could not remarry and many of her rights were still bound to her missing spouse.

Abandoned women could appeal to state agencies. As seen in previous chapters, women could go to the mayor to request information about or a search for missing relatives abroad. Some received answers which provided definitive word that their husbands were not returning, but others never got a response or were told that the consulate was unable to locate their spouse. These women were left in limbo. Some continued sending requests through official agencies, and no doubt also sent letters or messages with relatives and friends traveling abroad in an attempt to search for their missing spouses. While it is impossible to know the exact number or percentage of abandoned wives, the petitions of women hoping to emigrate reveal the circumstances of some of these unfortunate women.

One woman from Armento was desperate; she had not heard from her husband and wanted to obtain a passport to go search for him herself. She requested a passport but was unable to obtain marital authorization because her husband had been away for eight years. She did have the option of going to court to have her husband declared absent, but that was not an action she took prior to her petition. In her request to the mayor, she wrote that she was "lamenting the abandonment and the lack of aid on the part of her husband."[44] She accused her spouse of infidelity and wanted him to return home, not having heard from him in some time. To make matters worse, she reported that their daughter, now sixteen years old, had been engaged in an illicit love affair (*illeciti amori*). She wanted to travel to South America to find her husband and make him return to comply with his marital and paternal duties. Although the mayor had denied her request for a *nulla osta*, she continued making her case to the prefect. The mayor knew that she was missing the correct documentation, but forwarded the request anyway, writing that before him he saw a poor mother (*una povera madre*) and he wanted to help her. The mayor intervened for this woman prior to sending the request to the prefect, adding his own comments to the request, concerned about a woman struggling to raise her family and control her teenage daughter. Like other women mentioned, she was also requesting a passport so she could go and find her husband herself. Despite having funds and a place to stay, she was not granted authorization.[45]

Though most women were illiterate, some were able to write their own requests. These letters were even more powerful, with women's pleas in what were surely their own words. Maria Antonia V., an abandoned wife from Pignola, wrote a letter to the prefect to plead her case. In it, she "humbly presented" herself to the prefect, explaining her situation. Her husband abandoned her seven years prior without sending her any money, only letters. She explained that she was a "poor woman with three children without the means to live."[46] Desperate for relief, she asked the prefect to issue her a passport so that she could emigrate to her husband in Montevideo. After refusing to issue the passport, the prefect offered a piece of advice that was often given to women who wanted to emigrate: "It would be better if you did not venture on a long and expensive voyage without being sure of the consequences."[47] However, the response did mention that if she happened to receive word from her husband and he sent his authorization, she could make a new request for a passport. The advice given to her by the prefect shows the attitude of the government toward women who remained behind. Officials saw emigration as an adventure and not appropriate for women to undertake on their own. Women would have no choice but to wait at home and to use government agencies to search for their husbands. While officials may have felt sympathy for abandoned wives, they could not do much without authorization and could not break the law.

Not all abandoned women were in Italy with husbands abroad. An article in the *Bollettino dell'Emigrazione* described how some emigrant women found themselves abandoned in a foreign country. In 1901, the *Commisariato Generale dell'Emigrazione* commissioned Amy Bernardy to report on female emigrants. Her piece provides an example of a man who divorced his wife, which cost $500, and then sent her back to Italy with the children. He then ran off with a younger woman.[48] In another reported case, a man in Denver abandoned his wife for another woman in Chicago. With the help of the police, the wife located her husband and forced him to return home. They lived together afterward, but constantly disagreed. In another case, a husband, Michelangelo C., left his wife and child in France and returned home to Italy. His wife's relatives in Italy informed officials in an attempt to compel Michelangelo to go and fetch his family.[49] While this woman was closer to home than those an ocean away in America, she was still in a foreign country with likely few acquaintances.

Women abandoned abroad were in a foreign environment, likely did not speak the language, and would have had difficulty communicating with local authorities. These women were in an even more vulnerable and helpless position. If abandoned in Italy, women could turn to their family, friends, and community for assistance. While that extended community and social network might exist abroad, women abandoned after emigration often had to rely on strangers, or possibly local aid societies, to assist them. Their best option was to return home to Italy, if possible.

Women also appealed to the consulate from abroad to locate husbands who had abandoned them. For instance, the husband of Carolina G. returned to Italy, leaving her in Buenos Aires, so she appealed to the Italian Foreign Ministry for help in locating him in Italy. Carolina and her young daughter were not able to repatriate without her husband's consent, so she was stuck living in poverty in Argentina, according to her letter. Authorities located her husband, Giuseppe M., in Muro Lucano, and the mayor met with him in person. He told the mayor that he was not married to Carolina, and the two only had an "illicit relationship." Thus, he stated that for this reason he does not feel obligated to provide for her repatriation.[50] Documentation would be needed to prove which of the two were telling the truth. While they bickered, Carolina was on her own an ocean away from home.

ILLEGAL EMIGRATION

Feeling as if they had nothing to lose, some desperate women turned to *emigrazione clandestina*, or illegal emigration. While frowned upon especially for women, *emigrazione clandestina* was an act of agency and the ultimate expression that they had some power over their own lives. If writing and trying to contact their husbands failed, some women resorted to these extreme measures. As shown above, abandoned married women had few options. They could not get a passport, could not legally work, and may have had to care for a number of children on their own. Women depended on help from others, but they also may not have wanted outsiders to know how distressing their situation was.

Emigrazione clandestina included any type of illegal emigration, such as sneaking out of the country or using a false passport. Since most emigrants were men, a majority of the illegal emigrants were men as well. Men generally emigrated illegally if they could not obtain a passport, were trying to evade the military draft, wanted to avoid paying debts, or escape prosecution or prison time. Married women might attempt illegal emigration if they did not have permission from their husbands for a proper passport, or if they simply wanted to run away and start a new life. Authorities caught a number of people who attempted illegal emigration before they could make their way out of the country. If detained, these migrants were transferred back to their hometown.[51] Emigration was free, and it was relatively easy to obtain a passport legally. So those attempting to migrate illegally more likely than not had a legal impediment that prevented them from emigrating.

Official documents reveal the mindset of some of the women who attempted to emigrate in this manner. Much of the documentation occurred between local authorities in Basilicata and officials in Naples, the nearest and largest port of emigration. Various agencies and officials, including prefects and mayors, exchanged telegrams to track down or try to impede clandestine emigrants. The reports contained information about the emigrants, as well as a physical description, in an attempt to detain them before departure. These migrants were of all ages, some traveling in groups, and others with families.

Officials often warned each other to remain on the lookout for individuals attempting to migrate illegally. Since most migrants likely took a train and then embarked on a passenger ship in Naples, local mayors and prefects sent telegrams containing warnings to the Police Headquarters in Naples (*Questura di Napoli*). For example, officials in the town of Colobraro sent out a bulletin about a woman, Gerolama T., who attempted to travel to America with an internal passport, not an international passport. She initially stated she planned to visit a daughter in Genoa, but really intended to travel to America. The bulletin listed the train she was traveling on and it asked that authorities detain her and send her back to her village.[52] A number of offices were involved in searching for this individual, in order to escort her home. However, this woman, like many others, was not ignorant of the law and was aware that deceit was the only way to overcome her legal limitations.

Many women may have left without even attempting to obtain a passport. A report from the mayor of Pietrafesa (now Satriano di Lucania) to the prefect stated that Arcangela C. disappeared on the first train overnight in an attempt to emigrate illegally to join her husband in America. The document does not state her age or if she had any children. The letter claimed she left various obligations in the town and she did not hold a passport to travel abroad. The mayor promptly sent out a bulletin informing the prefect about her disappearance and asking his office to send a telegraph to Naples, where authorities could detain her and return her to the village before she was able to depart the country.[53] This instance shows the chain of command among officials policing emigration and demonstrates they were on the lookout for illegal emigrants and worked together to find them. Authorities found her a few days later in Tito, a neighboring town. Her case is interesting however because she was a "*signora*," a member of the upper class. Not limited to the poorest or most desperate, prominent women were also abandoned or had a difficult time obtaining proper paperwork, and nonetheless attempted to migrate.[54]

Some women attempted to emigrate illegally not just on their own, but with their children. Desperate to join her husband, authorities stopped a woman with her two sons on a ship leaving for America. They had passports for Genoa but had no intentions of traveling there. When caught, Gaetana G. said that she was going to Genoa for work.[55] Deceiving authorities, as they have done in other circumstances, was not out of the question for women who tried to leave without proper passports.

As examined in previous chapters, when men emigrated, women undertook responsibilities that far exceeded their legal role. They had more access to money and finances, had more contact with and relied upon the government and government agencies, and became largely responsible for the well-being of their families with the head of the household abroad. The role wives played in the decision to migrate varied from family to family, yet the decision was one that impacted women both while their husbands were away and after they returned. Their husbands may have come back claiming their old position in the home and family, relegating women to their previous subordinate roles. In many cases, wives may have gone from being the head of the household in practice to once again having inferior status. Despite men returning to the same house, the circumstances, roles, and worldviews of each spouse and even their children were greatly altered by migration. Other husbands may have called wives abroad to emigrate with the children, never again planning on returning to Italy. Some men completely abandoned the family, either financially, physically, or both, leaving women legally helpless and in desperate circumstances.

Although constituting a small percentage of migrants, women's experiences differed greatly than those of men. Married women were not free to migrate on their own and depended on their husbands to authorize their journey. The situation was worse for those who could not obtain this permission. Emigrating illegally was further proof of the desperation that some women may have felt being left on their own. They may no longer have been able to cope with their situation and felt they had nothing to lose by trying to emigrate. All of these circumstances show that women did not just sit back and passively accept their fate. They took initiative, requesting assistance from mayors, the prefect, and the Foreign Ministry to find their spouses abroad, and some even went so far as to attempt to illegally emigrate in search of their husbands. Whether migrating legally or illegally, the emotional impact on women who left their homes and families to settle in a new part of the world is undeniable.

NOTES

1. The Immigration Commission, "Emigration Conditions in Europe," (Washington, DC: Government Printing Office, 1911), 41.

2. Gianfausto Rosoli and Francesco Balletta, *Un secolo di emigrazione italiana 1876–1976* (Rome, 1978), 348–349; Richard J. Bosworth, *Italy and the Wider World 1860–1960* (London: Routledge, 1995), 115.

3. Adolfo Rossi, "Vantaggi e danni dell'emigrazione nel mezzogiorno d'Italia (Note di un viaggio fatto in Basilicata e in Calabria dal R. Commissario dell'Emigrazione)," *Bollettino dell'Emigrazione* 13 (1908): 1577.

4. Francesco Cerase, *L'emigrazione di ritorno: innovazione o reazione?* (Rome: Università, 1971), 74.

5. See: Bosworth, *Italy and the Wider World 1860–1960*; Mark Choate, *Emigrant Nation: The Making of Italy Abroad* (Cambridge, MA: Harvard University Press, 2008); Dino Cinel, *The National Integration of Italian Return Migration, 1870–1929* (New York: Cambridge University Press, 1991); Richard Alba, *Italian Americans: Into the Twilight of Ethnicity* (Englewood Cliffs, NJ: Prentice-Hall, 1985).

6. John Torpey, *The Invention of the Passport: Surveillance, Citizenship and the State* (New York: Cambridge University Press, 2000), 103.

7. ASP, Atti di Pubblica Sicurezza, Cat. 6, Busta 40.

8. The introduction of compulsory military service for all young men was an important change after Unification. Once a young male reached eighteen years of age, he was required to report to the local military office, where he would be examined and given a designation based on his ability to serve. Many looked upon this as a way to "make Italians," to forge a sense of nationalism and create unity among younger generations. This imposition was, however, resisted by many southern Italians for a long time.

9. ASP, Atti di Pubblica Sicurezza, Cat. 6, Busta 40.

10. "Atti del ministero degli affari esteri e del commissariato dell'emigrazione," *Bollettino dell'Emigrazione* 9 (1905): 37–38.

11. "Atti del ministero degli affari esteri e del commissariato dell'emigrazione," *Bollettino dell'Emigrazione* 9 (1905): 709–710.

12. ASP, Atti di Pubblica Sicurezza, Cat. 6. Busta 40.

13. ASP, Atti di Pubblica Sicurezza, Cat. 6. Busta 40.

14. ACS, Polizia Giudiziaria, Busta 290.

15. Maria Falvella, "Flussi migratori della Basilicata: situazioni e dimensioni nel periodo 1861–1940," *Basilicata Regione Notizie* 98 (2001): 90.

16. "Tutela e protezione degli emigranti," *Bollettino dell'Emigrazione* 11 (1904): 47.

17. "Relazione del Commissario Generale dell'Emigrazione," *Bollettino dell'Emigrazione* 7 (1904): 11.

18. The Immigration Commission, "Emigration Conditions in Europe," 115.

19. Augusta Molinari, "Porti, Trasporti, Compagnie," in *Storia dell'emigrazione Italiana*, eds. Piero Bevilacqua, Andreina de Clemente, and Emilio Franzina (Rome: Donzelli, 2001), 249.

20. Giuseppe Masi, "Tra spirito d'aventura e ricerca 'dell'agognato peculio:' linee di tendenza dell'emigrazione calabrese tra ottocento e novecanto," in *Emigrazione e storia d'Italia*, ed. Matteo Sanfilippo (Cosenza: Pellegrini, 2003), 123–124.

21. The Immigration Commission, "Emigration Conditions in Europe," 77, 114.

22. ASP, Atti di Pubblica Sicurezza, Cat. 6. Busta 40.

23. ASP, Atti di Pubblica Sicurezza, Cat. 6. Busta 40.

24. ASP, Atti di Pubblica Sicurezza, Cat. 6. Busta 40.

25. ASP, Atti di Pubblica Sicurezza, Cat. 6. Busta 40.

26. ASP, Atti di Pubblica Sicurezza, Cat. 6. Busta 40.

27. ASP, Atti di Pubblica Sicurezza, Cat. 6. Busta 40.

28. ASP, Atti di Pubblica Sicurezza, Cat. 6. Busta 40.

29. ASP, Atti di Pubblica Sicurezza, Cat. 6. Busta 41.

30. ASP, Atti di Pubblica Sicurezza, Cat. 6. Busta 40.

31. ASP, Atti di Pubblica Sicurezza, Cat. 6. Busta 40.

32. Falvella, "Flussi migratori della Basilicata," 90.

33. Bernardy, "Sulle condizione delle donne e dei fanciulli italiani negli Stati Uniti del centro e dell'ovest della confederazione del Nord-America," 31. See also: Donna Gabaccia, *From the Other Side: Women, Gender and Immigrant Life in the US 1820–1990* (Bloomington, IN: Indiana University Press, 1995).

34. Bernardy, "Sulle condizione delle donne e dei fanciulli italiani negli Stati Uniti del centro e dell'ovest della confederazione del Nord-America," 154.

35. ASP, Atti di Pubblica Sicurezza, Cat. 6. Busta 42.

36. ASP, Atti di Pubblica Sicurezza, Cat. 6. Busta 42.

37. ASP, Atti di Pubblica Sicurezza, Cat. 6. Busta 42.

38. ASP, Atti di Pubblica Sicurezza, Cat. 6. Busta 42.

39. ASP, Atti di Pubblica Sicurezza, Cat. 6. Busta 43.

40. Maria Schirone, "Le donne e l'emigrazione," *Basilicata Regione Notizie* (1998): 111.

41. Schirone, "Le donne e l'emigrazione," 111–112.

42. Carlo Levi, *Christ Stopped at Eboli* (Turin: Eunaudi, 1945), 94.

43. Codice Civile, 1865, Titolo III.

44. ASP, Atti di Pubblica Sicurezza, Cat. 6. Busta 40.

45. ASP, Atti di Pubblica Sicurezza, Cat. 6. Busta 40.

46. ASP, Atti di Pubblica Sicurezza, Cat. 6. Busta 40.

47. ASP, Atti di Pubblica Sicurezza, Cat. 6. Busta 40.

48. Amy Bernardy, "Sulle condizione delle donne e dei fanciulli italiani negli Stati Uniti del centro e dell'ovest della confederazione del Nord-America," *Bollettino dell'Emigrazione* 1 (1911): 167–169.

49. ASP, Atti di Pubblica Sicurezza, Cat. 6. Busta 40.

50. ASP, Atti di Pubblica Sicurezza, Cat. 6. Busta 41, Busta 43.

51. ASP, Atti di Pubblica Sicurezza, Cat. 6. Busta 40.

52. ASP, Atti di Pubblica Sicurezza, Cat. 6. Busta 40.

53. ASP, Atti di Pubblica Sicurezza, Cat. 6. Busta 44.

54. ASP, Atti di Pubblica Sicurezza, Cat 13, Categoria 6, Fascicolo 3, Busta 44-Emigrazione Clandestina.

55. ASP, Atti di Pubblica Sicurezza, Cat. 6. Busta 44.

Conclusion

Emigration touched the lives of millions of Italians between 1876 and 1914. It appealed to those experiencing economic hardship, provided a chance for a temporary escape, or gave residents the opportunity to leave the village permanently and live in a new part of the world. By the outbreak of World War I in 1914, large-scale emigration from Italy had been occurring for over forty years. During that time great movements of populations occurred both within and outside of Italy, large sums of money were added into the economy, and ideas and influence arrived from abroad. Emigration, however, not only affected the people in motion. Family, friends, and home communities—especially wives—were largely influential in, and greatly impacted by, the decision to migrate. The women who remained behind were left on their own to survive with their husbands abroad, a circumstance which led to innumerable changes in their lives.

Reconstructing what life was like for the women who remained behind has been challenging due to limited extant sources. Very few women left records or were the subject of written accounts. For many contemporaries, these women were invisible. Nonetheless, this book used various available primary and archival sources to piece together and imagine what their lives might have been like in order to argue that their experiences were important—who they were, how they lived, what they thought—and matter in telling the larger story of Italian emigration and Italian history.

During the Liberal Period, married women experienced various political, economic, social, and legal limitations: they could not vote, could not conduct economic activity, were viewed as the inferior sex, and legally were subordinate to men. Husbands and male members of the extended family closely guarded women and controlled their actions. Their social role was one centered on marriage and family; a woman's place was in the home and

153

men were responsible for providing for their families. Emigration largely transformed the traditional roles of women, changed the value of their labor, altered their roles in the private sphere and as mothers, and shook many of the ideals and practices of daily life in the communities of Basilicata. The subordinate legal status of women was meaningless when practicality and survival were more important, as women became heads of household when their husbands were gone.

The manner in which women dealt with emigration alters the stereotypical image of rural, southern Italian women as backward, passive, apolitical, and unchanging. Women did not passively wait for men to return. They took care of their families and became the main parental figures for their children. In many cases, the survival of the family rested on their shoulders, and they took on this extended responsibility. They were not silent when in trouble or in need of assistance. Despite what some have argued, the state was present in their lives, not a far-off and disconnected entity in Rome. Government and local authorities assisted inhabitants of the small towns of Basilicata, and women petitioned officials when in need of support or if they felt cheated. A new relationship formed between rural women and the burgeoning Italian state. Not only did the state eventually come to regulate and assist departing emigrants, it was also sympathetic to women, and supported those in need on a local level. Through interactions with the state, women became modern citizens.

Emigration also had an emotional impact on women and affected each in a unique way. With their husbands gone, some women felt like they had more freedom, but others experienced hardships if their spouses did not send money to support them. Some might have escaped an unhappy marriage or duties to someone they did not love, while others experienced feelings of despair and loneliness. Some women were eager about the opportunity to learn to read and write and to have an increased role outside the home, while others resented their husbands for leaving them on their own to take on more economic duties and physical labor, a role they were not used to and for which they had not been prepared. Even so, due to the high rate of return migration, sometimes estimated at about 50%, many women knew that their changed role would not be permanent. The emotional and psychological implications of emigration, such as depression, anxiety, and even suicide, would be a fascinating area of further study.

The prospect of return also demonstrates a unique connection between emigrants and the home, family, friends, and towns left behind. Inhabitants of Basilicata were constantly emigrating and returning, introducing new ideas and goods into their small towns. This exchange and interaction continued for generations over the course of the late nineteenth and early twentieth centuries, and demonstrates the true transnational nature of emigration. The women who remained behind lived in a society with mixed elements of the traditional and the modern. Inhabitants of Basilicata were not enclosed and isolated in small villages, but were influenced by factors that transcended borders, and were exposed to ideas, cultures, people, and goods from all over the world. Furthermore, women were not confined to the private or domestic sphere, but acted in the public sphere as needed. They may have lived in towns with only a few thousand inhabitants, but their world was far more international and globalized than ever before. These realities help further the argument that women living in the Italian south did not conform to the various stereotypes of women as ignorant and uneducated, coming from a homogeneous, backward, and unchanging society. Using emigration as a lens to examine life for women in the south and the overall Southern Question results in a more nuanced understanding of how society contained elements of old and new, local and foreign, and a heterogeneous mix of ideas and people. Despite living in a more modern world, tradition persisted, such as a strong honor culture, but even these elements were impacted by emigration and mixed with modern influences from abroad. In Basilicata, emigration created a mixture of tradition and modernity.

Basilicata itself is an important setting for this study, as the region is rarely the focus of individual examination. One of the poorest and least populated regions of Italy, Basilicata had high rates of emigration, making it a unique area to survey. The landscape and the weather, combined with little government interest and persistent stereotypes about the south overall, made it a largely disadvantaged region. Residents turned to emigration in an attempt to improve their lives and continue to do so today.

Over one hundred years after the time period discussed here, Basilicata has become a success story, and the image of the region has changed drastically. It has experienced economic growth, particularly with crude oil production and manufacturing, including the opening of a large FIAT plant in Melfi. In recent years, *agriturismo* has become popular in all of Italy, including the many towns of Basilicata. The same lands that were at one time not profitable or plentiful are now providing a source of revenue due to tourism. Travelers wishing to avoid big and crowded cities like Rome, Venice, and Florence, favor small villages where they can experience a more "authentic" Italy. Tourism is on the rise not only to rural areas and towns but also to the beautiful beaches that line the southern coast of the region on the Ionian Sea, and still offer a peaceful escape from large, commercial tourist developments in other areas of the Italian coastline. Potenza is the capital of the region today and is still a relatively small city, but it is Matera that has received much attention in recent years. The Sassi or ancient caves carved into the mountainside just outside the city center were inhabited by people for millennia until the 1950s, when the government forced out residents. The Sassi had a reputation for being places of crime, poverty, and deplorable living conditions, where families and animals lived together in windowless caves. In the last sixty years, the image of the Sassi has changed immensely. In 1994, they were declared a UNESCO world heritage site, and today, they are the home to boutique hotels, shops, and restaurants. Matera was even selected as the 2019 European capital of culture. Despite major changes over the past hundred years, the population of the region is still sparse. There is little opportunity for young people in small towns, and many residents still migrate to northern Italy or abroad to find work, continuing the mindset from the period examined in this book that those who wish to be successful must leave the region.

Despite increased outside interest in the region, it still is not represented in studies on Italian history or the history of migration. Basilicata merits further examination not just because of its unique characteristics regarding migration but also to help complicate our overall understanding of this period of mass Italian emigration during the late nineteenth and early twentieth centuries. Furthermore, emigration, from this region and from all of Italy, should continue to be integrated into and considered a major part of national history, and those connections should be further explored. Marriage, family, economics, and nation building were highly affected by emigration. The phenomenon impacted all the people and places involved, even the country and the people left behind, a fact which should be reflected in historical accounts. It was a phenomenon with deep implications and conceptualizing it in this way can help reframe social, political, economic, and legal issues in the study of Liberal Italy.

During the time period covered in this study, a little over one hundred years ago, anxiety over too much emigration was widespread. Citizens worried that all the young and able-bodied would emigrate, leaving no one to till the fields, harvest crops, or care for livestock. Officials, local priests, and citizens alike expressed concern that towns would be abandoned and worried about how they could possibly survive with the seemingly endless mass exodus. In recent years, Italy has been experiencing a different phenomenon: concern about too much immigration. When Italians left and migrated by the millions to places abroad, especially the United States, they were seen as an inferior and undesirable race. Many Americans, for example, did not welcome them with open arms, and immigrants faced much discrimination and hardship. Ironically, present-day immigrants to Italy from Eastern Europe, the Middle East, and North and sub-Saharan Africa receive similar treatment.

Another interesting parallel to the present day is the gendered aspect of migration for many groups. Between 1876 and 1914, men tended to be the pioneers, and they largely emigrated in search of jobs in industrial labor. Today, immigration from present-day Latin America to the United States, Eastern Europe to Western Europe, and Ireland to England feature "birds of passage," who engage in some of the same economic and family tactics as migrant groups from over a century ago. In contrast to the earlier period studied here, however, it is common with some present-day groups for women to be the pioneers and emigrate first. They arrive in the host country, find a job, often in the domestic service industry, and send money back home to their husbands and families. The men and children either follow or the women return home after saving money.

While the reasons and direction may be different, migration is a phenomenon that continues in Italy today. Never an easy decision, it affects the lives of migrants, those in receiving countries, and those who remain behind. It is important to continue to tell the stories of these migrants, especially those who are often overlooked, such as the women highlighted in this study. Even though it has been challenging to find them, the women who remained behind had a voice and their actions when left on their own contributed to them gaining a new social and economic role, and becoming more active citizens in a new Italian state.

Additional examinations of the women who remained behind in other regions of Italy during the same period would be exceptionally fruitful. A comparative approach would help view the emigration experience from various Italian regions and provide a more nuanced understanding of emigration from Italy as a whole. What about women who did not emigrate? How did their lives differ? Archives in other regions, where the number of migrants was significantly higher, might have better preserved documentation regarding women's petitions to local authorities. Lack of source material has made it difficult to examine the subjects of this study, but comparisons between groups of women from various other regions would indicate another aspect of their changing role in Italy in this period. The migration of children is another area in need of more examination. What was their experience like, as either migrants themselves or as individuals who remained behind and saw their parents and siblings emigrate? Also, did the family situation and the role of the wives left behind alter depending on whether or not they had children? The answers to these questions and many others would continue to expand our understanding of the migration experience.

While this study has focused on one region, it more broadly shows that gender and emigration were fundamental to the creation of citizens in a modern, secular state. Government involvement in emigration allows us to rethink the separation of public and private spheres and state interaction in women's lives during the Liberal Period. Overall, this study has shown the complexities of emigration and the consequences of it on young married women who remained at home. Though not emigrating themselves, they were affected just as much as the migrants, and their lives changed in innumerable ways. Gender roles, relationships between husbands and wives, and motherhood all transformed in varying degrees as a result of emigration. Women's relationships to the economics, politics, and community of the new Italian state also were impacted. Many suffered and experienced incredible hardships; others survived just fine on their own. This study has pieced together those various experiences, showing that women, even in the most wretched situations, acted, spoke up, and had a voice.

In returning to Arcangela's story from the Introduction, and the stories of all the women at the beginning of each chapter, it is clear that migration deeply impacted and transformed their lives. Arcangela's husband migrated and left her with young children, no economic support, and little hope of him ever returning. The chapters of this book give insight into how she may have coped with this difficult situation. She had a new role in her household and became the unofficial head of the family. She raised her children without her husband and found ways to support them when he did not send remittances home. Perhaps family or members of the community or church assisted her. Arcangela did not migrate and could not migrate without the permission of her husband, so she could not leave the village. Yet, despite her husband being gone for years, she did not wait idly for him to return. Arcangela actively sought for news of him, petitioning the mayor requesting various searches for her husband abroad. Not content with her husband's continued inaction, she persistently requested information and financial assistance from him. Her story, like those of the many women highlighted here, demonstrate how emigration truly impacted the women who remained behind. On the surface, her petitions might evoke sadness or empathy because of her husband's abandonment. Yet, as seen throughout this book, she stood up for her rights and found a way to survive on her own.

Bibliography

"Adunanza del 15 giugno 1906." *Bollettino dell'Emigrazione* 1 (1907): 67–72.

Alba, Richard. *Italian Americans: Into the Twilight of Ethnicity.* Englewood Cliffs, NJ: Prentice Hall, 1985.

"Allegati alla relazione sui servizi dell'emigrazione." *Bollettino dell'Emigrazione* 7 (1904): 186–243.

"An Italian Railway Disaster." *The New York Times.* Oct. 22, 1888.

Archivio Centrale dello Stato-Rome (ACS) Collections: Archivio Crispi, Direzione Generale Sanità, Polizia Giudiziaria.

Archivio di Stato-Potenza (ASP) Collections: Atti di Pubblica Sicurezza, Corte d'Assise, Prefettura.

Archivio di Stato-Matera (ASM) Collections: Atti Notarili, Corte d'Assise.

Archivio Storico-Ministero degli Affari Esteri.

Arena, Pasquale. *L'Infanticidio per ragion d'onore: Studio giuridico-sociologico.* Napoli: R. Tipografia de Angelis & Bellisario, 1896.

Armiero, Marco and Marcus Hall, eds. *Nature and History in Modern Italy.* Athens, OH: Ohio University Press, 2010.

Arru, Angiolina, Daniela Luigia Caglioti, and Franco Ramella, eds. *Donne e Uomini Migranti: Storie e geografie tra Breve e Lunga Distanza,* Rome: Donzelli, 2008.

Arru, Angiolina and Franco Ramella. *L'Italia delle Migrazioni interne: donne, uomini, mobilità in età moderna e contemporanea.* Rome: Donzelli, 2003.

Astarita, Tommaso. *Between Salt Water and Holy Water: A History of Southern Italy.* New York: W.W. Norton & Company, 2005.

"Atti del ministero degli affari esteri e del commissariato dell'emigrazione." *Bollettino dell'Emigrazione* 9 (1905): 23–62.

Atti Parlamentari, Camera dei Deputati, Disegni di Legge, 1880–1914.

Baily, Samuel. *Immigrants in the Land of Promise: Italians in Buenos Aires and New York, 1870–1914.* Ithaca, NY: Cornell University Press, 2004.

Baines, Dudley. "European Emigration, 1815–1930: Looking at the Emigration Decision Again." *The Economic History Review* 47, no. 3 (August 1994): 525–544.

Baldassar, Loretta and Donna Gabaccia, eds. *Intimacy and Italian Migration: Gender and Domestic Lives in a Mobile World*. New York: Fordham University Press, 2010.

Balletta, Francesco and Gianfausto Rosoli. *Un Secolo di Emigrazione Italiana, 1876–1976*. Rome: Centro Studi Emigrazione, 1978.

Banfield, Edward C. *The Moral Basis of a Backwards Society*. New York: Free Press, 1958.

Barbagli, Marzio and David Kertzer. *Italian Family History, 1750–1950*. Greenwich, CT: JAI Press, 1990.

Barca, Fabrizio. "New Trends and the Policy Shift in the Italian Mezzogiorno." *Daedalus* 130, no. 2 (Spring 2001): 93.

Bavione, Giuseppe. "Lettere dall'Argentina: Le colpe della Madre Patria." *La Stampa*. Nov 1, 1910.

Beauclerk, William Nelthorpe. *Rural Italy: An Account of the Present Agricultural Condition of the Kingdom*. London: Richard Bentley and Son, 1858.

Bell, Rudolph. *Fate, Honor, Family and Village: Demographic and Cultural Change in Rural Italy since 1800*. Chicago: Chicago University Press, 1976.

Ben-Ghait, Ruth and Stephanie Malia Ham, eds. *Italian Mobilities*. New York: Routledge, 2015.

Bernardy, Amy. "Sulle condizione delle donne e dei fanciulli italiani negli Stati del centro e dell'ovest della confederazione del Nord-America." *Bollettino dell'Emigrazione* 1 (1911): 3–171.

Bevilacqua, Piero. *Breve Storia dell'Italia Meridionale*. Rome: Donzelli Editore, 1992.

Bevilacqua, Piero, Andreina de Clementi and Emilio Franzina, eds. *Storia dell'Emigrazione Italiana*. Roma: Donzelli, 2002.

Bideau, Alain, Bertrand Desjardins, and Hector Perez Brignoli, eds. *Infant and Child Mortality in the Past*. New York: Oxford University Press, 1997.

Bosworth, Richard J. *Italy and the Wider World, 1860–1960*. New York: Routledge, 1996.

Boyd Carioli, Betty. *Italian Repatriation from the US, 1900–1914*. New York: Center for Migration Studies, 2008.

Brettell, Caroline. *Men Who Migrate, Women Who Wait: Population and History*. Princeton: Princeton University Press, 1986.

Cagli, Cesare. "L'emigrazione e l'agricolutra in Basilicata." *Nuova Antologia* CXLVIII (July–Aug 1910): 135–157.

Caglioti, Daniela Luigia. "Elite Migrations in Modern Italy: Patterns of Settlement, Integration and Identity Negotiation." *Journal of Modern Italian Studies* 13, no. 2 (2008): 141–151.

Campolongo, Francesco. *La delinquenza in Basilicata*. Rome: Uniche Cooperativa, 1904.

Canella, Maria, Luisa Dodi and Flores Reggiani. *Si consegna questo figlio: l'assistenza all'infanzia e alla maternità dall Ca' Grande alla provincial di Milano: 1456–1920*. Milan: Università degli studi di Milano, 2008.

Capano, Antonio. "La Lunga Storia della Viabilità del Potentino Nord Occidentale: La Strada Tito-Atena Nell'800." *Basilicata Regione Notizie* 119–120 (2008): 116–126.

Caserta, Giovanni, ed. *Viaggiatori stranieri in terra di Lucania Basilicata*. Venosa: Osanna Edizioni, 2005.

Cenedella, Cristina and Laura Giuliacci. *La vita fragile: infanzia, disagi e assistenza nella Milano del lungo Ottocento: convegno di studi, Milano, Fondazione Stelline*. Milano: Vita e pensiero, 2013.

Cerase, Francesco Paolo. *L'Emigrazione di Ritorno: innovazione o reazione?* Rome: Università, 1971.

Choate, Mark. *Emigrant Nation: The Making of Italy Abroad*. Cambridge, MA: Harvard University Press, 2008.

Cinel, Dino. *The National Integration of Italian Return Migration, 1870–1929*. New York: Cambridge University Press, 1991.

Ciuffoletti, Zeffiro and Maurizio Degl'Innocenti. *L'emigrazione nella storia d'italia, 1868–1974: storia e documenti*. Firenze: Vallecchi, 1978.

Clò, Clarissa and Teresa Fiore. "Unlikely Connections: Italy's Cultural Formations between Home and the Diaspora." *Diaspora* 10, no. 3 (2001): 415–440.

Cohen, Robin. *Global Diasporas: An Introduction*. New York: Routledge, 2004.

Colucci, Michele and Michele Nani, eds. *Lavoro mobile, migranti, organizazioni, conflitti*. Palermo: New Digital Frontiers, 2015.

Colucci, Michele and Matteo Sanfilippo, eds. *Guido allo Studio dell'Emigrazione Italiana*. Viterbo: Sette Città, 2010.

"Contro l'analfabetismo." *Primavera Lucana*. Sept. 30, 1907.

Cordasco, Francesco. *Italian Mass Emigration and the Exodus of a Latin People*. Totowa, NJ: Rowman and Littlefield, 1979.

Cornelisen, Ann. *Women of the Shadows: Wives and Mothers of Southern Italy*. South Royalton, VT: Steerforth Press, 1976.

Corti, Paola. "Donne che vanno, donne che restano. Emigrazione e comportamenti femminili." *Annali dell'Istituto 'Alcide Cervi'* 12 (1990): 213–235.

Corti, Paola. *Temi e problem di storia delle migrazioni italiane*. Viterbo: Sette Città, 2013.

Corti, Paola and Maddalena Tirabassi, eds. *Racconti dal mondo: narrazioni, memorie, e saggi delle migrazioni*. Torino: Fondazioni Agnelli, 2007.

Corti, Paola and Michele Sanfilippo, eds. *L'Italia e le migrazioni*. Rome: Laterza, 2012.

"Current Foreign Topics." *The New York Times*. Oct. 24, 1888.

D'Andrea, Giampolo and Francesco Giasi, eds. *La Scoperta del Mezzogiorno: Zanardelli e la questione meridionale*. Rome: Edizioni Stadium, 2015.

Davis, John A. *Conflict and Control: Law and Order in Nineteenth Century Italy*. Atlantic Highlands, NJ: Humanities International Press, 1988.

Davis, John A. *Italy in the Nineteenth Century: 1796–1900*. New York: Oxford University Press, 2000.

Davis, John A. *Naples and Napoleon: Southern Italy and the European Revolution 1780–1860*. Oxford: University of Oxford Press, 2006.

Davis, John A. and Paul Ginsborg, eds. *Society and Politics in the Age of the Risorgimento: Essays in Honor of Denis Mack Smith*. New York: Cambridge University Press, 1991.

Davis, John. *Land and Family in Pisticci.* New York: Humanities Press, 1973.

De Giorgio, Michela. *Le Italiane Dall'Unità a Oggi: Modelli Culturali e Comporamenti Sociali.* Rome: Laterza, 1992.

De Giorgio, Michela and Christiane Klapisch-Zuber, eds. *Storia del Matrimonio.* Rome: Laterza, 1996.

De Grand, Alexander. *The Hunchback's Tailor: Giovanni Giolitti and Liberal Italy from the Challenge of Mass Politics to the Rise of Fascism, 1882–1922.* Westport, CT: Praeger, 2001.

"Della emigrazione Italiana." *La Civiltà Cattolica* XI, no. 916 (1888): 385–403.

DeRosa, Gabriele, Antonio Cestaro and Dinu Adamesteanu, eds. *Storia della Basilicata,* 4 vols. Rome: Laterza, 2006.

Dickie, John. *Darkest Italy: The Nation and Stereotypes of the Mezzogiorno, 1860–1900.* New York: St. Martin's Press, 1999.

di Maria, Salvatore. *Towards a Unified Italy: Historical, Cultural, and Literary Perspectives on the Southern Question.* New York: Palgrave Macmillan, 2018.

DiGiorgio, Michela. "Women's History in Italy." *Journal of Modern Italian Studies* 1, no. 3 (1996): 377–389.

Direzione Generale della Statistica. *Annuario statistico italiano: 1895.* Rome: Tipografia Nazionale di G. Bertero, 1896.

Direzione Generale della Statistica. *Annuario Statistico Italiano, 1905–1907.* Rome: Tipografia Nazionale di G. Bertero, 1908.

Direzione Generale della Statistica. *Annuario statistico italiano: 1912.* Rome: Tipografia Nazionale di G. Bertero, 1913.

Direzione Generale della Statistica. *Statistica della Emigrazione Italiana per l'estero negli anni 1904 e 1905.* Rome: G. Bertero E.C., 1906.

DiScala, Spencer. *Italy from Revolution to Republic, 1700 to the Present.* Philadelphia: Westview Press, 1995.

"Discusione dei disegni di leggi: stati di previsione dell'entrata e della spesa del Fondo dell'emigrazione per l'esercizio finanziario 1905–906 e assestamento degli stati medesimi per l'esercizio 1904–905." *Bollettino dell'Emigrazione* 15 (1905) 34–73.

Di Tolla, Anna Maria. "La Presenza dei Lucani in Nord Africa." *Basilicata Regione Notizie.*1–2 (1998): 37–44.

Domenico, Roy Palmer. *The Regions of Italy: A Reference Guide to History and Culture.* Westport, CT: Greenwood, 2002.

Douglass, William A. *Emigration in a South Italian Town: An Anthropological History.* New Brunswick: Rutgers University Press, 1984.

Duggan, Christopher. *Francesco Crispi: 1818–1901 from Nation to Nationalism.* Oxford: Oxford University Press, 2002.

Duggan, Christopher. *The Force of Destiny: A History of Italy since 1796.* New York: Houghton Mifflin, 2008.

Dunnage, Jonathan. *Twentieth Century Italy: A Social History.* New York: Pearson, 2002.

"Entire Mountain Falling." *The New York Times.* Mar. 3, 1907.

Falvella, Maria. "Flussi migratori della Basilicata: situazioni e dimensioni nel periodo 1861–1940." *Basilicata Regione Notizie* 98 (2001): 87–96.

Fazio, Ida. "The Family, Honor and Gender in Sicily: Models and New Research." *Modern Italy* 9, no. 2 (November 2004): 263–280.

Fiume, Giovanna. "Women's History and Gender History: The Italian Experience." *Modern Italy* 10, no. 2 (November 2005): 207–231.

Foerster, Robert F. *Italian Emigration of our Times*. Cambridge: Harvard University Press, 1919.

Franzina, Emilio. *Traversate: le grandi migrazioni transatlantiche e i racconti italiani del viaggio per mare*. Foligno, PG: Editoriale Umbra, 2003.

Fuchs, Rachel. *Abandoned Children: Foundlings and Child Welfare in 19th Century France*. Albany: State University of New York Press, 1984.

Gabaccia, Donna. *From the Other Side: Women, Gender and Immigrant Life in the US 1820–1990*. Bloomington: Indiana University Press, 1995.

Gabaccia, Donna. *Italy's Many Diasporas*. Seattle: University of Washington Press, 2000.

Gabaccia, Donna and Franca Iacovetta, eds. *Women, Gender and Transnational Lives: Italian Workers of the World*. Toronto: University of Toronto Press, 2002.

Gabaccia, Donna and Frasser Ottanelli. "Diaspora or International Proletariat?" *Diaspora* 6, no. 1 (1997) 61–84.

Gatti, Anna Maria. "La mortalità infantile tra ottocento e Novecento." La Sardegna nel panorama Italiano (2002). http://veprints.unica.it/445/1/q2_02.pdf.

Gibson, Mary. *Prostitution and the State in Italy, 1860–1915*. New Brunswick, NJ: Rutgers University Press, 1986.

Gorni, Maria Grazia and Laura Pellegrini. *Un Problema di Storia Sociale: L'Infanzia Abbandonata in Italia nel Secolo XIX*. Florence: La Nuova Italia Editrice, 1974.

Grandi, Casimira. *Donne Fuori Posto: l'Emigrazione Femminile Rurale d'Italia Postunitaria*. Ann Arbor: University of Michigan, 2008.

Green, Nancy and François Weil, eds. *Citizenship and Those who Leave: The Politics of Emigration and Expatriation*. Chicago: University of Illinois Press, 2007.

Green, Nancy L. "The Politics of Exit: Reversing the Immigrant Paradigm." *Journal of Modern Italian Studies* 77 (Jun 2005): 263–289.

Guglielmo, Jennifer. *Living the Revolution: Italian Women's Resistance and Radicalism in New York City*. Chapel Hill, NC: University of North Carolina, 2010.

"Havoc by Falling Mountain." *The New York Times*. Mar. 4, 1907.

Hearder, Harry and Jonathan Morris, eds. *Italy: A Short History*. New York: Cambridge University Press, 2001.

Hughes, Steven P. *Politics of the Sword: Dueling, Honor and Masculinity in Modern Italy*. Columbus: Ohio State University Press, 2007.

"I locali della scuola normale." *La Vita Lucana*. Dec 23, 1905.

The Immigration Commission. "Emigration Conditions in Europe." Washington, DC: Government Printing Press, 1911.

Ipsen, Carl. *Italy in the Age of Pinocchio: Children and Danger in the Liberal Era*. New York: Palgrave Macmillan, 2006.

Isabella, Maurizio. *Risorgimento in Exile: Italian Emigres and the Liberal International in the Post- Napoleonic Era*. New York: Oxford University Press, 2009.

"Istruzione Popolare in Basilicata." *La Vedetta*. Nov. 1895.

"Italian Emigration: How It Will be Affected by the Crispi Bill." *The New York Times.* Jul 5, 1888.

"Italian Village Destroyed." *The New York Times.* May 16, 1901.

"Italy Stops Emigration." *The New York Times.* Sept 24, 1911, C4.

"IV: Cose Varie." *La Civiltà Cattolica* 3, no. 1298 (1904): 252–256.

Kertzer, David. *Sacrificed for Honor: Italian Infant Abandonment and the Politics of Reproductive Birth Control.* Boston: Beacon Press, 1993.

Kertzer, David and Marzio Barbagli, eds. *The History of the European Family: Family Life in the Long 19th Century (1789–1913).* New Haven, CT: Yale University Press, 2002.

Kertzer, David and Marzio Barbagli, eds. *The History of the European Family: Family Life in the Twentieth Century.* New Haven, CT: Yale University Press, 2003.

Kertzer, David and Richard P. Saller, eds. *The Family in Italy from Antiquity to the Present.* New Haven: Yale University Press, 1991.

"La delinquenza nei fanciulli." *La Provincia: Quindicinale Cattolico di Potenza.* May 24, 1908.

Lacava, Pietro. "L'analfabetismo in Basilicata." *Primavera Lucana.* May 7, 1907.

Lacava, Pietro. "Sulle condizioni economico-sociali della Basilicata." *Nuova Antologia.* vol CXXVIII (March–April 1907): 105–133.

Lafranceschina, Felice. "I lucani in Argentina, Brasile, e Cile." *Basilicata Regione Notizie* 94 (2000): 73–80.

"L'emigrazione dei fanciulli." *La Stampa.* Aug 13, 1909.

"L'emigrazione italiana per l'estero nell'anno 1906." *Bollettino dell'Emigrazione* 11 (1907): 9–26.

"L'emigrazione delle donne e dei fanciulli dalla provincia di Caserta." *Bollettino dell'Emigrazione* 13 (1913): 3–23.

"L'emigrazione in Basilicata." *Primavera Lucana.* Dec 25, 1906.

"L'emigrazione italiana delle provincie tedesche del Reno e della Westfalia." *Bollettino dell'Emigrazione* 10 (1902): 3–15.

"L'emigrazione transoceanica ed i proposti del governo." *Primavera Lucana.* Feb 12, 1907.

"Le ombre nel quadro della nostra emigrazione." *Bollettino dell'Emigrazione* 15 (1907): 168–176.

Lerra, Antonio. *Chiesa e società nel Mezzogiorno: dalla "ricettizia" del secolo XVI alla liquidazione dell'Asse ecclesiastico in Basilicata.* Venosa: Edizioni Osanna, 1996.

Levi, Carlo. *Christ Stopped at Eboli.* Torino: Eunaudi, 1945.

Lisanti, Nicola. "L'Emigrazione lucana dall'Unità alfascismo." *Lucani Nel Mondo* n. 1-2 (1998): 11–20.

"L'istruzione fa divenire la donna maliziosa." *La Stampa.* Oct 7, 1887.

Livi-Bacci, Massimo. *A History of Italian Fertility during the Last Two Centuries.* Princeton, NJ: Princeton University Press, 1977.

Luconi, Stefano. "Emigration and Italians' Transnational Radical Politicization." *Forum Italicum* 47, no. 1 (May 2013): 96.

Luconi, Stefano and Maria Varricchio, eds. *Lontane di casa: donne italiane e diaspora globale dall'inizio del Novecento a oggi.* Torino: Academia University Press, 2015.

Lumley, Robert and Jonathan Morris, eds. *The New History of the Italian South.* Exeter: University of Exeter Press, 1997.

Lupo, Salvatore. *The Two Mafias: A Transatlantic History, 1888–2008.* New York: Palgrave Macmillan, 2013.

Lyttelton, Adrian. *Liberal and Fascist Italy: 1900–1945.* New York: Oxford University Press, 2002.

Maggio, Monica. "Banditi Lucani: Antropologia Storica della Dissidenza." *Basilicata Regione Notizie* 101 (2002): 87–90.

"Mali e dolori dell'emigrazione." *La Stampa.* Jan 5, 1907.

Moe, Nelson. *The View from Vesuvius: Italian Culture and the Southern Question.* Berkeley: University of California Press, 2002.

Moretti, Enrico. "Social Networks and Migrations: Italy 1876–1913." *International Migration Review* 33, no. 3 (Autumn 1999): 640–657.

Nitti, Francesco Saverio. *Scritti sulla questione meridionale. Saggi sulla storia del Mezzogiorno.* Bari: Laterza, 1958.

Pace, Aldo. *Banco di Napoli: l'emigrazione e le rimesse emigranti.* Naples: Istituto Banco di Napoli, 2007.

Palazzi, Maura. *Donne Sole: Storie dell'altra Faccia dell'Italia tra Antico Regime a Società Contemporanea.* Torino: B. Mondadori, 1997.

Parati, Graziella and Anthony Julian Tamburri, eds. *The Cultures of Italian Migration.* Lanham, MD: The Rowman & Littlefield Publishing Group, 2011.

Patriarca, Silvana. "Gender Trouble: Women and the Making of Italy's 'Active Population,' 1861–1936." *Journal of Modern Italian Studies* 3, no. 2 (1998): 144–163.

Petrusewicz, Marta. *Come il Meridione Divenne una Questione.* Catanzaro: Rubbettino, 1998.

Petrusewicz, Marta. *Latifundium: Moral Economy and Material Life in a European Periphery.* Ann Arbor: University of Michigan Press, 1996.

Piselli, Fortunata. *Parentele ed Emigrazione: mutamenti e continuità in una communità calabrese.* Torino: Einaudi, 1981.

Pollard, John. *Catholicism in Modern Italy: Religion, Society and Politics since 1861.* New York: Routledge, 2008.

Pozzetta, George E. *The Italian Diaspora: Migration across the Globe.* Toronto: Multicultural History Society of Ontario, 1992.

Protasi, Maria Rosa. *I fanciulli nell'emigrazione Italiana: una storia minore, 1861–1920.* Isernia: C. Iannone, 2010.

Quine, Maria Sophia. *Italy's Social Revolution: Charity and Welfare from Liberalism to Fascism.* London: Palgrave Macmillan, 2002.

Raciopi, Giacomo. *Storia dei Popoli della Lucania e della Basilicata.* Torino: E Loescher, 1889.

Racioppi, Giacomo. *Sui Tremuoti di Basilicata nel Dicembre 1857.* Napoli: Tipografico della Gazzetta dei Tribunali, 1858.

"Rassegna di Statistica, Le Scuole." *La Vedetta.* Nov 1895.

Reeder, Linda. *Widows in White: Migration and the Transformation of Rural Italian Women, Sicily, 1880–1920.* Toronto: University of Toronto Press, 2003.

Reeder, Linda. "Women in the Classroom: Mass Migration, Literacy and the Nationalization of Sicilian Women at the Turn of the Century." *Journal of Social History* 32, no. 1 (Autumn 1998): 101–124.

"Relazione del Commissario Generale dell'Emigrazione." *Bollettino dell'Emigrazione* 7 (1904): 9–184.

Rettaroli, Rosella. "Age at Marriage in Nineteenth-Century Italy." *Journal of Family History* 15, no. 4 (October 1990): 409–425.

Riall, Lucy. "Which Road to the South? Revisionists Revisit the Mezzogiorno." *Journal of Modern Italian Studies* 5, no. 1 (2000): 89–100.

Rocca, Giancarlo."Congregazioni Religiose Femminili e la Chiesa in Italia." Dizionario Storico Tematico La Chiesa in Italia, Vol II-Dopo l'unità nazionale. http://www.storiadellachiesa.it/glossary/congregazioni-religiose-femminili-e-la-chiesa-in-italia-2/.

Rodogna, Adele. *Le solitudini delle donne molisane ai tempi della prima grande migrazione.* Milan: Meltemi, 2018.

Rosoli, Gianfausto and Francesco Balletta, eds. *Un secolo di emigrazione italiana, 1876–1976.* Rome: Centro Studi Emigrazione, 1978.

Rossi, Adolfo. "Vantaggi e danni dell'emigrazione nel mezzogiorno d'Italia (Note di un viaggio fatto in Basilicata e in Calabria dal R. Commissario dell'Emigrazione)" *Bollettino dell'Emigrazione* 13 (1908): 3–110.

Sanfilippo, Matteo, ed. *Emigrazione e storia d'Italia.* Cosenza: Pellegrini, 2003.

Sanfilippo, Matteo, ed. *Problemi di Storiografia dell'Emigrazione Italiana.* Cosenza: Pellegrini, 2002.

Schirone, Maria. "Le Donne e L'emigrazione." *Basilicata Regione Notizie.* 1-2 (1998): 111–112.

Schneider, Jane, ed. *Italy's 'Southern Question': Orientalism in One Country.* New York: Berg, 2001.

Schneider, Jane and Peter Schneider. *Festival of the Poor: Fertility Decline and the Ideology of Class in Sicily.* Tuscon: University of Arizona Press, 1996.

Sergi, Pantaleone. *Storia del Giornalismo in Basilicata: per passione e per potere.* Roma: Laterza, 2006.

Seymour, Mark. *Debating Divorce in Italy: Marriage and the Making of Modern Italians 1860–1974.* New York: Palgrave Macmillan, 2006.

Sharpe, Pamela. *Women, Gender and Labour Migration.* New York: Routledge, 2001.

Snowden, Frank M. *Naples in the Time of Cholera, 1884–1911.* Cambridge: Cambridge University Press, 1995.

Snowden, Frank M. *The Conquest of Malaria: Italy, 1900–1962.* New Haven: Yale University Press, 2006.

Solimena, Vincenzo. *Educhiamo la donna: Conferenza letta al circolo degli artigiani.* Rionero in Vulture, Tipografia di Torquato Ercolani, 1888.

Soresina, Marco. "Italian Emigration Policy during the Great Migration Age, 1888–1919: The Interaction of Emigration and Foreign Policy." *Journal of Modern Italian Studies* 21, no. 5 (2016): 723–746.

Stato Civile: Collections: Atti di Nascita, Atti di Matrimonio Marsiconuovo, Potenza, Picerno.

Strazza. Michele. "I piccoli 'desaparacidos' Lucani dell'800." *Basilicata Regione Notizie* 117 (2008): 62–67.

Strazza, Michele, ed. *Le Donne nella Storia della Basilicata.* Lagonegro: Zaccara, 2010.

Sturino, Franc. *Forging the Chain: A Case Study of Italian Migration to North America 1880–1930.* Toronto: Multicultural History Society of Toronto, 1990.

Teti, Vito. *Il senso dei luoghi: memoria e storia dei paesi abbandonati.* Rome: Donzelli, 2014.

"Tornando dalla Basilicata." *La Stampa.* Oct 26, 1890.

Torpey, John C. *The Invention of the Passport.* New York: Cambridge University Press, 2000.

"Tutela degli emigranti in patria e durante il viaggio transatlantico." *Bollettino dell'Emigrazione* 14 (1905): 27–39.

"Tutela e protezione degli emigranti." *Bollettino dell'Emigrazione* 11 (1904): 40–106.

"Un lembo ignorato d'Italia: La Basilicata, VI." *La Stampa.* Oct 3, 1887.

"Un lembo ignorato d'Italia: La Basilicata, VIII." *La Stampa.* Oct 7, 1887.

"Un lembo ignorato d'Italia: La Basilicata IX." *La Stampa.* Oct 11, 1887.

Verdicchio, Pasquale. *Bound by Distance: Rethinking Nationalism through the Italian Diaspora.* London: Cranbury, 1997.

Vetritti, Giovanni. *Francesco Saverio Nitti: Un Profilo.* Soveria Mannelli, Cosenza: Rubbettino, 2013.

Willson, Perry. "From Margin to Centre: Recent Trends in Modern Italian Women's and Gender History." *Modern Italy* 11, no. 3 (November 2006): 327–337.

Willson, Perry. *Gender, Family and Sexuality: The Private Sphere in Italy, 1860–1945.* New York: Palgrave Macmillan, 2004.

Willson, Perry. *Women in Twentieth-Century Italy.* New York: Palgrave Macmillan, 2010.

Zanotti-Bianco, Umberto. *La Basilicata: Storia di una regione del Mezzogiorno dal 1861 ai primi decenni del 1900.* Venosa: Edizioni Osanna, 2000.

Zucchi, John E. *Little Slaves of the Harp.* Quebec: McGill-Queens University, 1992.

Index

About the Author

Victoria Calabrese received her PhD in modern European history from the Graduate Center at the City University of New York. Her research focuses on modern Italian history, gender, migration, and nation building. In addition to the women who remained behind, she has written articles on infanticide and traveling child musicians. She is currently an adjunct professor, teaching courses in early modern and modern European history, as well as world civilizations. In her free time, Victoria loves travel, genealogy research, and following her favorite sports teams.

www.ingramcontent.com/pod-product-compliance
Lightning Source LLC
Chambersburg PA
CBHW022314280326
41932CB00010B/1093